MARKETING IN A
REGULATED ENVIRONMENT

SERIES ON MARKETING MANAGEMENT

Series Editor: **FREDERICK E. WEBSTER, JR.,**
The Amos Tuck School of Business Administration,
Dartmouth College

Marketing in a Regulated Environment

GEORGE S. DOMINGUEZ

A RONALD PRESS PUBLICATION

JOHN WILEY & SONS, New York • Chichester • Brisbane • Toronto

Other Publications by the Same Author

PRODUCT MANAGEMENT
MARKETING IN A SHORTAGE ECONOMY
BUSINESS, GOVERNMENT AND THE PUBLIC INTEREST
HOW TO BE A SUCCESSFUL PRODUCT MANAGER
GUIDE BOOK: TOXIC SUBSTANCES CONTROL ACT

Library of Congress Cataloging in Publication Data

Dominguez, George S.
  Marketing in a regulated environment.

  (Series on marketing management)
  "A Ronald Press publication."
  Bibliography: p.
  Includes index.
  1. Marketing—United States. 2. Product management.
3. Industry and state—United States. I. Title.
HF5415.1.D65   658.8'00973   77-22099
ISBN 0-471-02402-3

Printed in the United States of America

10 9 8 7 6 5 4 3 2 1

To my wife Shirley
my son George
and my daughter Tee
who no doubt had to contend with a great deal
the least of which was the clacking typewriter at 5 A.M.

Series Editor's Foreword

Marketing management is among the most dynamic of the business functions. On the one hand it reflects the everchanging marketplace and the constant evolution of customer preferences and buying habits, and of competition. On the other hand, it grows continually in sophistication and complexity as developments in management science are applied to the work of the marketing manager. If he or she is to be a true management professional, the marketing person must stay informed about these developments.

The Wiley Series on Marketing Management has been developed to serve this need. The books in the series have been written for managers. They combine a concern for management application with an appreciation for the relevance of developments in such areas of management science as behavioral science, financial analysis, and mathematical modeling, as well as the insights gained from analyzing successful experience in the marketplace. The Wiley Series on Marketing Management is thus intended to communicate the state-of-the-art in marketing to managers.

Virtually all areas of marketing management will be explored in the series. Books now available or being planned cover advertising management, industrial marketing research, brand loyalty, sales management, product policy and planning, public relations, overall marketing strategy, and financial aspects of marketing management. It is hoped that the series will have some effect in raising the standards of applied marketing management.

FREDERICK E. WEBSTER, JR.

Hanover, New Hampshire
June 1977

Preface

In my earlier publications I admitted to writing the preface after writing the book—something I strongly suspect most authors do. This time the preface is a true one in that it not only precedes the book, it was actually written before the book was.

In approaching the subject of government regulation—policy and practice —which has created what I now call a regulated environment, the task looms awesome but patently necessary. The media and the literature—professional, lay, and all the shades of pseudo between—are replete with discussion, review, and analysis of business and government action and interaction. Condemnation or commendation of business or government abounds, depending on which perspective or basis is expressed.

Nothing can or should be said against this as an expression of free will, the natural and reasonable consequence of the public interest, and democracy in action; however, the practical problems are that all too often these are far from constructive or of help to business, government, or the public; they are ultimately at least confusing; and they create external pressures often leading to "knee-jerk" reactions.

Given the extent to which existing regulation (based on present legislation) and the prospects of far more rather than less future regulation (based on actual proposed and logically projected legislation) and its effect on the conduct of the business, this would seem to be a subject in need of comprehensive and cohesive treatment. Such treatment should not be, for our purposes, from the viewpoint of the regulators (whose problems we recognize and admit are many and varied), but from that of the regulated. There are several obvious differences but one that is at first not so apparent is, in fact, of major concern. While the regulators have to deal only with their one specific area of interest and authority—that is, within

the statutory limits of the legislation that establish their regulatory authority
—business must respond to, contend with, and comply with all of the regulatory
requirements of all the agencies.

Our problem is quite different not only because we are simultaneously the
subject and object of regulation but because we must deal with the individual
regulation or agency as well as with the totality. We must be concerned also with
the cumulative effect of not the singular but the additive, an additive that must be
examined in terms of its ultimate cumulative effect. When explored in this light,
the problems of industry that are regulatorily derived take on yet another dimension. This is a vital distinction that does not seem to be recognized by the
bureaucracy. What it means to business in more specific terms and what can be
done are among the many things this book is all about.

In examining this regulatory matrix—or better yet, web—and its effects from
the perspective of the regulated, several approaches could logically have been
undertaken: the effect on the total corporate entity and its existence, corporate
policy, growth, socioeconomics; the relationship between federal, state, and
municipal regulation; or the role of the public interest advocates and the media in
the direction and creation of legislation and regulation. All of these are vital and
valid concerns. If, however, we were even to attempt to address all of them even
superficially, an entire library, not a single volume, would be required.

A sharper and more pragmatic focus is desirable. Marketing is the logical
focus because marketing is a dominant element in corporate activity, both as the
active visual operational component and as *the* essential activity for existence,
survival—corporate success or failure. Additionally, because many of the regulatory actions and decisions bear directly or indirectly on marketing operations,
the logic for considering marketing and·regulation as our basic point of reference
is reinforced.

Such functional separation is at best, arbitrary. Some discussion of effect on
overall corporate activity, policy, business planning, capital formation—to mention but a few elements—is not only inevitable but—to place some effects in
their proper perspective—essential.

The basic direction of this book is derived from the impacts and effects on
marketing and the ensuing action and interactions that are required for continued
marketing success under the regulatory burdens. To do this I examine each key
marketing function—for example, sales, advertising and promotion, product
management—in these terms. There are certain practical limitations, and hence,
I attempt only to examine federal regulatory effects, explore only major
agencies/regulations, and consider general regulatory policy and overall effect
since each and every regulation could not possibly be considered. I hope that
these constraints will not be looked upon as too limiting because I do not feel that
they will detract from our basic intention and purpose: what effects regulations

and regulators have on marketing and, equally important, how one markets in a regulated environment.

The concept is then founded on examining effects on marketing with the intention to translate this into practical recommendations and strategies. There is a heavy emphasis on what can be and how it should be done.

To accomplish this the book essentially is divided into three sections. The first—Chapters 1–5—deal with major aspects and examine the history, evolution, and present conditions as they apply to marketing and to total business conduct. In the second section—Chapters 6–8—I deal with the "micro" effects more specifically focused on marketing and provide both practical strategical considerations and broader and longer-term theoretical approaches. The concluding section—Chapters 9–11—is focused on "macro" business elements such as the need for total integration of regulatory concerns within the company and how to achieve it with some prognostications of the regulatory future.

Marketing, more than any other organizational function, operates in the real-world environment of the give and take of the market/customer dynamic. Government official or bureaucrat, business executive or manager, public interest advocate or blue-collar worker, we are all the same in that we are all consumers. In approaching marketing in a regulated environment we should not lose sight of the ultimate objective of the regulatory and business activity: to satisfy our customers' wants and needs, actual or perceived. Although the regulators and regulated are providing goods and services that differ, their intent is common. Factors of business conduct, such as obligations to shareholders, the concern for profits, and similar economic and financial needs, of course, set government and industry apart because such corporate "needs" do not exist in government. Looked at from the broader viewpoint of the dynamics of interaction with the consumer, whether regulator or regulated, we are all tried by public reaction. We should not overlook this aspect and its implications—as marketing managers will clearly realize.

I started from the premise that a thorough treatment of marketing in a regulated environment is needed. I hope that this book, which cannot pretend to have all the answers, will at least provide a foundation—a foundation to meet existing regulatory challenges from a marketing viewpoint in a practical way and as a foundation to be built upon by others as further refinements in knowledge and experience provide additional insights and solutions. To those who would take up the baton, I can only wish success. To those who have a more practical or perhaps better phrased more immediate business survival need, may this book serve its intended purpose which is to provide some practical guidance to marketing in a regulated environment.

GEORGE S. DOMINGUEZ

Wilton, Connecticut
September 1977

Preface Update

This book has two prefaces. The first preface was actually drafted before the book was written. As stated therein, I felt strongly that the writing of the preface should be completed before the book, rather than after as so often is the case. However, since government activities, like most events in contemporary society, move with a rapidity that is constantly accelerating my original preface reflects some already outdated materials.

The most significant event is the election of a new president, Jimmy Carter. As a consequence, Gerald Ford's previous legislative agenda, which is contained in its entirety in Chapter 11, is in one sense obsolete. Nevertheless, it is still pertinent in the context of the book—even though any legislative agenda proposed by Mr. Carter is bound to have its own characteristics. Ford's proposals reflect the scope, nature, general thrust, and direction of legislative activity that can be expected.

The events of recent months, such as President Carter's announced energy and environmental programs, the Consumer Product Safety Commission's ban on the flame retardant Tris, the proposed FDA ban on saccharin, and renewed Congressional interest in the Consumer Protection Act, serve to reaffirm my basic contention that, despite avowed federal concern with excess legislation and regulation, and with regulatory reform proposals, the marketing manager will in the short term continue to encounter more, rather than less, government imposition in marketing management, and decision making.

G.S.D.

Acknowledgments

Like any author of a major publication, I owe a debt of gratitude to many who have assisted by virtue of discussion, both before and after the writing of this book, as well as to several who also reviewed the manuscript. While the list is long, I especially thank Ronald Lang, Synthetic Organic Chemicals Manufacturers Association; George W. Ingle, Manufacturing Chemists Association; Robert Barnard, Cleary, Gottlieb, Steen and Hamilton; John McGraw and Dr. Rolf Bernegger, CIBA-GEIGY Corporation. Thanks must also be given to Ronald Brennan, Valda Aldzeris and Judith Loebl of the John Wiley & Sons staff, all of whom provided immeasurable help in improving the book and accelerating its publication.

All of these efforts notwithstanding, the author, as always, must take sole final responsibility for the opinions, positions, and recommendations contained in the book. In this context it should also be clear that the opinions, conclusions, and recommendations made here are not necessarily those of my employer, CIBA-GEIGY Corporation, Ardsley, New York, and there should be no inference that this necessarily represents their position in any particular area.

G.S.D.

Contents

MARKETING IN A REGULATED ENVIRONMENT

ONE
The Historical
Context

Most articles or books dealing with the government start out with a recitation of statistics that either prove or disprove the enormity of government size, expenditure, and proliferation. This book will not break the mold and so, we too examine the size, expenditures, and proliferation of government: however, because our main concern is the effect of government intervention on business in general and marketing in particular, we deal with these statistical details later. For now let us assume that the statistics will stand on their own and undoubltedly support the patent fact of government size and cost. Size and cost alone, however, do not tell the story or prove the facts of intervention, incursions, dominance, and control. Size and cost alone do not demonstrate benefit or loss, and they do not validate need or excess. To explore these concerns and to look to the question of government effects on marketing we need to examine not so much the statistics of government as the functions, reach, and actions of government.

The contemporary regulatory environment did not spring forth full grown. Like business, it evolved and is continuing its evolution. Both points are important to remember. That government evolved and that policies, statutes, rules, and regulations, developed with it tells us that it was not static and that much of the effort resulted from some preceived need. What some of these preceived needs were are still important to us, not only because they resulted in laws that still affect us, but because they are illustrative of the legislative and regulatory process. That government, and with it legal and regulatory activity, is still evolving is perhaps more important; for this is the continuation of the process. The onward manifestation of the action/reaction pattern continues on basically the same premise of preceived need. The need may differ, the preception may alter, the role of government may change, but all of this occurs not in a vacuum but in the real

world with real-world consequences. Part of our challenge as marketing executives therefore lies in knowing the laws, rules, and regulations as well as in
knowing something about how they came into being and where we and they are
likely to go. Note should be taken of the phrase *likely to go;* for clearly we want
to have a say in where this evolutionary process goes; we want in fact to go rather
than be taken. Too often we in marketing management see business ''follower-
ship'' rather than leadership in dealing with the government and its actions.

Our objectives are many: to study government policy and growth, to examine
effects of federal legislation and regulation on marketing, to determine what can
and what should be done before and after legislative or regulatory fact, to
develop specific business practices and strategies—in short, the determination of
how to market in a regulated environment. Considering each of these alone
would be no mean task; taken collectively they represent a vast effort. To
approach this task some concessions have to be made. The most important of
these is that we can of necessity deal with only federal legislation and regulation.
The role of the states and their activities are no less important, and they must
always be kept clearly in mind and carefully considered, analyzed, and incorporated in the evaluations and proposals that we will be making. Fortunately, the
basic logic examined and the recommendations made regarding marketing actions and reactions are as applicable to state as to federal actions. The second
major concession is that time and space do not permit dealing with all federal
agencies or departments, laws or regulations, and so only major examples, some
in relatively abbreviated form, are cited. This should not, however, prove to be a
significant limitation; the major examples are of universal concern, and the more
limited and specific instances are no doubt already well-known and keenly felt by
those that are directly affected.

BUSINESS AND GOVERNMENT

Since his transition from the primoridal state to even the most unstructured
socially primitive one, man has effected some semblance of organization and
thus some semblance of both business and government. Although the earliest
forms of business and government were no doubt unplanned and unintentional,
they did occur, and with them came specialization and eventual separation.
Specialization appeared in what eventually came to be formally recognized as
business or government as well as in the broader construction of each of these
forces as social entities. Eventually two clearly separate, but interrelated and
interdependent, social forces evolved—business and government.

From earliest times there has been a distinction of function and to some extent
a separation of interests and activities. Both forces followed separate but equally

important progressions. The first person in business was probably some individual whose natural or acquired skill made him or her most proficient in some essential task, which led to some position of recognition leading eventually to the use of the skill for some purpose other than self protection, satisfaction, or needs fulfillment. Obviously, even this simplest of steps was essentially an unconscious progression, but from it evolved far more complex forms of "business" activity from early bartering systems to rudimentary entrepreneurships and on to complex corporations of national and international scope. Each country and each time saw its variations. The growth of specialized industries and proficiencies resulted in national distinctions that remain with us at least as images and reputations even if not in fact. Characteristics of nations—industrialized or nonindustrialized, agricultural or mechanical—developed and remain.

At the same time there was a shift in the emphasis of business and its role in society in general. When business was essentially an individual activity the effect of business action and conduct was essentially individual—limited and on a one-to-one basis. As entrepreneurships and business effects grew, the outreach of the business grew. Such outreach brought with it broader effects, which can be either beneficial or harmful. When business later grew still larger, the effects became not only correspondingly larger but reached a transition point, a point at which the effects of the business activity were at least potentially disruptive. That is, the activities and decisions of the business—insofar as their effects on people in specific and society in general were concerned—exceeded what could be clearly delineated as the legitimate rights and prerogatives of the business activity and encroached on the broader scale of social events, social values, and social interests. The corporation was not only a business but a social institution. Although this was evolutionary, not conscious or intentional, it was clearly factual.

When transporting wares involved carrying them on one's back from door to door, there was one dimension of the shipping problem. When railroads (the classical example of argued need and regulatory action) dominated the domestic transportation scene in the late 1800s, the problems were obviously quite different; and the rights and responsibilities of the business, government, and the public correspondingly were quite different. What this meant and what it led to or will lead to, we are only now beginning to see clearly. The issue for the moment, then, is not one of actual actions but rather of the evolution of business and its eventual emergence as a force that went and goes beyond its normal or even intentioned bounds, by virtue of its size, effect, and social importance.

While this was going on, government also changed. The changes were different in degree, nature, and intent; and they varied greatly from country to country, leading to a wide diversity of expression and representation. The recognition that society required rules of conduct, both for itself and its institutions, and that these had to be imposed by some for the benefit of all led to institutionalization and formalization: a body of government and with it a body of law. A system, with organization and authority, must be based on a determination of what the government and the law should be and must effect its establishment and enforcement and allow for both its perpetuation and needed change—evolution. Thus came about organized representation and authority with the means to attain social ideals, the public well-being, and a guarantee of stability and equality.

In the United States this of course led to the democratic form of government that was developed in our early history, resulted in our Constitution, and constitutes our existing form of government and legislation. Our early legislative history is important as a part of our heritage and because it establishes the foundation of our present system of government and legal system. Laws establish and in some cases define our relationships as individuals and, for our purposes here, businesses as social institutions. As they are the result of dynamic forces, so too are they dynamic. They are not fixed, are not immutable; they are changeable and changing. This subject is discussed at some length in later portions of the book, for these past relationships and perspectives have changed. These changes have brought about and will continue to bring about new relationships and with them laws, rules, and regulations that go towards redefining not only business in relationship to government but business in relationship to society. The whys and hows of this should be clear if we look to another concurrent development.

As is often said in marketing, the company does not exist in a vacuum; the market determines. So too the evolution of business and government does not occur in a vacuum, either intellectual or economic. Both elements are significant to us because dominant social forces develop from these intellectual and economic demands or, conversely, from their satisfaction. These social forces come into play in shaping, directing, and altering society, business, and government. These forces have always been in motion even if not so clearly labelled or perceived. They have been the undercurrents, or in some instances, rivers, that have resulted in determining the nature and conduct of society and its institutions. For in the ultimate analysis business and government are social institutions. What this means is that there is a third force that must be appreciated to understand fully this evolutionary process. The third force also contains a number of elements that range from the selfish motivations of the single individual who espouses only his private cause to those of the most sophisticated altruist and his advocacy for universal economic and spiritual liberation of all of mankind. What comes out of this is the public force that eventually translates itself into actions that directly or indirectly control the efforts, authorities, relationships, and responsibilities of business and government and even those social forces themselves.

THE PUBLIC INTEREST

The public interest can be seen as both a driving and limiting force behind the social institutions of business and government. The importance of this cannot be overstated because from it stems our understanding of the role of business and government in society and the evolved relationship among the three (a perspective first articulated in my *Business, Government and the Public Interest,* American Management Association, 1976).

As a conscious entity, discretely identified and with a clear advocacy of its own, the public interest evolved after business and government. It is an element of only comparatively recent isolation, although it has made the most progress in the shortest period of time. As in most evolutionary systems, as the systems matures and develops means for expression and resolution, later entries have the benefits of older elements and, therefore, in many ways they start with an advancement that the others had to labor long to achieve. The public interest groups have in fact achieved far greater recognition and effect by and on business and government than other social forces in as short a time.

Looking back over the comparatively recent history of U.S. business shows us clearly that in our recent past business was a dominant element in the entire social construct. Through business we attained our posture of national and international prominence. Through business we achieved an unrivaled standard of technological development and living. We looked to business for leadership and we found it. We looked to business for prosperity and progress and we found it. We looked to business for international development and we found it. At the same time we looked to government for a system in which certain securities could be attained and preserved—the need for consolidated action as a nation; the establishment of the relationship between states and the central government, between people and each other, and people and their government; the need for money, banking, stability, protection, and economic infrastructure. All this and more we sought and found. From the comparative government and economic chaos of the founding settlements in Virginia and Plymouth, through the initial but uncoordinated efforts at stabilization throughout the colonies to the Constitution and the attainment of total U.S. consolidation ran the unifying theme of attaining economic and political security for the purpose of public safety and satisfaction.

As these purposes were achieved, however, a relationship between business and government resulted that clearly reflected a certain mutuality of interest and interdependency. Neither could go too far without the other. As time and circumstances progressed, however, and as the public began to feel adversely effected—that is, as the satisfaction of the public interest was not achieved and in some instances was subversed and abused by both business and government-

—this relationship began to change. While it is not my purpose to write a lengthy history of abuses either by government or by business, it is important to our understanding of the present regulatory environment and the reason for public activists' condemnation of business, and some of the further restrictions they have sought and the government seems to favor, to examine at least one example in more detail as it exemplifies the principle.

THE FIRST FEDERAL BUSINESS CONTROL

On July 4, 1828, the last surviving signer of the Declaration of Independence, Charles Carrol, put a spade into the ground, symbolic, or otherwise, to mark the beginning of the first passenger railway in the United States—the Baltimore and Ohio Railroad. This marked the true start of railroads in this country, although there had been interest as early as 1813 which for many reasons had not been acted upon. It was an historic moment, one of those many transitions that had one objective which it obtained but which also has an unplanned result. For while this event initiated railroads in the United States, with all of their subsequent importance in trade, commerce, opening of the states, and transcontinental trade, it also marked the beginning of a business operation that was to lead to the creation of the first Federal Commission charged with the control of business in the "public interest." With government support (an irony unto itself), the railroad developed, prospered and acquired—acquired land, money, resources, and power. By the 1840s railroads were increasing the number of road miles; the 1850s was a period of vigorous expansion. By 1860 railroads where the backbone of transportation in the North, central regions, and part of the South. As if these accomplishments were not enough, the railroads were clearly instrumental in opening the great western states and finally in connecting the east and west coasts. Much, if not all of this, was supported by federal grants in the form of direct monetary subsidies and rights of way and large tracts of land.

So far as all of this went towards the development of much needed transportation and the interconnection of remote rural with coastal or central urban portions of the states and territories, with the inevitable growth and economic prosperity that accompanied it, so good. However, by the late 1880s the railroads had become too important, too dominating, and too powerful. That they were able to control the markets they were intened to serve soon became apparent. At least that was the perception of many, a perception that resulted in the control of their activity by several states. Between the years 1869 and 1874 several laws were enacted on a state-by-state basis to regulate the railroads. This involved the historically famous series of Granger Laws. Initially the Supreme Court upheld these decisions, which involved the railroads and other business activities because, as the court said, these businesses, while private, did have important effects on the general public and the public interest. In 1877 it reversed its stand, stating that only Congress could control interstate commerce. Although the court judged that there was justification in the control of interstate commerce, it was pointing out that such control had to come not from the states but from the Congress. In striking down the decisions of the state courts and establishing the principle of congressional or federal control, it marked the beginning of an era, whose full time was yet to come. For the moment, however, it did lead to the creation of the first federal regulatory body the Interstate Commerce Commission (ICC). This Commission, despite its initial difficulty in actually implementing control over the railroads, nevertheless represented a landmark in U.S. history. It established the precedent that business regulation is not only justified but essential in certain instances. It also established the legal foundation by which the Federal Government could effectively control and regulate business that involved interstate commerce when this was considered to be in the "public interest." As we shall see, this premise has gone much further in recent years. Now the Congress feels it in order not only to regulate interstate commerce but, in certain instances where the public health and welfare are concerned, intrastate commerce.

WHERE DOES THIS TAKE US?

The example cited is a classical one. It is one not only of abuse of private power and ultimate justification for regulation, but one of pattern and, from many viewpoints, repetion. Later years saw the emergence of a number of other commissions, statutes, rules, and regulations all of which move from the same point—protection of the public—until we reach the present position of virtually omnipresent federal intervention and control of business. Allowing that much of this in its earliest stages of development and enactment may have been necessary, even desirable, serious questions as to the present need for new legislation and regulation have to be raised. In subsequent chapters some of these questions are posed, especially as we examine the negative effects on cost, products, productivity, innovation, international trade, and economic welfare and growth. All of this does not deny, however, that there is a public benefit, social-welfare aspect that has to be considered in public and private decisions. The ledger is not all one-sided. What has to be sought, however, is some balance. Ultimately the public must be served. Business regulation is only one of many techniques to achieve public well-being that is available to the government and that can rightfully be examined within this broader concern of public benefit.

It is, however, too often an area of relatively easy control because over the years there has been a tremendous erosion of public confidence in business and its activities. No discussion of business, society, and government could even pretend at responsible treatment without recognizing the existence of this phenomena. At one time business was held in the highest regard; of late it has plunged from the zenith of public opinion and confidence to its nadir. Should any in the business community doubt this, they have but to look to any number of independent surveys and analyses, one of the most recent and important of which was the 1976 Study of American Opinion by the marketing department of the *U.S. News and World Report,* as summarized in two of their articles "Why Business Has a Black Eye" and "Americans Speak Out on Inflation...Politicians...Bureaucracy" (September 6 and 13, 1976, issues of *U.S. News and World Report).* What interests us here is that business got low marks on controlling pollution, helping solve social problems, conservation of natural resources, honesty in advertising and product claims, concern for the consumer, and business ethics. None of these criticisms can leave the marketing manager with much enthusiasm. However, the public was not in favor of additional general business regulation, but did favor additional government regulation of business for product safety and to provide safe working conditions.

One of the conclusions reached by W. E. Robertson, Assistant to the President and Director of Marketing, *U.S. News and World Report* in his interpretative statement is very revealing and very important:

The public seems to be saying to business: We believe in free enterprise. Your profits are not too high. We respect your many accomplishments. BUT we are not sure how much we can trust you, and how much you really care about us. If we were to sum up the mood of America, business certainly has its problems—but the outlook is not all that bad. The major problems of business are problems that business can control, and problems that business can correct.

While there are those who might not agree with these conclusions, they are encouraging and by and large correct. The main question is that of business' responsiveness to the challenge and its willingness to "correct." Many of the practical recommendations made in this book start from the premise reflected in the conclusions reached by the *U.S. News and World Report* study. While the problems are many, more even than those identified in the survey, they are not ipso facto insoluable. First, we must be made aware, and second, we must make efforts to correct. This is not to imply that the problems are all one sided—clearly this is not so.

What starts out as a regulation in the public interest may and often does become an excess. The cumulative effect of regulations, while perhaps not completely obliterating the free enterprise system, certainly has cast more than a shadow over it. Has government gone too far in protecting the public interest? Have these excesses been disadvantageous to the public? As members of the business community and as members of society we can and should raise these questions. We are told that the cost of federal regulation is approximately $1800 to $2000 per year per family in the United States, which translates, for instance, into an additional cost of $2.00 per electric coffee percolater. This is a compelling reason to question wisdom, need, and justification.

The issue for the moment is not who is right or who is wrong; it is exploration of the issues. We must be fully aware of all sides of the question. No longer are there only two sides, that of business and that of government, there is the rightful, legitimate, and welcome view of the public. Ultimately only people and organizations that serve the public interest survive and prosper.

WHERE ARE WE TODAY?

The shift in perception from business and government to business, government, and the public interest is permanent. However this implies nothing more than the logical extension of the evolution we have been describing. It is another opportunity. To be taken as such, however, implies responsible knowledgeable action on all sides, a matter we will address in several instances in this book. To understand better where we are and where we are going we must still examine some of the key distinctions between past events and emphasis on present ones.

We have seen that the ICC, for example, was created to rectify a perceived public abuse by the railroads. Similarly, other Commissions and Agencies were created, and enabling legislation enacted to control, rectify, or prevent abuses in other areas of perceived public need. The focus in the past was on the general need to control corporate size and conduct, particularly as it related to the activities of companies between each other and in the market place (antitrust, unfair trade practices, etc.); in more recent years there has been a broadening of legislation and business regulation to encompass other aspects of business conduct. While some of these are of only indirect impact on the marketing manager, they are important for at least two reasons: They have indirect effects on the marketing manager (added costs, increased complexity in doing business, additional restraints); and they exemplify the broader social concerns and influences of the public interest groups as they are brought to bear on the business activity, and they point to the logic of future restraints.

While not completely accurate, we can distinguish regulatory focus and effect into two main periods—the pre-1970 and the post-1970 period.

THE PRE-1970 PERIOD

In the pre-1970 period of social concern and regulatory effort there was a preoccupation with general business conduct, competitive activity, control of monopoly and monolistic practices, including pricing and unfair trade practices and restraint of trade. Other legislation most familiar to marketing managers have been issues of social concern, such as child labor, work practices, misbranding, and mislabeling. From a legal viewpoint, the other important aspect was liability. Throughout this period the corporation was the object of such legislation as well as the subject of liability and penalty for proven violation.

THE POST-1970 PERIOD

In the post-1970 period a whole new host of concerns and restraints were introduced. The focus of legislation and regulation has now shifted from the general conduct of the corporation to the product, the process, and work place. Legislation aimed at control of processes, product and work place—for example, the Occuaptional Safety and Health Act of 1970 (OSHA), the Federal Water Pollution Control Act (FWPCA), the Clean Air Act (CAA)—aimed at processes, product, add work place, was enacted during this period. In addition, products and market-oriented legislation such as the Consumer Product Safety Act (CPSA) and several socially oriented laws such as the Equal Employment Opportunity Act (EEOA) and the Employee Retirement Income Security Act (ERISA) were enacted. This legislation, and in some cases the commissions or agencies created to administer them, such as the Environmental Protection Agency (EPA), the Occupational Safety and Healthy Administration (OSHA), and Equal Employment Opportunity Commission (EEOC), had a new direction and a new tenet. Society had a right to effect controls and sanctions on business not only in the marketplace but also in the business place.

There is now a clear distinction between the objectives of the past and those of the present—a distinction some of the legislators themselves have recognized and elaborated upon—although the distinction is by theme rather than by time: regulation of business conduct versus legislation and regulation with a social or safety objective. We will return to this point later because although many persons agree that there may be some alterations in government's efforts towards further controls of overall business practices, that would be legislation and regulation of the first type, there is little expectation of relief in the latter area. In fact the probability is for more legislation and regulation. This is particularly the case as government moves in the direction of greater assumption of responsibility for "protection" of the individual and as society at large looks to its delegation of personal responsibility to government. This is another concern and quite possibly another example of the social evolutionary process. From our vantage as marketing managers, however, the points are: Government is taking on an ever-increasing role in the overall conduct of business; such controls now extend beyond practices in the market place to product, process, and work place; and there is little anticipation of alteration in both direction and rate of federal activity in this socially oriented legislation.

Another difference is that the focus and object of pre-1970 legislation was the corporation. The liability was corporate. In the post-1970 period the focus and the liability has changed to the individual. Most of the new statutes involve personal liability—that is, liability attaching to the corporate officer and not only to the corporation. As if this were not enough, many of the statutes also impose penalties that are not only civil but criminal. Therefore, the corporate officer faces the potential of both personal civil and criminal liability for knowing or willful violations of these statutes.

Added to this alteration of focus and intention, we must consider the vast growth of government agencies and commissions and overall employment. What this means from a practical viewpoint is that business faces a significant force with vast resources aimed specifically at its control and regulation. This change is also reflected in another difference between the pre- and post-1970 period. In the past legislation and regulation was directed at specific industries with essentially an agency or commission created for enforcement of it, vis-à-vis a specific industry or sector.

The ICC, for example, was created to control railroads and later was expanded to encompass trucking. The Civil Aeronautical Board (CAB) was created to control aviation, and the Food and Drug Administration (FDA) to regulate the pharmaceutical industry. The new approach is generic rather than industry-oriented, and hence one agency or department cuts across business lines to reach specific activities—for instance, the Occupational Safety and Health Administration to administrate the Occupational Safety and Health Act (OSHA) or the Environmental Protection Agency to administer several environmentally oriented acts. This development has not been incidental or one that is necessarily derived from the basic thrust of the legislation. It is intentional in that there are cross-cutting issues to resolve in these areas. Moreover, it attempts to resolve one of the earlier and most severe criticisms of past regulatory agencies—namely, that they became the pawns of the industries they were intended to regulate.

When the relationship of the agency was essentially one-to-one with an industry, there was a certain logic to this argument. Indeed, one could assert that after a time they needed each other. However, in the area of safety and health or the socially oriented legislation and regulation, one agency deals with issues, not industries, and there is little likelihood and less motivation for any expressed or implied compact between any agency and any industry. Without attempting to side with people who wish to argue the previous relationships one way or the other, the compelling logic of the present situation is that is is vastly different from that of the past.

WHERE DOES THIS LEAVE US?

The objective in this chapter is not to be discouraging or pessimistic. Rather it has been an attempt to set out on the broadest scale some of the past, present, and future considerations the marketing manager must address. While many ironies have been pointed to with regard to business, government, and the public interest, clearly two of the most ironic are:

1. Marketing managers, who are both directly and indirectly affected by all of this, are often the least involved in their companies with many of the legislative and regulatory activities that influence their marketing activities. This is an issue that will be addressed at some length throughout the book. Many suggestions for changing this situation are made. I hope the reasons will be clear and compelling to both the marketing manager and the executive general management.

2. Business is a social institution. It is in fact one of the most important and necessary of all the social institutions. This is an argument more for the public and the government than for the businessman (at least most businessmen seem to recognize this). How to get the message of business need and business value as a social institution to the public is one of the many questions that are examined.

The control and regulation of business by government, no matter how motivated, is not an issue of academic concern. For any particular business it can well be one of survival. For government it can be one of economics and for society one of basic political and social effect.

Because our concern is clearly from the vantage point of the marketing manager and to place into some perspective what we have seen of government incursions into business conduct and practice we close this chapter with what is also a fitting introduction to the next chapter. This is a statement by Guy Vander Jagt, Congressman from Michigan, in which he deals with the question of government regulation and the more basic tenet of the need to preserve our free enterprise system—a system that is severely threatened by all we have discussed and that from subsequent discussion we will see is even more severely threatened. How we may cope with this and alter it in the public interest is the subject of much subsequent discussion.

PRESERVATION OF A FREE MARKET ECONOMY

This is where America stands today after nearly 50 years of the erosion of our free enterprise system: one out of every six Americans works for government; one out of every three Americans is dependent for his livelihood on a check from the government; one-third of the land is owned by government. We will pay more this year in interest on the national debt than it took to run the whole government, exclusive of defense, as recently as 1955.

This year you can take every penny that is paid in income tax by two-thirds of the American people—every penny of it—and it doesn't do anything but pay the interest of the national debt!

In 1930, government took 12 percent of the gross national product—the fruits of the labor of a free people. In 1930, government took 12 percent of our total production and left the people who produced it 88 percent. This year government will take 38 percent of our GNP and our President told us in his State of the Union message that unless trends are reversed government will take over half of our gross national product by 1985. And if we've been inching away from free enterprise over the last half century, we're galloping away from it this year in this Congress.

Those who control Congress, or at least those who control the caucus that controls Congress, really believe that government is wiser and more just than free enterprise and they sincerely believe that government should reallocate our wealth and redistribute our resources. They genuinely believe that America is great because of what government does for people and they, therefore, always want more government, greater federal intervention, and increased federal spending and regulation.

Those of us in the minority say that is nonsense. America is not great because of what government did for people but because of what government permitted a free people to do for themselves. And we, therefore, want less government and a reduction in federal spending and involvement in private enterprise. We still believe the consumer's best hope in the long run lies in competition.

We who believe in free enterprise believe that the mightiest force ever unleashed on the face of this earth—a force greater evan than the energy from the split atom—was the force that was released in 1776 when a free people were told: You may enjoy the fruits of your labor. You may enjoy and keep the rewards of your initiative and ability and your ambition and your work.

TWO

THE PRESENT

Regulatory
Environment

In Chapter 1 we mentioned that some statistics would be unavoidable. Many of those that are presented later focus on the more limited effects of particular legislation or regulation on a specific business or area. Table 2.1: Statistical Information—A Miscellanea, however, sets the stage for what follows, for here we take an overview of the economic and social dimensions of government and some perspectives as to how big an entity we are dealing with. Many people seem concerned with "big business' and make much of bigness alone. Fortunately, many of them have perception enough not to stop there, for as we shall see, the size of business, measured by the federal scale, becomes small by comparison. If size, budget, funding, employment, control, effect, or deficits are to be among the criteria for judging an activity, proponents of the "big is bad" philosophy had better not look too closely at the very big brother that is usually called in to right the wrong, redress the inequity, or exercise its other powers of control or limitation.

To anyone who has been even slightly involved with the government many of these facts and figures will come as no surprise. To those who have had only the remotest contact, the fact that government is vast is no revelation but exactly how large it is, may be. The degree and extent of its employment; budgets; and the numerical dimensions of agencies, departments, commissions, councils, laws, rules, and regulations is enough to make one stand in awe without even considering what all this means substantially. In the succeeding chapters we examine the agencies, laws, and regulations and their effects on marketing and market. What

TABLE 2.1   STATISTICAL INFORMATION—A MISCELLANEA

Government employment	1965	1974
Federal civilian	2,588,000	2,874,000
State, local	8,000,000	11,794,000

Government payroll	1965	1974
Federal civilian	$1.5 billion	$3.3 billion
State, local	$3.4 billion	$8.8 billion

Government employment (federal, state, and local) = approximately 20% of all employed (1974).

Federal spending recently has equaled approximately 25% of the gross U.S. GNP.

Federal expenditures for business regulations (fiscal years, in millions of dollars):

Agency	1974	1975	1976
Agriculture	$ 330	$ 376	$ 381
Health, Education and Welfare	145	173	189
Interior	59	74	79
Justice	270	345	383
Labor	231	343	397
Transportation	178	212	234
Treasury	246	306	320
Civil Aeronautics Board	89	85	85
Commodity Future Trading Commission	—	—	11
Consumer Product Safety Commission	19	43	37
Equal Employment Opportunity Commission	42	54	60
Federal Communications Commission	33	127	208
Federal Energy Administration	38	49	50
Federal Power Commission	27	37	36
Federal Trade Commission	32	41	45
International Trade Commission	7	9	10
Interstate Commerce Commission	38	47	50
National Labor Relations Board	55	63	70
National Transportation Safety Board	8	10	10
Nuclear Regulatory Commission	80	139	198
Securities and Exchange Commission	35	45	49
All Other	17	21	23
Total	$1,979	$2,599	$2,925

In 1974 approximately 25,000 federal regulations were issued.

TABLE 2.1 (*continued*)

Federal laws enacted:

1964	409	1967	249	1970	505	1973	248
1965	349	1968	391	1971	224	1974	285
1966	461	1969	190	1972	483	1975	209

By best count there are 5146 (as of 6/30/74) federal forms (no one seems to know for sure just how many there really are).

Completing federal forms requires approximately 130.5 million work hours per year.

While no one knows for sure, the estimates were that federal paper work cost about $40 billion a year to complete. While again no one yet knows with certainty, estimates now are increased to $60 billion (1976 government estimate).

Government regulation requirements added an average $320 per automobile due to 1968/1974 requirements thus amounting to a total of approximately $3 billion additional cost in 1974.

Regulatory costs to consumers are $60 to $300 per year per person.

Government regulations add approximately $2 to the average cost of each electric percolator sold (1976 estimate).

There are approximately 50 federal agencies that have 20 or more presidentially appointed commissioners or board members.

There are 1250 (as best one can tell as of 12/31/73) Federal advisory boards, committees, commissioners, and councils.

Federally mandated fringe benefits amount to approximately $35 billion (1972).

87 Federal agencies have been created within the past two years (1974, 1975).

Federal financial deficit was:

1970	$ 2.8 billion
1971	23.0 billion
1972	23.2 billion
1973	14.3 billion
1974	3.5 billion
1975	34.7 billion (estimate)

TABLE 2.1 (*continued*)

From 1906 through 1968, 24 federal consumer protection laws were enacted. However, between 1969 thru 1974 there were 65.

In 1930 government required 12% of GNP. In 1975 38%, and President Ford estimates it will require over 50% by 1985.

Congressional activity for 1973, 1974, 1975:

	1973	1974	1975
Bills signed by the president	247	281	205
Bills vetoed by the president	10	17	17
Vetoes overridden	1	4	4
Public bills and resolutions introduced	17,528	8,691	17,015

we want to do now is to provide a broad overview of government, social concern, legislation, and regulation so that what is subsequently described in more limited terms will have the benefit of perspective and context. As we consider specific aspects of legislative and regulatory effects or even specific rules we must recognize that they are part of a larger pattern of government action and that this in turn fits into a broader pattern of social reaction to public perceptions. Only by having this foundation can we fully appreciate not only the whys of the present situation but also how we got there and gain the ability to make predictions of where we will go in the future. We also discuss the effects on business overall and marketing in particular. Our position is to some extent a relatively narrow interpretation; and because we are businessmen, an inherent bias in our position will occasionally show despite our efforts at impartiality. We tend to look at only the effects on the business side of the equation and not, as we point out later in many cases, to the benefit side in any depth or detail. This should not be misconstrued as an attempt to deny that benefits occur or that there can be beneficial and socially desirable results from some legislation and regulation. We must, however, leave these evaluations essentially to those who advance them; we must highlight the effects side, which is often negative or at least complex, insidious, and perhaps difficult to understand or even suspect.

In analyzing and describing effects, in most cases we draw no conclusions as to whether they actually are negative or positive, beneficial or detrimental. This may come as a disappointment to some readers, but our position is not that every effect of government is adverse. The determination of whether an effect is positive or negative is a judgment. Any particular action, visualized from the business viewpoint, might appear to be negative. The cost might be high and the ultimate price born by the consumer correspondingly undesirable. However, from the viewpoint of both the consumer and the government, it may be worthwhile in accomplishing some socially desired objective; measured against this criterion the action may be considered inexpensive.

What this all comes down to is that many of the ultimate judgments will have to be made by society and not by government or business. Part of the current social transformation clearly reflects this need and mood. However, both government and business are obliged to inform the public fully so that such social choices can be made in full light, with the full knowledge of direct and indirect effect, and with no illusions. As we examine these effects, learn to identify and quantify them, we must also learn how to communicate them to government and the public in new and more believable and less seemingly self-serving ways. We approach all of these aspects in the next chapters as we attempt to meet all of these objectives.

THE INTENDED AND THE UNINTENDED

We examine government, then, from the viewpoint of the intended and unintended effects of its actions on business. Many of the effects that we can and do identify are not necessarily intended. The basic premise of government in initiating and finally issuing any legislation or regulation is that of ultimate benefit to the public, or at least the largest possible segment of it that can be assisted or benefited. Sometimes there is a clear recognition that this may be costly or that it may have some other negative influences. Usually these are justified as the necessary consequences of actions that have as their intention a larger "good," or as being only temporary disruptions that will eventually be reabsorbed into the larger scheme of events. Taken from this vantage point, negative influences are only the price that has to be paid for advancement.

Without even attempting to argue the merits of this concept in any specific case, but assuming it to be true and valid, there is still the factor of the unintended negative or disruptive effect—the one that resulted but was not foreseen, not planned for, and does not have as its justification that it is only the price to be paid or is of such a transitory nature as to be only one of the ripples that occasionally bestir the calm waters, which ultimately regain equilibrium. More important might be the instances in which the unintended effects are undetected until later, and worse may be neither minor nor temporary. Such costly and permanent effects must be of paramount concern. Because they may be long term and require an expert knowledge of business economics, they are not readily identifiable by the public and government. These do fall within the realm of business and economic effects. Yet government and the public are responsible for the legislation or regulation, the effect, and, more fundamentally, the social judgment that has to be made as to whether costs, disruptions, or displacements are socially acceptable and desirable. Who can and should identify the indirect consequence of federal action that can lead to long-term structural alterations in markets or business actions? Who should bring them to the attention of government and public? The answers to these and similar questions are clear. This must be done by those best able to make the determinations. Is this not part of the social responsibility of business? We must learn what the effects are or can be, how to understand them, and how and where to communicate our concerns. While doing this, however, we must also conduct a viable and profitable business. This is an obligation to our employees and our shareholders, and in a very real sense it is a social obligation. To conduct our business effectively in these times of legislative and regulatory entanglement requires many modifications in organization, attitude, conduct, investment, and day-to-day judgment. The necessity of these changes brings us to the main theme of the book: how to market in a regulated environment. All of the topics covered ultimately relate to this objective.

We have many reasons to be looking at government. There are also many *ways* in which we can look at it because it plays many roles in relationship to business. Although government can be identified as a partner, a competitor, a customer, a financier, or even as a business entrepreneur itself (TVA, CON RAIL, etc.,), we must limit ourselves to examining the role of government as the controller and regulator of business.

EVOLUTIONARY ASPECTS OF LEGISLATIVE AND REGULATORY ACTIVITY

We did not arrive at our present position instantaneously. Given that the United States has historically held business in high regard and that in the not too distant past there was a close and vital working relationship between business and government, the contemporary situation, which often borders on an adversary relationship, may seem to be both startling and incredible. But it is true in most instances. The alteration in this relationship may seem to be more abrupt than our earlier comments on evolution might imply; to many the transition seems to have occurred more precepitiously than gradually. The growth of government size, employment, economic strength, authority, and power has accelerated and in part at least this acceleration has both paralleled and been caused by the expanded role of government in regulating business. Somewhat along the lines of a simultaneous cause and effect, as the power base increases to exercise power, the structure takes on a life and substance of its own and continues to feed on itself and to feel internal pressure to maintain its expansion and therefore tends to extend its own size and authority (the growth of the bureacracy). In doing this there are concurrent changes: size and rate. In many respects this is completely consistent with other social and cultural alterations and the total behavior experience in all disciplines—the rapid rate of innovation, the explosion of publications, the burgeoning of communications: Mankind from a crawl, to a walk, to a full gallop.

Accurate as these observations may be, however, we must guard against taking them to a too rapid conclusion. To assess contemporary social structural relationships fully and therefore to be in a better position to predict the future, we must appreciate that in reality the foundations for all of this control were formally laid down in the earliest U.S. history. At least as they obtained in the United States, these foundations date back to the Articles of Confederation and the Constitution. That one of the objectives of our founding fathers was to escape both religious and economic and business oppression is ironic. Moreover, our Revolutionary War was also one of fundamental economic and business rights (British Colonialism versus domestic merchantilism and subsequent industrialism). Recognizing that the intention of the Constitution was to provide social and class equalities as well as to attend to questions of business freedom, even if only indirectly, it nevertheless did establish the basic rights of government in the control of business (interstate commerces, money supply, etc.). So basic are these to the earlier concepts of business government relationships that legal historians have indicated that business was the prime mover behind the adoption of the Constitution and constitutional government and away from the prior Articles of Confederation which still allowed state separatism and the business effects inherent in that system. For better or worse, business interests then supported federal centralization and broad economic and regulatory powers. That, as needed, they may have far exceeded original expectations is now at issue. This approach involved a close working relationship and mutual respect. Somehow these have been lost.

How we moved away from such clear perceptions of interrelationships is a subject of considerable interest and importance. Before we examine it, however, we must pause to think about the corporation although many people consider it an item that is essentially form and formality. The question involves the individual's right to form corporations and the utilization of the corporate form of operation, both legally and organizationally. Because there are major distinctions between the legal and organizational aspects of the corporation and because both are well known, we do not propose to address either. Rather, we briefly discuss the origin of the corporation in America, the relationship between "doing business" and the Constitution, and the essential question of relationships.

That these issues are important, no one will deny. That they derive essentially from the transition from small to big business and that this in turn derives from the ability to form corporations is perhaps not so clear. We have previously reflected on the fact that as the business enterprise enlarges, its actions can result in social and economic effects that are at least equivalent to its "business" effects if not disproportionate to them. The individual entrepreneur individually, or even most entrepreneurs collectively, could not have this influence or effect. That business was able to exert such influence was derivative of its ability to form aggregate organizations whose size and economic viability put them into this position. This was the consequence of the ability to form corporations, and hence the legal right to establish corporations is one of central interest.

Thus, the social importance of business was accidental and incidental to its original purpose. The precise point of transition is unknown—that is, the point at which employment, monetary effects, investment effects, and vestments are such that they cause effects on the extrinsic socially necessary infrastructures, which are separate from the primary business purpose of the enterprise. Consequences change from those solely affecting the corporation to those affecting the community and, ultimately, the state. This was true when we were dealing solely with large national corporations; it is even more evident now that we are confronted with international and multinational corporations.

However, in expressing all of these concerns, we must be extremely careful, for there is nothing intrinsically sinister, undesirable, or necessarily harmful about any of this; it too is an evolutionary phenomenon. It is also a mechanism of social accommodation to allow for the accomplishment of social needs, ranging from the most basic of sustenance to the most ethereal of self-actualization. That it requires careful and reasoned judgments in all actions taken by all sides because of the very effects and events that they put into motion is, of course, our fundamental contention.

This right originally was the closely restricted privilege of the government (in whatever form prevailed). Business charters were bestowed upon only the chosen few—and few they were. Only in the early 1800s was the authority for private incorporation in the United States established by the government via appropriate legislation. That this was bitterly contested was not unexpected. The fact remains, however, that such legislation was enacted, and since then we have had private corporations. What it led to was perhaps one of those unexpected developments that we mentioned before. The effect was the growth of large business entities that intentinally or not have the economic and social impacts we have described. With typical irony, another result was the alteration in the business, government, and public relationships and interactions that are our basic concern now.

The fact that private individuals on their own initiative could establish corporations provided a new opportunity for the creation of "big" business. Combined with the technical, social, and economic events of the times, which include the industrial revolution, we have a set of circumstances that catalyzed the momentous growth of the corporate form and the corporation. Relating this back to our consideration of the Constitution at this time is important, for one of the contentions (which was contested) was that the corporation would be considered as a person for purposes of establishment of rights under the Constitution. Early decisions established that it was for aspects such as guarantee of due process. This elevated the corporation to the status of the person and gave it some of the protections and rights of the Constitution. That this is not academic becomes apparent when we realize that questions in this area still exist and that, for instance, only in late 1976 did a court decision establish that for purpose of constitutional protection over double jeopardy the corporation is considered to be a person. It is also still an issue of legal and practical consequence because most previous statutes did not go beyond the corporation for purposes of penalties and liability and therefore they are effective only against the corporation and not individuals within those corporations. We will see that this has changed radically.

What happened to alter this harmonious relationship? Everything was not completely in accord, and there were significant questions of responsibilities and relationships. However, no one clearly foresaw the full implications, so when corporations and their effects grew so did public and government reactions. We will not discuss the abuses that led to early government intervention—rates, routes, tariffs, monopolies, labor, and so on. We admit that these occurred, but even more important the indirect and unintended effects remain. Some of them may be negative, but all must be taken into consideration.

Being a dynamic body, society responded to this perceived need and reacted to business growth/effect through the establishment of limitations. Although the corporation could not be dismantled its activities could be restricted or controlled. The limitations were aimed at controlling the effect—direct and indirect, intentional and unintentional—of the corporation on the market and, quite logically, the individual and society. To be effective the route to limitation and restriction was the only one that could collectively be followed at that time—namely, through the medium of the government. For a relatively long time this was the approach. The public, through the government, expressed its concerns and reactions to business and business practices through sanctions and controls that were established and enforced by government. To a minor degree they also imposed direct sanctions as they exercised their personal options in the marketplace.

The last is important, for as the public became disenfranchised with the government—as it did—the consumer shifted to a three-fronted attack on the problem. He or she continued to utilize the vehicle of the government, but added to this greater collective assertion of purchasing power—or more to the point, the withholding thereof—while also pressuring for alteration in the conduct and the form of the government itself. Most recently consumers advocate more quintessential alterations in the structure of business and the body politic. These, which entail such fundamental changes in our society, economics, and political forms, are far beyond our charter. This does not mean that they are far beyond our concern. Quite the contrary, they are not only provocative statements, not only rhetoric; they are the harbingers of social reform.

To condense these events quickly, we can say that business and the corporation grew and flourished when it was deemed suitable to the public purpose. Limitations were imposed when it was deemed to be abusive. When even these limitations were deemed insufficient, and when those who are responsible for imposing them are themselves suspect, even more fundamental structural alterations have been proposed and effected. This, in the barest outline, is not only the retrospective but the prospective.

OTHER CONCURRENT EVENTS

During these transitions there were, of course, other alterations. Once mechanisms—such as restraint of trade, control of monopolies and unfair trade practices as time and circumstances permitted—were in place to control market and personal purchasing abuses attention was diverted to other areas such as labor, the environment, safety and health, and most recently social egalitarianism both in the community at large and in the business place.

To effect these changes legalities had to be provided; they took the form of the maze of statutes and regulations that comprise the majority of what we are about to address. Behind them are the reasons and the force of public opinion action and reaction, which point us in the direction of future events and validate the probability of their occurrence. As we examine them in depth later we will see that the result has been the creation of individual civil and criminal liability within the corporation, the ability for citizens to petition government action under specific statutes and to file suit against it and the company. This has resulted in one of the important phenomena that we will allude to—namely, the increasing power of the courts as a determinant in legislative intent and in public policy. This too may be one of the hidden effects. As we move into an era of litigation, we may well have moved into an era where by default we have allowed of the establishment of naitonal goals, priorities, and policy not by the Congress but by the courts. We may well talk about the separation of powers, but what is to be said or done about the separation of effects?

Many of these changes, of course, are the result of satisfying the so-called public interest. This appellation has come to be deprecated in some quarters, but we should not really encourage or allow this. While there may be some misperceptions and disagreements as to what constitutes the actual best for the public—and by extension the public interest—there can be no denial that this is a valid concern that we all share. Our admonition is justification, rational action, and ultimate benefit. We caution against the ad hominum and advocate the substantive. Here again is a message that must be carried forward by industry, and industry also must learn to communicate in positive terms.

Public interest as perceived by one individual or group does not in fact represent the public interest; often it might better be described as a special interest. Unfortunately, there are all too many of these, some of which do in reality correspond with the public interest and some of which, alas, do not. We accept that there are many and varied interests, and no one would deny that there must be a forum for their rightful expression. The problem then comes in rating them all equally, assigning equal priority, allowing equal reaction. It is more than a wheat and shaft argument, for too many are not a one-time, one-effect situation. The longer-term as well as unintended factors must be recognized. In our extremely complex and yet closely interrelated societal and economic structure, there is bound to be some reaction in some sector to an action in what is seemingly some remote or unrelated area. This, of course, is the same problem that we were alluding to before when assessing other government effects, whether they be self-initiated or the consequence of ''public-interest'' activities.

THE EFFECTS OF THE MATERIALS AND ENERGY CRISES

As if all of this were not enough, we must give attention to other elements in the construct of the present and future mentality of the public. Historically, concerns over business and government were made in the absence of concerns over materials, resources, energy. Everyone assumed that we had absolute ability for infinite growth, progress, and wealth. Coupled with an explicit expectation for science and technology to overcome any temporary obstacles this attitude became a ''faith.'' This faith has long since been undermined, both implicitly and explicitly. Furthermore, our ability to cope with these obstacles individually or collectively has suffered, as has our innate confidence in national supremacy and lack of international independency. We have now shifted to at least a tacit acknowledgement of our international interdependency as well as our international vulnerability. Although we need not dwell on these, we must realize that they have made their mark on the public psyche and will be an indelible element in the perspectives and approaches of future generations.

There are clear signals for those of us who will read them. As responsible members of business, we must heed and respond to them and—better yet——anticipate and resume our earlier position of public responsibility and leadership. Marketing as an instrument that reaches out of the corporation is in the unique position to accomplish this. Despite what some may think of advertising and promotion, public relations, and the media, and with all due respect to all of them, the product is what ultimately makes or breaks the company. Having the ability to create products that are responsive to existing perceived needs will be the cornerstone of both marketing success and the reassertion of responsible business leadership. Obviously, there is more to the problem than that but this is not the place in which to deal with all of the broader issues of socially responsible corporate conduct or the totality of the present and future position of the corporation in society. It is enough for our purposes here to show that marketing can perform an absolutely essential function in these accomplishments.

THE LEGISLATIVE AND REGULATORY PERSPECTIVE

Having considered all of these elements, we now turn our attention to the nature of the regulated environment. Obviously, by a regulated environment we refer to the prevailing extent, nature, and form of federal restriction. These combine to create many effects, including serious limitations that apply not only to marketing but to the full roster of business activities. Later we examine many of these, but again our principal attention is devoted to those whose primary thrust and effect is on marketing. During the evolutionary process we have experienced the transition was from essentially economic controls—trade, competition, and market—to essentially social controls—safety, health, environment, civil rights, and equity. Coupled with these have been changes in liability and intent on the part of the Congress and the courts. To better equip ourselves to survive in this new environment we must understand these changes and the new laws, regulations, and agencies of government that create and sustain, implement, and enforce them. To do so involves in-depth review of at least the majority of the most significant new laws and agencies that have been created to accomplish this. We must also examine the new legal framework in which all of this operates and the alternatives and options that are open to us. Arbitrary as it is, we focus on the pre-1970 period as a point of departure in terms of some substantial alterations in statutory provision and congressional intent and court involvement. Although we deal mainly with post-1970 activity, we must realize that the main body of previous law, regulation, and agency involvement in the more traditional concept of government involvement (e.g., anti-trust or labor relations) is as active as ever. There has not been a replacement of concern so much as an addition. Eventually, as we face new challenges, even those that seem today to be so new and demanding may become as institutionalized as are the older economically oriented restrictions. However, we must guard against complacency and an attitude of resignation. We can change that which is not truly in the public interest. Alterations are possible. It is up to us.

THE FREE ENTERPRISE SYSTEM

We as a nation still retain our commitment to, and endorsement of a free market system. However, it has suffered many encroachments and limitations. In fact there are those who feel that the free enterprise system is already dead, that it is a verbal mirage. To some measure this is true, if to define *free enterprise* we harken back to prior days of strictly constructed laissez faire—the "the business of business is business" attitude. This can no longer be so. However, this does not mean the opposite extreme—that all business functions, activities, and authorities must be controlled, regulated, and directed by some external agency, which in this case would be the government. Rather, it means that laissez faire, like other concepts and social institutions is undergoing its evolution. That what many of us knew as free enterprise is no longer prevalent is undeniable. However, that all is gone or forsaken is as fallacious as the thought that some balance cannot be restored. In fact one of our greatest challenges is the preservation of the principal, however modified, of free enterprise while still satsifying the legitimate demands of social concern and social responsibility.

LEGISLATION, RULE, AND REGULATION

Having established some framework, supported upon our early foundations of historical exploration we can turn attention meaningfully to the mechanisms of legislation and regulation. After this, in Chapter 3, we will look at government, and how it uses these important laws and regulations as the device by which to accomplish the social purposes we have been discussing. To do this the first aspect to clarify is the distinction between legislation and regulation.

Legislation. Legislation represents those laws that are enacted by the Congress that impose specific requirements or establish the authority by which designated agencies can, by regulation, accomplish this. The orientation may vary, but the basic procedures and intentions are the same. The legislation then, after proposal and enactment, becomes the "law of the land" and is the basis for the agency to issue its regulations and the courts to render their decisions. Because understanding this procedure is so necessary "How a Bill Becomes a Law," which describes the legislative process, is provided (Table 2.2). This is particularly important because of its description of the procedure and because it provides many insights into opportunities for business to become involved in the legislative process procedurally as well as conceptually and ideolgically.

Rule and Regulation. These terms which are often conjoined as they are in this book by virtue of convention, are in actuality synonymous. What they represent, after being duly promulgated by an agency, are the procedures or standards that regulate operation and conduct of the business. Although they are not laws in the

TABLE 2.2   HOW A BILL BECOMES LAW

The following explanation of how a bill becomes law incorporates the changes made in the legislative process by the Legislative Reorganization Act of 1970. The act, which cleared Congress Oct. 8, 1970, was designed to improve the operations of Congress in committee and on the floor, to provide Congress with better means of evaluating the federal budget and with improved resources for research and information.

INTRODUCTION OF BILLS

A House member (including the resident commissioner of Puerto Rico and nonvoting delegates of the District of Columbia, Guam and the Virgin Islands) may introduce any one of several types of bills and resolutions by handing it to the clerk of the House or placing it in a box called the hopper. A senator first gains recognition of the presiding officer to announce the introduction of a bill. If objection is offered by any senator the introduction of the bill is postponed until the following day.

As the next step in either the House or Senate, the bill is numbered, referred to the appropriate committee, labeled with the sponsor's name, and sent to the Government Printing Office so that copies can be made for subsequent study and action. Senate bills may be jointly sponsored and carry several senators' names. In the House, until 1967, each bill carried the name of one sponsor only; however, the House April 25, 1967, voted to allow cosponsorship of bills, setting a limit of 25 cosponsors on any one bill. A bill written in the Executive Branch and proposed as an administration measure usually is introduced by the chairman of the congressional committee which has jurisdiction.

Bills—Prefixed with "HR" in the House, "S" in the Senate, followed by a number. Used as the form for most legislation, whether general or special, public or private.

Joint Resolutions—Designated H J Res or S J Res. Subject to the same procedure as bills, with the exception of a joint resolution proposing an amendment to the Constitution. The latter must be approved by two-thirds of both houses and is thereupon sent directly to the administrator of general services for submission to the states for ratification rather than being presented to the President for his approval.

Concurrent Resolutions—Designated H Con. Res. or S Con. Res. Used for matters affecting the operations of both houses. These resolutions do not become law.

Resolutions—Designated H Res or S Res. Used for a matter concerning the operation of either house alone and adopted only by the chamber in which it originates.

COMMITTEE ACTION

A bill is referred to the appropriate committee by a House parliamentarian on the speaker's order, or by the Senate president. Sponsors may indicate their preferences for referral, although custom and chamber rule generally govern. An exception is the referral

Source: Reprinted from *Congressional Quarterly Almanac 1976* by permission of Congressional Quarterly Service, Washington, D.C.

27

TABLE 2.2 *(continued)*

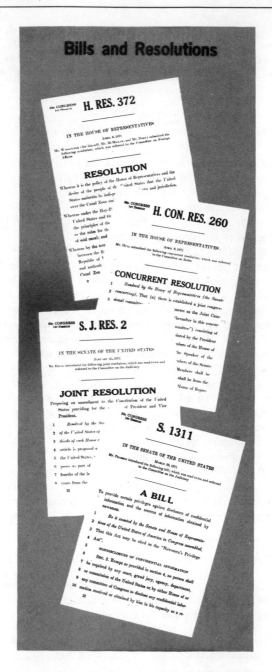

TABLE 2.2 *(continued)*

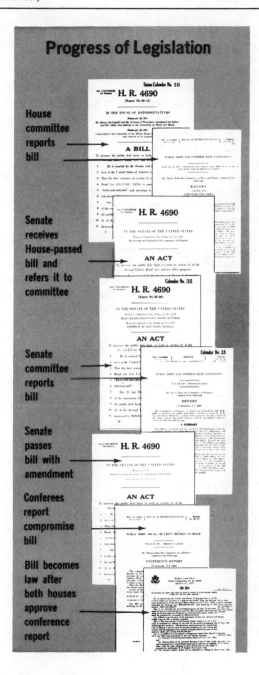

TABLE 2.2 *(continued)*

of private bills, which are sent to whatever group is designated by their sponsors. Bills are technically considered "read for the first time" when referred to House committees.

When a bill reaches a committee it is placed upon the group's calendar. At that time it comes under the sharpest congressional focus. Its chances for passage are quickly determined—and the great majority of bills fall by the legislative roadside. Failure of a committee to act on a bill is equivalent to killing it; the measure can be withdrawn from the group's purview only by a discharge petition signed by a majority of the House membership on House bills, or by adoption of a special resolution in the Senate. Discharge attempts rarely succeed.

The first committee action taken on a bill usually is a request for comment on it by interested agencies of the government. The committee chairman may assign the bill to a subcommittee for study and hearings, or it may be considered by the full committee. Hearings may be public, closed (executive session), or both. A subcommittee, after considering a bill, reports to the full committee its recommendations for action and any proposed amendments.

The full committee then votes on its recommendation to the House or Senate. This procedure is called "ordering a bill reported." Occasionally a committee may order a bill reported unfavorably; most of the time a report, submitted by the chairman of the committee to the House or Senate, calls for favorable action on the measure since the committee can effectively "kill" a bill by simply failing to take any action.

When a committee sends a bill to the chamber floor, it explains its reasons in a written statement, called a report, which accompanies the bill. Often committee members opposing a measure issue dissenting minority statements which are included in the report.

Usually, the committee proposes amendments to the bill. If they are substantial and the measure is complicated, the committee may order a "clean bill" introduced, which will embody the proposed amendments. The original bill then is put aside and the "clean bill," with a new number, is reported to the floor.

The chamber must approve, alter, or reject the committee amendments before the bill itself can be put to a vote.

FLOOR ACTION

After a bill is reported back to the house where is originated, it is placed on the calendar.

There are five legislative calendars in the House, issued in one cumulative calendar titled Calendars of the United States House of Representatives and History of Legislation. The House calendars are:

The Union Calendar
to which are referred bills raising revenues, general appropriation bills and any measures directly or indirectly appropriating money or property. It is the Calendar of the Committee of the Whole House on the State of the Union.

The House Calendar to which are referred all bills of a public character not raising revenue or appropriating money or property.

TABLE 2.2 (*continued*)

The Consent Calendar to which are referred bills of a noncontroversial nature that are passed without debate when the Consent Calendar is called on the first and third Mondays of each month.

The Private Calendar to which are referred bills for relief in the nature of claims against the United States or private immigration bills that are passed without debate when the Private Calendar is called the first and third Tuesdays of each month.

The Discharge Calendar to which are referred motions to discharge committees when the necessary signatures are signed to a discharge petition.

There is only one legislative calendar in the Senate and one "executive calendar" for treaties and nominations submitted to the Senate. When the Senate Calendar is called, each senator is limited to five minutes' debate on each bill.

Debate

A bill is brought to debate by varying procedures. If a routine measure, it may await the call of the calendar. If it is urgent or important, it can be taken up in the Senate either by unanimous consent or by a majority vote. The policy committee of the majority party in the Senate schedules the bills that it wants taken up for debate.

In the House, precedence is granted if a special rule is obtained from the Rules Committee. A request for a special rule is usually made by the chairman of the committee that favorably reported the bill, supported by the bill's sponsor and other committee members. The request, considered by the Rules Committee in the same fashion that other committees consider legislative measures, is in the form of a resolution providing for immediate consideration of the bill. The Rules Committee reports the resolution to the House where it is debated and voted upon in the same fashion as regular bills. If the Rules Committee should fail to report a rule requested by a committee, there are several ways to bring the bill to the House floor—under suspension of the rules, on Calendar Wednesday or by a discharge motion.

The resolutions providing special rules are important because they specify how long the bill may be debated and whether it may be amended from the floor. If floor amendments are banned, the bill is considered under a "closed rule," which permits only members of the committee that first reported the measure to the House to alter its language, subject to chamber acceptance.

When a bill is debated under an "open rule," amendments may be offered from the floor. Committee amendments are always taken up first, but may be changed, as may all amendments up to the second degree, i.e., an amendment to an amendment to an amendment is not in order.

Duration of debate in the House depends on whether the bill is under discussion by the House proper or before the House when it is sitting as the Committee of the Whole on the State of the Union. In the former, the amount of time for debate is determined either by special rule or is allocated with an hour for each member if the measure is under consideration without a rule. In the Committee of the Whole the amount of time agreed on

31

TABLE 2.2 *(continued)*

for general debate is equally divided between proponents and opponents. At the end of general discussion, the bill is read section by section for amendment. Debate on an amendment is limited to five minutes for each side.

Senate debate is usually unlimited. It can be halted only by unanimous consent by "cloture," which requires a three-fifths majority of the entire Senate except for proposed changes in the Senate's rules. The latter require a two-thirds vote.

The House sits as the Committee of the Whole on the State of the Union when it considers any tax measure or bill dealing with public appropriations. It can also resolve itself into the Committee of the Whole if a member moves to do so and the motion is carried. The speaker appoints a member to serve as the chairman. The rules of the House permit the Committee of the Whole to meet with any 100 members on the floor, and to amend and act on bills with a quorum of the 100, within the time limitations mentioned previously. When the Committee of the Whole has acted, it "rises," the speaker returns as the presiding officer of the House and the member appointed chairman of the Committee of the Whole reports the action of the committee and its recommendations (amendments adopted).

Votes

Voting on bills may occur repeatedly before they are finally approved or rejected. The House votes on the rule for the bill and on various amendments to the bill. Voting on amendments often is a more illuminating test of a bill's support than is the final tally. Sometimes members approve final passage of bills after vigorously supporting amendments which, if adopted, would have scuttled the legislation.

The Senate has three different methods of voting: an untabulated voice vote, a standing vote (called a division) and a recorded roll call to which members answer "yea" or "nay" when their names are called. The House also employs voice and standing votes, but since January 1973 yeas and nays have been recorded by an electronic voting device, eliminating the need for time-consuming roll calls.

Another method of voting, used in the House only, is the teller vote. Traditionally, members filed up the center aisle past counters; only vote totals were announced. Since 1971, one-fifth of a quorum can demand that the votes of individual members be recorded, thereby forcing them to take a public position on amendments to key bills. Electronic voting now is commonly used for this purpose.

After amendments to a bill have been voted upon, a vote may be taken on a motion to recommit the bill to committee. If carried, this vote removes the bill from the chamber's calendar. If the motion is unsuccessful, the bill then is "read for the third time." An actual reading usually is dispensed with. Until 1965, an opponent of a bill could delay this move by objecting and asking for a full reading of an engrossed (certified in final form) copy of the bill. After the "third reading," the vote on final passage is taken.

The final vote may be followed by a motion to reconsider, and this motion itself may be followed by a move to lay the motion on the table. Usually, those voting for the bill's passage vote for the tabling motion, thus safeguarding the final passage action. With that,

TABLE 2.2 (*continued*)

HOW A BILL BECOMES LAW

This graphic shows the most typical way in which proposed legislation is enacted into law. There are more complicated, as well as simpler, routes, and most bills fall by the wayside and never become law. The process is illustrated with two hypothetical bills, House bill No. 1 (HR 1) and Senate bill No. 2 (S 2).

Each bill must be passed by both houses of Congress in identical form before it can become law. The path of HR 1 is traced by a solid line, that of S 2 by a broken line. However, in practice most legislation begins as similar proposals in both houses.

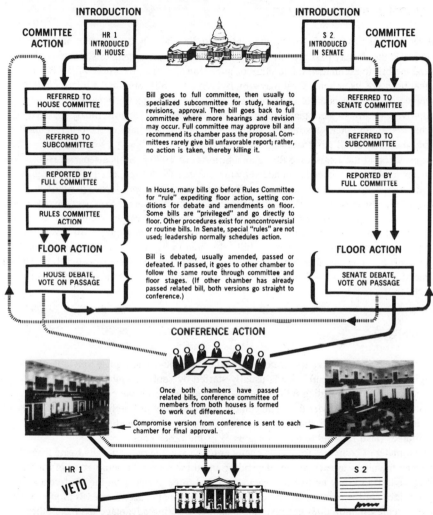

INTRODUCTION

COMMITTEE ACTION

HR 1 INTRODUCED IN HOUSE

INTRODUCTION

S 2 INTRODUCED IN SENATE

COMMITTEE ACTION

REFERRED TO HOUSE COMMITTEE

REFERRED TO SUBCOMMITTEE

REPORTED BY FULL COMMITTEE

RULES COMMITTEE ACTION

FLOOR ACTION

HOUSE DEBATE, VOTE ON PASSAGE

Bill goes to full committee, then usually to specialized subcommittee for study, hearings, revisions, approval. Then bill goes back to full committee where more hearings and revision may occur. Full committee may approve bill and recommend its chamber pass the proposal. Committees rarely give bill unfavorable report; rather, no action is taken, thereby killing it.

In House, many bills go before Rules Committee for "rule" expediting floor action, setting conditions for debate and amendments on floor. Some bills are "privileged" and go directly to floor. Other procedures exist for noncontroversial or routine bills. In Senate, special "rules" are not used; leadership normally schedules action.

Bill is debated, usually amended, passed or defeated. If passed, it goes to other chamber to follow the same route through committee and floor stages. (If other chamber has already passed related bill, both versions go straight to conference.)

REFERRED TO SENATE COMMITTEE

REFERRED TO SUBCOMMITTEE

REPORTED BY FULL COMMITTEE

FLOOR ACTION

SENATE DEBATE, VOTE ON PASSAGE

CONFERENCE ACTION

Once both chambers have passed related bills, conference committee of members from both houses is formed to work out differences.

Compromise version from conference is sent to each chamber for final approval.

HR 1
VETO

S 2

Compromise version approved by both houses is sent to President who can either sign it into law or veto it and return it to Congress. Congress may override veto by a two-thirds majority vote in both houses; bill then becomes law without President's signature.

TABLE 2.2 (*continued*)

the bill has been formally passed by the chamber. While a motion to reconsider a Senate vote is pending on a bill, the measure cannot be sent to the House.

ACTION IN SECOND HOUSE

After a bill is passed it is sent to the other chamber. This body may then take one of several steps. It may pass the bill as is—accepting the other chamber's language. It may send the bill to committee for scrutiny or alteration, or reject the entire bill, advising the other house of its actions. Or it may simply ignore the bill submitted while it continues work on its own version of the proposed legislation. Frequently, one chamber may approve a version of a bill that is greatly at variance with the version already passed by the other house, and then substitute its amendments for the language of the other, retaining only the latter's bill designation.

A provision of the Legislative Reorganization Act of 1970 permits a separate House vote on any nongermane amendment added by the Senate to a House-passed bill and requires a majority vote to retain the amendment. Previously the House was forced to act on the bill as a whole; the only way to defeat the nongermane amendment was to reject the entire bill.

Often the second chamber makes only minor changes. If these are readily agreed to by the other house, the bill then is routed to the White House for signing. However, if the opposite chamber basically alters the bill submitted to it, the measure usually is "sent to conference." The chamber that has possession of the "papers" (engrossed bill, engrossed amendments, messages of transmittal) requests a conference and the other chamber must agree to it.

Conference

A conference undertakes to harmonize conflicting House and Senate versions of a legislative bill. The conference is usually staffed by senior members (conferees), appointed by the presiding officers of the two houses, from the committees which managed the bills. Under this arrangement the conferees of one house have the duty of trying to maintain their chamber's position in the face of amending actions by the conferees (also referred to as "managers") of the other house.

The number of conferees from each chamber may vary, the range usually being from three to nine members in each group, depending upon the length or complexity of the bill involved. There may be five representatives and three senators on the conference committee, or the reverse. But a majority vote controls the action of each group so that a larger representation does not give one chamber a voting advantage over the other chamber's conferees.

Theoretically, conferees are not allowed to write new legislation in reconciling the two versions before them, but this curb sometimes is bypassed. Many bills have been put into acceptable compromise form only after new language was provided by the conferees. The 1970 Reorganization Act attempted to tighten restrictions on conferees by forbidding them

TABLE 2.2 (*continued*)

to introduce any language on a topic that neither chamber sent to conference or to modify any topic beyond the scope of the different House and Senate versions.

Frequently the ironing out of difficulties takes days or even weeks. Conferences on involved appropriation bills sometimes are particularly drawn out.

As a conference proceeds, conferees reconcile differences between the versions, but generally they grant concessions only insofar as they remain sure that the chamber they represent will accept the compromises. Occasionally, uncertainty over how either house will react, or the positive refusal of a chamber to back down on a disputed amendment, results in an impasse, and the bills die in conference even though each was approved by its sponsoring chamber.

Conferees sometimes go back to their respective chambers for further instructions, when they report certain portions in disagreement. Then the chamber concerned can either "recede and concur" in the amendment of the other house, or "insist on its amendment."

When the conferees have reached agreement, they prepare a conference report embodying their recommendations (compromises). The reports, in document form, must be submitted to each house.

The Legislative Reorganization Act of 1970 provides that Senate and House conferees must jointly prepare an explanatory statement for every conference report and that all conference reports and accompanying statements must be printed in both houses.

Previously conference reports were printed in the House with an explanatory statement prepared by the House conferees only.

The conference report must be approved by each house. Consequently, approval of the report is approval of the compromise bill. In the order of voting on conference reports, the chamber which asked for a conference yields to the other chamber the opportunity to vote first.

Final Steps

After a bill has been passed by both the House and Senate in identical form, all of the original papers are sent to the enrolling clerk of the chamber in which the bill originated. He then prepares an enrolled bill which is printed on parchment paper. When this bill has been certified as correct by the secretary of the Senate or the clerk of the House, depending on which chamber originated the bill, it is signed first (no matter whether it originated in the Senate or House) by the speaker of the House and then by the President of the Senate. It is next sent to the White House to await action.

If the President approves the bill he signs it, dates it and usually writes the word "approved" on the document. If he does not sign it within 10 days (Sundays excepted) and Congress is in session, the bill becomes law without his signature.

However, should Congress adjourn before the 10 days expire, and the President has failed to sign the measure, it does not become law. This procedure is called the pocket veto.

A President vetoes a bill by refusing to sign it and before the 10-day period expires, returning it to Congress with a message stating his reasons. The message is sent to the

TABLE 2.2 *(continued)*

chamber which originated the bill. If no action is taken there on the message, the bill dies. Congress, however, can attempt to override the President's veto and enact the bill, "the objections of the President to the contrary notwithstanding." Overriding of a veto requires a two-thirds vote of those present, who must number a quorum and vote by roll call.

Debate can precede this vote, with motions permitted to lay the message on the table, postpone action on it, or refer it to committee. If the President's veto is overridden by a two-thirds vote in both houses, the bill becomes law. Otherwise it is dead.

When bills are passed finally and signed, or passed over a veto, they are given law numbers in numerical order as they become law. There are two series of numbers, one for public and one for private laws, starting at the number "1" for each two-year term of Congress. They are then identified by law number and by Congress—i.e.; Private Law 21, 90th Congress; Public Law 250, 90th Congress (or PL90-250).

---

strict sense, they have the force of law and are enforceable. This has given rise to the expression "forth branch" in respect to regulatory aspects of agency authority.

Unfortunately, we cannot provide any absolute flow chart summarizing the process by which rules and regulations are developed and promulgated because, despite some basic similarities in procedures, there are a number of variables in statutory provisions and agency practices. Since the regulations issue on the basis of such statutory authority the specifics of the development and promulgation procedures differ. However, we can describe in general some common elements that will provide insights into business participation in the regulatory process. These elements are summarized in Table 2.3

COURTS AND THEIR IMPORTANCE

The effect of the courts in the legislative and regulatory process is a vastly significant area of concern. Once the law has been enacted the courts take action in cases involving litigation. The interpretations of the courts are important to the outcome of each individual case and to establish precedents to be employed in later decisions. This, however, is not the complete story, for the courts have taken on a new role: In making their judgments they often establish policy. This policy, which admittedly is an indirect consequence of their decision-making authority, is important. We examine this in more detail later as we proceed with discussion of some specific statutes and subsequent litigation and adjudication. For now, the following information about the role of litigation and the courts is important. It will be useful in understanding the reasoning behind some of the suggestions and approaches discussed later.

TABLE 2.3 SEQUENCE OF EVENTS IN DEVELOPMENT AND PROMULGATION OF A REGULATION

REGULATION CONTEMPLATED

↓

PROPOSED REGULATION PUBLISHED FOR COMMENT AND/OR PUBLIC HEARING

↓

COMMENTS OR HEARING PERIOD

↓

CONSIDERATION OF COMMENTS AND/OR HEARING RECORDS

↓

PUBLICATION OF FINAL REGULATION

↓

FINAL REGULATION TAKES EFFECT AFTER INTERIM PERIOD

Notes
1. Business can participate before proposed regulation is published in some instances through agency contact.
2. Business can participate after publication of the proposal by:
   (a) Written comments
   (b) Oral statements during the hearings
   (c) Written posthearing comments
3. The final rule can be legally challenged after promulgation and therefore business does have an opportunity to participate even after final rule-making.
4. This highly oversimplified diagram, while possibly not accurate in any given case, does reflect the general sequence of events and opportunities.
5. The reason no one procedure can be outlined is basically because most of the enabling legislation has specific rule-making procedures stipulated which varies from statute to statute. Where procedures are not stipulated, the Administrative Procedures Act is followed.
6. While the specific differences are important procedurally in any given case, particularly if there are to be subsequent challenges to the rule-making on either procedural or substantive grounds, the key is to establish the record. Business can accomplish this only by involvement and active participation either directly or through appropriate representation (council, trade, or professional association).

1. Litigation can lead to specific court decisions that
   (a) Have a direct effect upon conviction or exoneration
   (b) Are important insofar as they establish precedents or contribute to case law
   (c) Can be important insofar as they establish interpretations and policy with regard to agency implementation of legislation (these cases involve challenges to agency action or inaction).
2. Actual litigation is often unnecessary and is merely used as a tactic employed frequently by certain factions.
3. For the case to come to actual judgment is also unnecessary sometimes because so-called consent agreements can be entered into by plaintiff and defendant (with court approval). These instances are important, however, because they are tantamount to the establishment of policy.
4. More and more often courts are being compelled to render decisions on technical and scientific matters, which are in fact not truly issues of law and are sometimes beyond the experience or expertise of the court. Therefore court decisions must be examined as they affect science as well as business and marketing. This is a question of such importance that it is receiving much attention not only in the business communities but also in academic, and government communities. The mechanism by which technical and scientific matters are decided by the courts may well change.
5. Because litigation is becoming more than a way of life—it is also a tactic of survival or a tool of accomplishment—industry could well learn to use it too in the accomplishment of its objectives.

Laws and regulations differ in both the mechanics of passage and the safeguards involved. For a bill to be enacted there are many procedural, constitutional, and remedial safeguards. Regulations are instituted by agencies, with far fewer safeguards and remedies; yet they have the full force and effect of law. True they can be brought to litigation, but to do this successfully requires knowledge of the procedures involved, participation, money and the establishment of a full and complete record of the regulatory proceeding. This explains the reasons we repeatedly draw attention to the need to participate, submit statements or testify—in other words, establish the record.

BUSINESS, GOVERNMENT, AND THE PUBLIC INTEREST

In Chapter 1 we drew attention to the need of some reexamination of the relationships between the three dominant sectors of society: business, government, and the public interest. Here we have expanded our discussion including how they have changed. In some ways change has been a deterioration, in others (or at least looked at differently), it has been an improvement. Certainly the alteration has called attention to societal demands that cannot be ignored and have allowed the participation of the public in a direct and important way. Business is learning about its impact on society in many and varied new ways, both intentional and unintentional. It is seeking an accomodation in an emerging new social dynamic. A whole set of new relationships will be required for this, however. Changes have to be made by business and government and by the public interest groups themselves. At the conclusion of this book we offer very specific suggestions for all three. The suggestions can be better appreciated after we have completed our examination of the contemporary situation, an appraisal of effects, and have had the benefit of some predictions of the future.

THREE

PRINCIPAL

Federal Agencies, Commissions, and Departments

AND THEIR MAJOR EFFECTS ON BUSINESS

In the present regulatory environment the broad and pervasive powers of the government are being applied to restrict business autonomy to an ever-increasing degree. From economics to social concern the government now enters into virtually every phase of business conduct and decision-making, up to and including in the public service sectors (communications, utilities, and transportation), two of the most basic precepts of free enterprise—namely, the right to enter and withdraw from markets. That this might be desirable in the public service sectors is hardly arguable. However, when this is extended into other nonessential public service business activities, as is being done, then to question need or desirability is legitimate.

Benefits do accrue, and the growth of the large corporation, both national and mutinational, requires that the role of "business" in the community, the country, and the world be reconsidered and redefined in socially acceptable terms. The essential quarrel is not really with need but extent, not with intent but with implementation, which ranges not only from (the sublime) of controlling market entry and withdrawal but to (the ridiculous) of setting standards for the height of toilet partitions. Perhaps the public does need to be protected, but one has to wonder about the degree, extent, and ultimate benefit of protection. In some cases one might even question from whom we need to be protected.

AGENCIES, DEPARTMENTS, AND COMMISSIONS

A basic understanding of the structure of government—the agencies, commissions, and departments that generate these rules and regulations and some of the major statutes that they are responsible for implementing—would be beneficial. This is not meant to be a primer on the U.S. Government, political science, politics, or the law. But, despite familiarity with the acronyms, jargon, and vocabulary of legislation and regulation, most of us do not know the basic organizaion, charter, and intended responsibility of many of the government agencies with which we must work. Accordingly, the following charts summarize basic organization of U.S. Government (Tables 3.1 to 3.4); basic organization of major agencies, commissions, and departments that have significant effect on business (Tables 3.5 to 3.26); origin and primary responsibilities of agencies, commissions, and departments that have significant effect on business (Table 3.27).

The list of organizations is long, and the responsibilities and coverage are both complex and extensive. Unfortunately, this only documents a portion of the problem when visualized from the business viewpoint; we must add several additional but important factors:

1. In many instances there are direct and in some case as yet unresolved agency overlaps and jurisdictional issues (e.g., EPA and FDA authority over public drinking water).

2. Many of the requirments of one agency duplicate those of others (e.g., multilple reporting requirements and data bank establishment authorities of EPA, OSHA on toxic materials).

3. The multiplicity of agencies and authorities cause confusion and sometimes outright conflict (e.g., confidentiality of school records vs. disclosure requirements for federal funding).

4. Some industries are subject to so many agencies and statutes that the effort required merely to keep track of their requirements, to say nothing of their compliance problems, represents a real but unrecognized burden (e.g., the

TABLE 3.1 BASIC ORGANIZATION OF THE U.S. GOVERNMENT: THE GOVERNMENT OF THE UNITED STATES

This chart seeks to show only the more important agencies of the Government. See text for other agencies.

THE CONSTITUTION

LEGISLATIVE

THE CONGRESS

Senate   House

Architect of the Capitol
General Accounting Office
Government Printing Office
Library of Congress
United States Botanic Garden
Cost Accounting Standards Board
Office of Technology Assessment
Congressional Budget Office

EXECUTIVE

THE PRESIDENT

Executive Office of the President

White House Office
Office of Management and Budget
Council of Economic Advisers
National Security Council
Federal Property Council
Office of the Special Representative
  for Trade Negotiations
Council on International Economic Policy

Council on Environmental Quality
Domestic Council
Office of Telecommunications Policy
Council on Wage and Price Stability
Energy Resources Council
Office of Drug Abuse Policy
Office of Science and Technology Policy

JUDICIAL

The Supreme Court of the
  United States

Circuit Courts of Appeals of the
  United States
District Courts of the United States
United States Court of Claims
United States Court of Customs and
  Patent Appeals
United States Customs Court
Territorial Courts
Federal Judicial Center
Administrative Office of the
  United States Courts
United States Tax Court

DEPARTMENT OF AGRICULTURE

DEPARTMENT OF STATE

DEPARTMENT OF COMMERCE

DEPARTMENT OF THE TREASURY

DEPARTMENT OF LABOR

DEPARTMENT OF DEFENSE

DEPARTMENT OF HEALTH, EDUCATION, AND WELFARE

DEPARTMENT OF JUSTICE

DEPARTMENT OF HOUSING AND URBAN DEVELOPMENT

DEPARTMENT OF THE INTERIOR

DEPARTMENT OF TRANSPORTATION

INDEPENDENT OFFICES AND ESTABLISHMENTS

ACTION
Administrative Conference of the U.S.
American Revolution Bicentennial Administration
Board for International Broadcasting
Civil Aeronautics Board
Commission o: Civil Rights
Commodity FuturesTrading Commission
Community Services Administration
Consumer Product Safety Commission
Energy Research and Development
  Administration
Environmental Protection Agency
Equal Employment Opportunity Commission

Export-Import Bank of the U.S.
Form Credit Administratic
Federal Communications Commission
Federal Deposit Insurance Corporation
Federal Election Commission
Federal Energy Administration
Federal Home Loan Bank Board
Federal Maritime Commission
Federal Mediation and
  Conciliation Service
Federal Power Commission
Federal Reserve System, Board of
  Governors of the

Federal Trade Commission
General Services Administration
Interstate Commerce Commission
National Aeronautics
  and Space Administration
National Foundation on the
  Arts and the Humanities
National Labor Relations Board
National Mediation Board
National Science Foundation
National Transportation Safety Board
Nuclear Regulatory Commission

Pension Benefit Guaranty Corporation
Railroad Retirement Board
Securities and Exchange Commission
Selective Service System
Small Business Administration
Tennessee Valley Authority
U.S. Civil Service Commission
U.S. Information Agency
U.S. International Trade Commission
U.S. Postal Service
Veterans Administration

TABLE 3.2 BASIC ORGANIZATION OF THE U.S. GOVERNMENT: EXECUTIVE OFFICE OF THE PRESIDENT

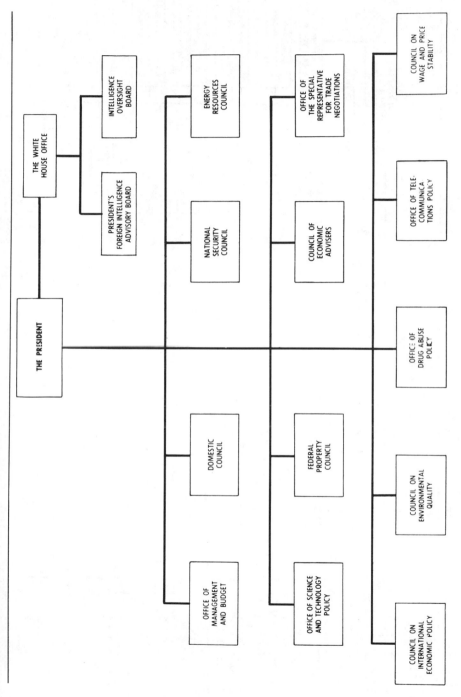

TABLE 3.3   BASIC ORGANIZATION OF THE U.S. GOVERNMENT: U.S. SENATE

THE VICE PRESIDENT
PRESIDENT PRO TEMPORE

SERGEANT AT ARMS OF THE SENATE

DEPUTY SERGEANT AT ARMS

Administrative Assistant to the Sergeant at Arms

Senate Chamber (Order in; furnishings; Pages, Doorkeepers)

Capitol Police Board (Member of; Chairman, odd years)

Capitol Police-Senate Side (Appointive authority for Senate detail)

Radio-TV recording studio (Radio tapes, video tape and TV filming)

Capitol Guide Board Chairman

Capitol Guides (Appointive and supervisory authority)

Cabinet Shop

Senate Post Office

Service Department (Office machines, supplies, repairs; warehouse; duplicating; speech folding; heavy documents)

Computer Center

Custodial Service (Senate side of Capitol)

Communications (Telephone and Telegraph)

Telephone Operators

Procurement and Auditing

Elevator Operators

Press
Press gallery, Radio-TV, Periodical, and Press Photogs gallery

SECRETARY FOR THE MAJORITY
Assistant Secretary

SECRETARY FOR THE MINORITY
Assistant Secretary

CHAPLAIN

LEGISLATIVE COUNSEL

ELECTED OFFICERS OF THE SENATE:
President Pro Tempore
The Secretary
The Sergeant at Arms
The Chaplain
Secretary for the Majority
Secretary for the Minority

SECRETARY OF THE SENATE

ASSISTANT SECRETARY

Disbursing Office

Library

Document Room

Stationery Room

Curator of Art and Antiquities

Senate Historian

Administrative Director Technical Advisor

Parliamentarian
Assistant Parliamentarians
Journal Clerk
Legislative Clerk
Assistant Legislative Clerk
2d Assistant Legislative Clerk
Executive Clerk
Legislative Information Clerk

Printing Clerk
Bill Clerk
Enrolling Clerk
Clerk of Enrolled Bills
Special Assistant
Deputy Assistant Clerks

Official Reporters of Debates

Senate Daily Digest

Office of Public Records

TABLE 3.4 BASIC ORGANIZATION OF THE U.S. GOVERNMENT: HOUSE OF REPRESENTATIVES

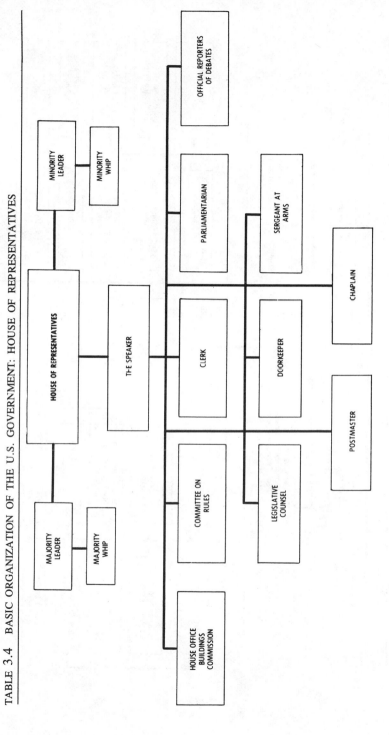

TABLE 3.5   BASIC ORGANIZATION OF MAJOR AGENCIES, COMMISSIONS, AND DEPARTMENTS: DEPARTMENT OF AGRICUL-
TURE

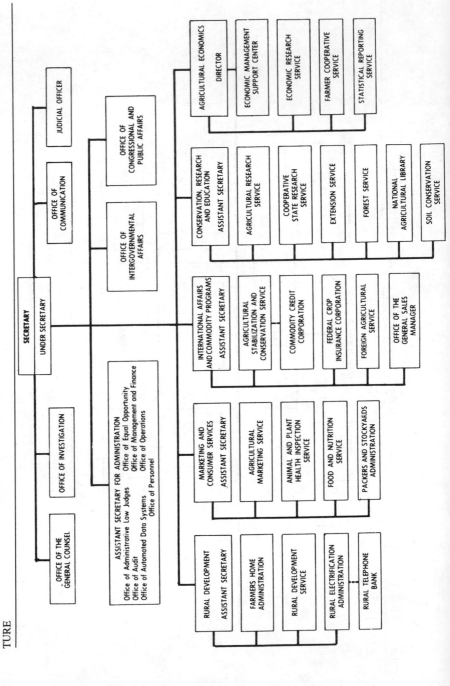

DEPARTMENT OF COMMERCE

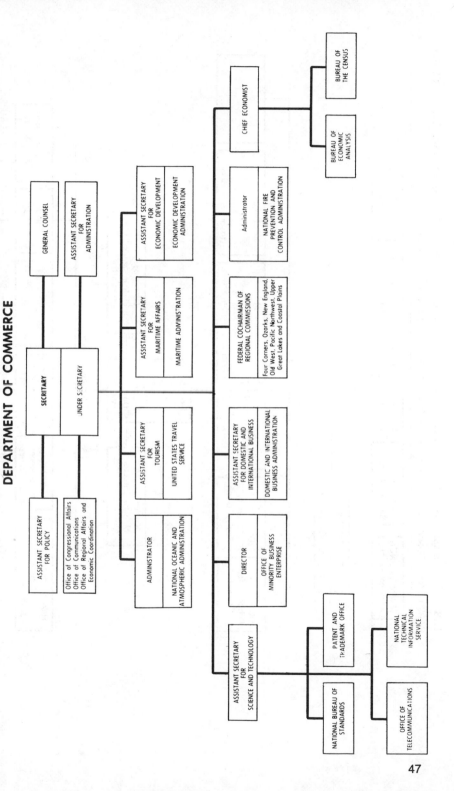

TABLE 3.7 BASIC ORGANIZATION OF MAJOR AGENCIES, COMMISSIONS, AND DEPARTMENTS: CONSUMER PARTMENTS: CONSUMER PRODUCT SAFETY COMMISSION ORGANIZATION CHART

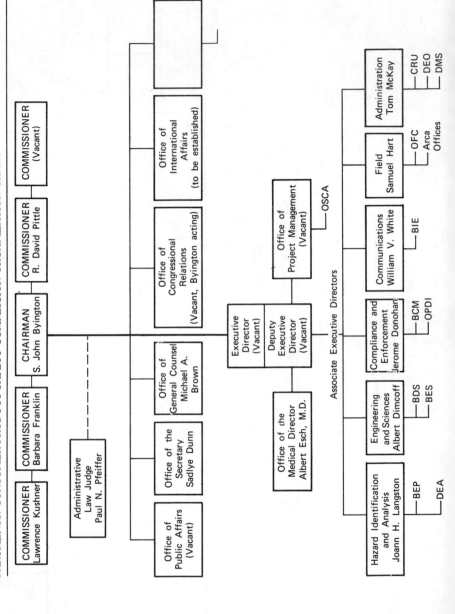

TABLE 3.8   BASIC ORGANIZATION OF MAJOR AGENCIES, COMMISSIONS, AND DEPARTMENTS: DEPARTMENT OF DEFENSE

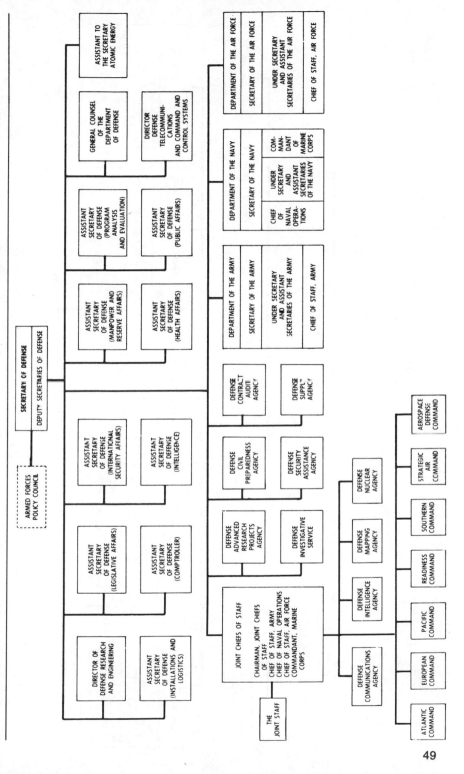

TABLE 3.9 BASIC ORGANIZATION OF MAJOR AGENCIES, COMMISSIONS, AND DEPARTMENTS: DEPARTMENT OF HEALTH, EDUCATION AND WELFARE

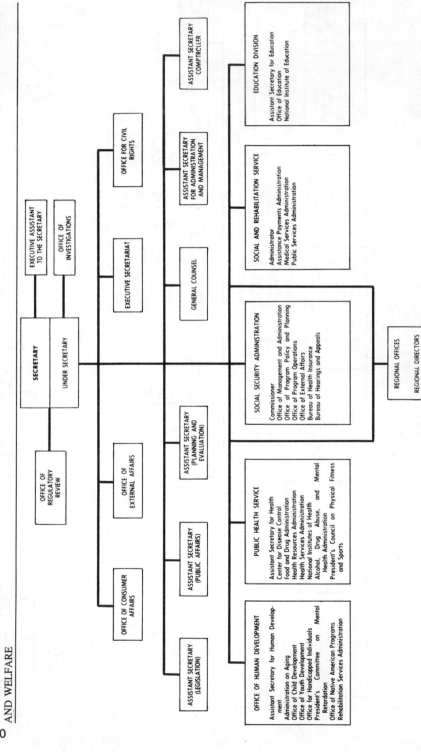

TABLE 3.10 BASIC ORGANIZATION OF MAJOR AGENCIES, COMMISSIONS, AND DEPARTMENTS: DEPARTMENT OF THE INTERIOR

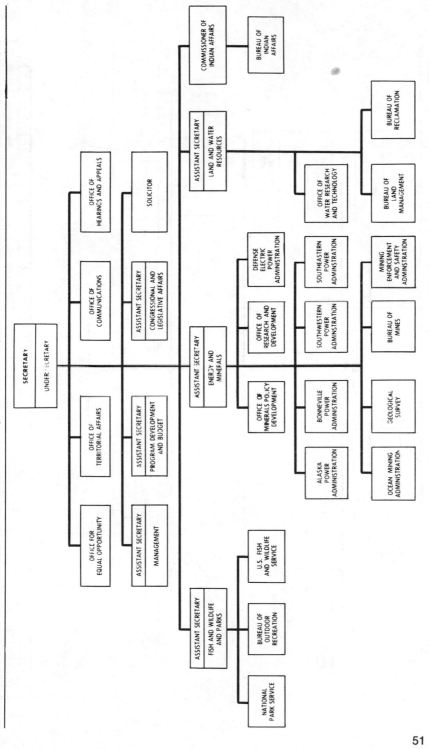

TABLE 3.11   BASIC ORGANIZATION OF MAJOR AGENCIES, COMMISSIONS, AND DEPARTMENTS: DEPARTMENT OF LABOR

TABLE 3.12   BASIC ORGANIZATION OF MAJOR AGENCIES, COMMISSIONS, AND DEPARTMENTS: DEPARTMENT OF JUSTICE

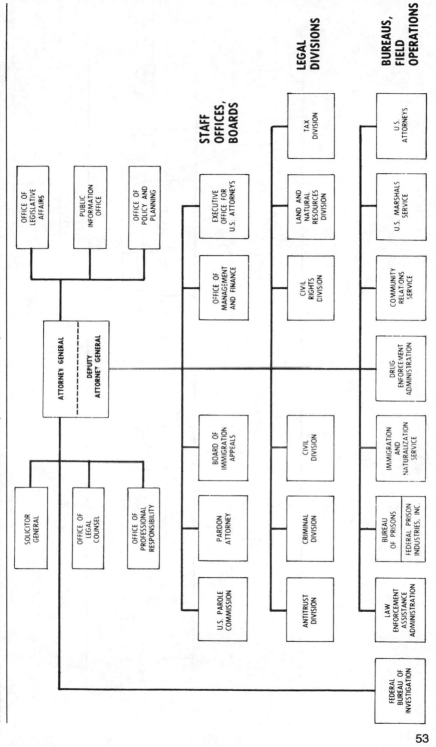

53

TABLE 3.13   BASIC ORGANIZATION OF MAJOR AGENCIES, COMMISSIONS, AND DEPARTMENTS: DEPARTMENT OF TRANSPORTATION

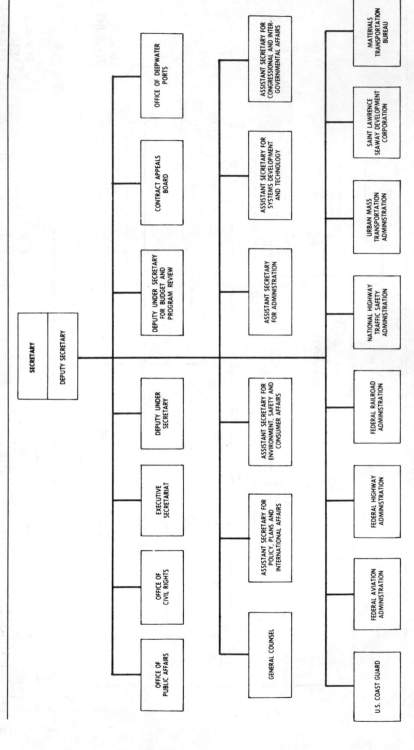

TABLE 3.14   BASIC ORGANIZATION OF MAJOR AGENCIES, COMMISSIONS, AND DEPARTMENTS: DEPARTMENT OF THE TREASURY

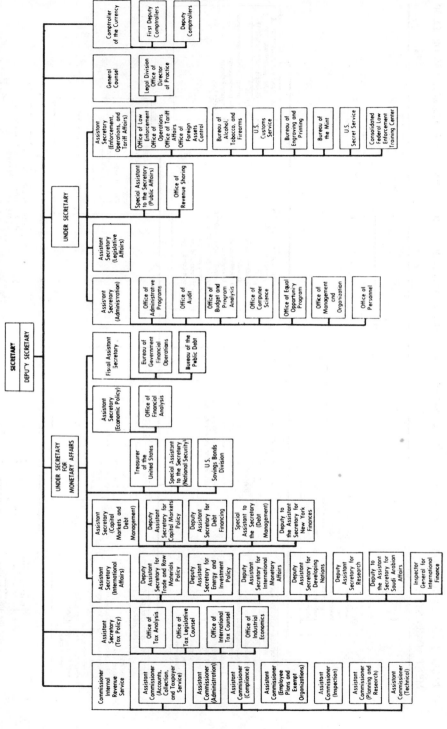

TABLE 3.15   BASIC ORGANIZATION OF MAJOR AGENCIES, COMMISSIONS, AND DEPARTMENTS: ENERGY RESEARCH AND DEVELOP-
MENT ADMINISTRATION

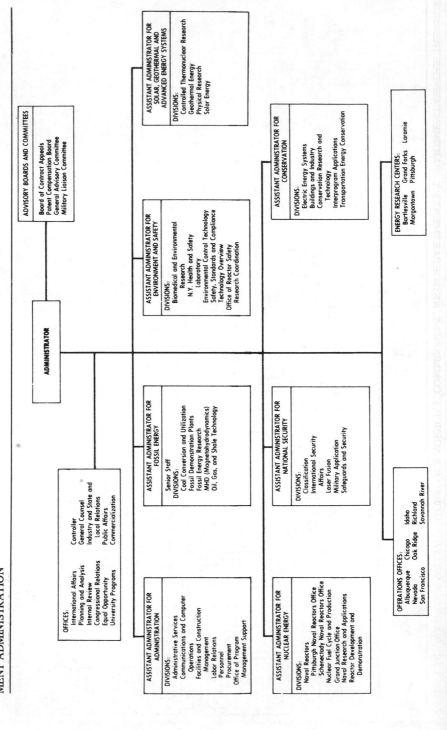

TABLE 3.16 BASIC ORGANIZATION OF MAJOR AGENCIES, COMMISSIONS, AND DEPARTMENTS: ENVIRONMENTAL PROTECTION AGENCY

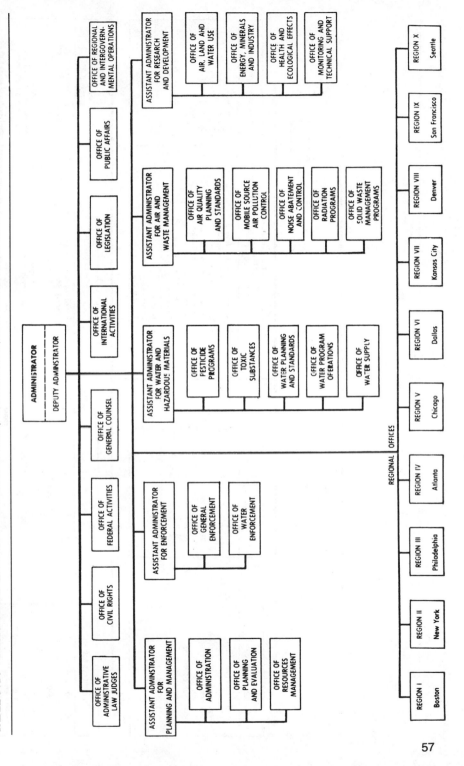

TABLE 3.17   BASIC ORGANIZATION OF MAJOR AGENCIES, COMMISSIONS, AND DEPARTMENTS: FEDERAL COMMUNICATIONS COMMIS-
SION

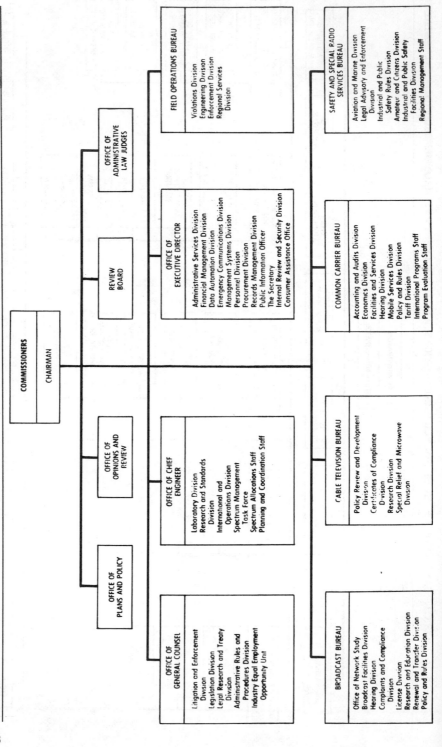

TABLE 3.18 BASIC ORGANIZATION OF MAJOR AGENCIES, COMMISSIONS, AND DEPARTMENTS: FEDERAL ENERGY ADMINISTRATION

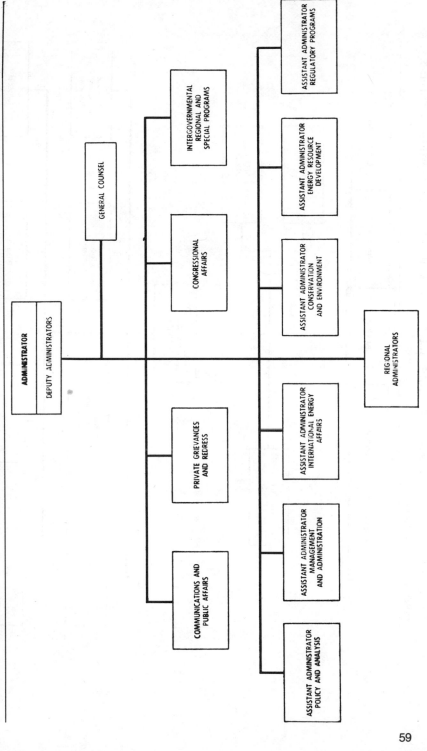

TABLE 3.19 BASIC ORGANIZATION OF MAJOR AGENCIES, COMMISSIONS, AND DEPARTMENTS: FEDERAL MARITIME COMMISSION

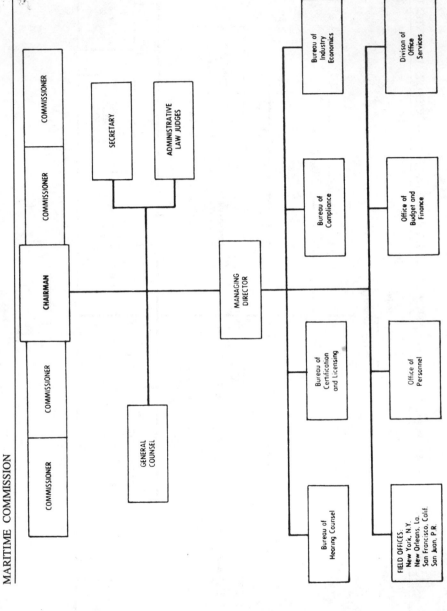

TABLE 3.20   BASIC ORGANIZATION OF MAJOR AGENCIES, COMMISSIONS, AND DEPARTMENTS: FEDERAL POWER COMMIS-
SION

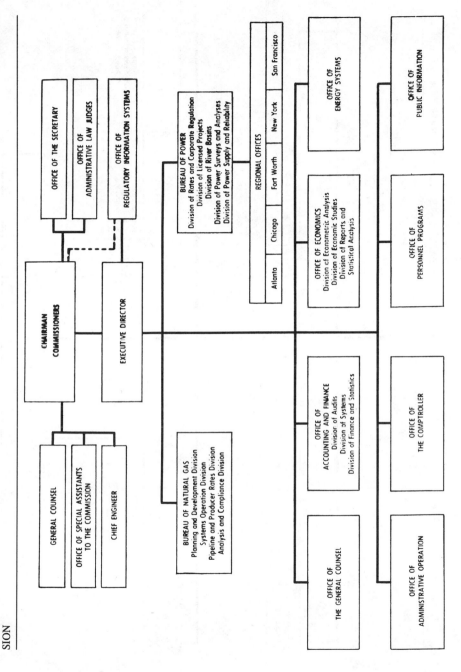

TABLE 3.21 BASIC ORGANIZATION OF MAJOR AGENCIES, COMMISSIONS, AND DEPARTMENTS: FEDERAL TRADE COMMISSION

TABLE 3.22   BASIC ORGANIZATION OF MAJOR AGENCIES, COMMISSIONS, AND DEPARTMENTS: INTERSTATE COMMERCE COMMISSION

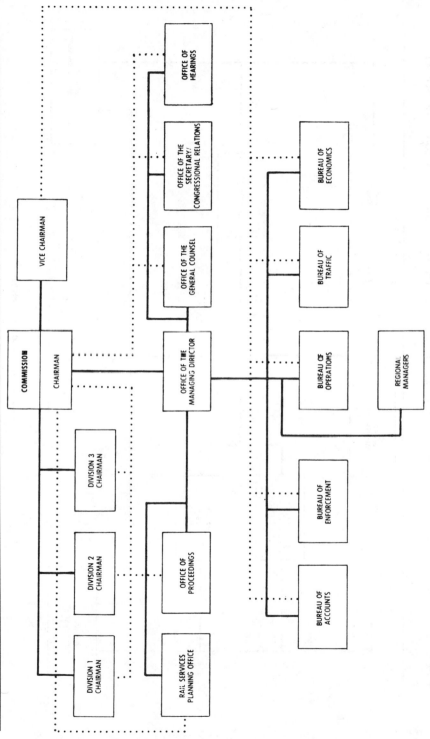

TABLE 3.23   BASIC ORGANIZATION OF MAJOR AGENCIES, COMMISSIONS, AND DEPARTMENTS: NATIONAL TRANSPORTA-
TION SAFETY BOARD

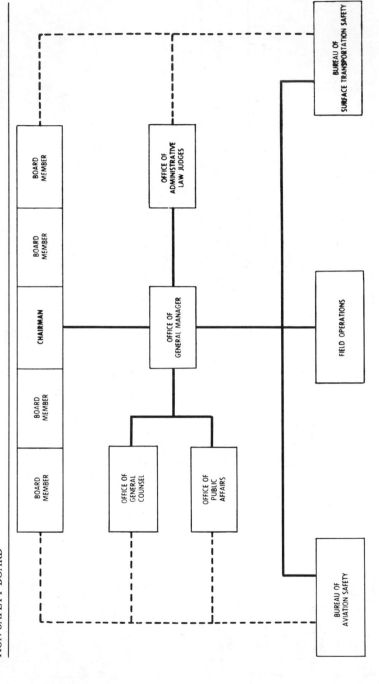

TABLE 3.24 BASIC ORGANIZATION OF MAJOR AGENCIES, COMMISSIONS, AND DEPARTMENTS: PENSION BENEFIT GUARANTY CORPORATION

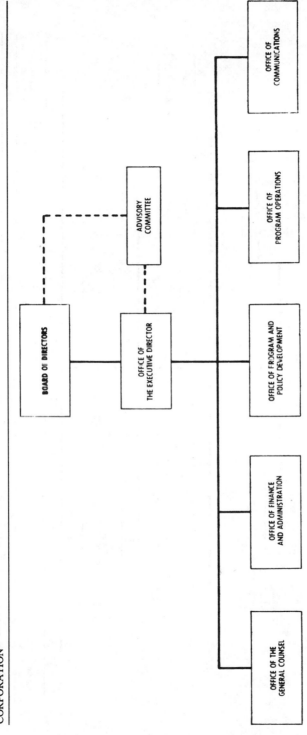

TABLE 3.25 BASIC ORGANIZATION OF MAJOR AGENCES, COMMISSIONS, AND DEPARTMENTS: SECURITIES AND EXCHANGE COMMISSION

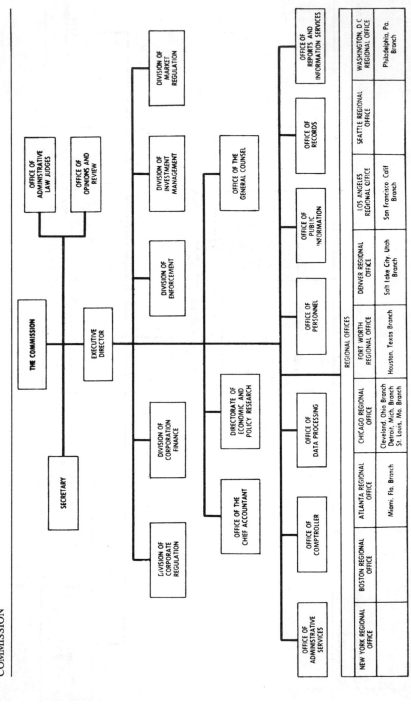

REGIONAL OFFICES							
NEW YORK REGIONAL OFFICE	BOSTON REGIONAL OFFICE	ATLANTA REGIONAL OFFICE	CHICAGO REGIONAL OFFICE	FORT WORTH REGIONAL OFFICE	DENVER REGIONAL OFFICE	LOS ANGELES REGIONAL OFFICE	SEATTLE REGIONAL OFFICE	WASHINGTON, D.C. REGIONAL OFFICE
		Miami, Fla. Branch	Cleveland, Ohio Branch Detroit, Mich. Branch St. Louis, Mo. Branch	Houston, Texas Branch	Salt Lake City, Utah Branch	San Francisco, Calif. Branch		Philadelphia, Pa. Branch

TABLE 3.26 BASIC ORGANIZATION OF MAJOR AGENCIES, COMMISSIONS, AND DEPARTMENTS: U.S. GENERAL ACCOUNTING OFFICE

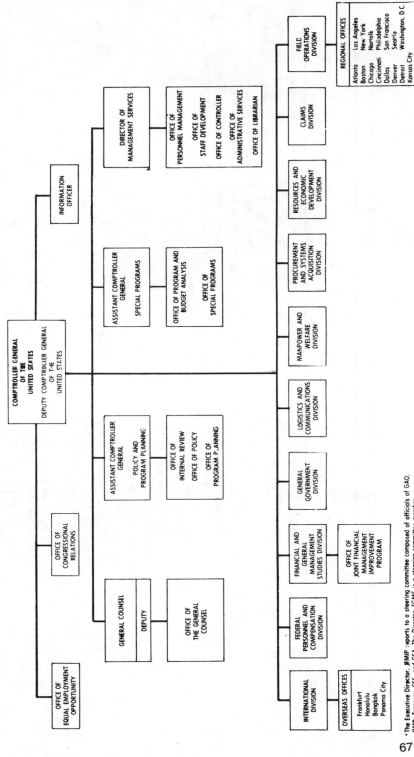

* The Executive Director, JFMIP reports to a steering committee composed of officials of GAO, OMB, Treasury, CSC, and GSA. The Director, FGMS is a steering committee member.

TABLE 3.27 ORIGIN AND PRIMARY RESPONSIBILITIES OF AGENCIES, COMMISSIONS, AND DEPARTMENTS (*continued*)

Title	Origin and Authority	Basic Responsibilities
Commission on Civil Rights	The Commission on Civil Rights was created by the Civil Rights Act of 1964 (78 Stat. 241), and subsequent legislation (81 Stat. 582: 86 Stat. 813. The Commission makes findings of fact but has no enforcement authority. Findings and recommendations are submitted to both the President and the Congress, and more than 60 percent of the Commission's recommendations have been enacted, either by statute, Executive order, or regulation. The Commission evaluates Federal laws and the effectiveness of Government equal opportunity programs. It also serves as a national clearinghouse for civil rights information.	The role of the Commission on Civil Rights is to encourage constructive steps toward equal opportunity for minority groups and women. The Commission investigates complaints, holds public hearings, and collects and studies information on denials of equal protection of the laws because of race, color, religion, sex, or national origin. Voting rights, administration of justice, and equality of opportunity in education, employment, and housing are among the many topics of specific Commission interest.

Consumer Product
Safety Commission

The Consumer Product Safety
Commission is an independent
Federal regulatory agency
established by act of October 27,
1972 (86 Stat. 1207).

The Commission has primary
responsibility for establishing
mandatory product safety
standards, where appropriate, to
reduce the unreasonable risk of
injury to consumers from
consumer products. In addition it
has authority to ban hazardous
consumer products.

The Consumer Product Safety
Act also authorizes the
Commission to conduct
extensive research on consumer
product standards, engage in
broad consumer and industry
information and education
programs, and establish a
comprehensive Injury
Information Clearinghouse.

In addition to the new
authority created by the act, the
Commission assumes
responsibility for the Flammable
Fabrics Act (67 Stat. 111; 15
U.S.C. 1191), the Poison

The purpose of the Consumer Product Safety Commission is to protect
the public against unreasonable risks of injury from consumer products;
to assist consumers to evaluate the comparative safety of consumer
products; to develop uniform safety standards for consumer products and
minimize conflicting State and local regulations; and to promote research
and investigation into the causes and prevention of product-related
deaths, illnesses, and injuries.

TABLE 3.27   ORIGIN AND PRIMARY RESPONSIBILITIES OF AGENCIES, COMMISSIONS, AND DEPARTMENTS (*continued*)

Title	Origin and Authority	Basic Responsibilities
Consumer Product Safety Commission	Prevention Packaging Act (84 Stat. 1670), the Hazardous Substances Act (74 Stat. 372; 15 U.S.C. 1261), and the act of August 2, 1956 (70 Stat. 953; 15 U.S.C. 1211) which prohibits the transportation of refrigerators without door safety devices. The act also provides for petitioning of the Commission by any interested person, including consumers or consumer organizations, to commence proceedings for the issuance, amendment, or revocation of a consumer product safety rule.	
Department of Agriculture (USDA)	The act of Congress, approved May 15, 1862, created the Department of Agriculture, which was administered by a Commissioner of Agriculture until 1889 (12 Stat. 387; U.S.C.	The Department of Agriculture (USDA) serves all Americans daily. It works to improve and maintain farm income and to develop and expand markets abroad for agricultural products. The Department helps to curb and to cure poverty, hunger, and malnutrition. It works to enhance the environment and to maintain our production capacity by helping landowners protect the soil, water, forests, and other natural resources.

Rural development, credit, and conservation programs are key resources for carrying out national growth policies. USDA research findings directly or indirectly benefit all Americans. The Department, through inspection and grading services, safeguards and assures standards of quality in the daily food supply.

511, 514, 516). By act of February 9, 1889, the powers and duties of the Department were enlarged. The Department was made the eighth executive department in the Federal Government, and the Commissioner became the Secretary of Agriculture.

Department of Commerce

The Department of Commerce encourages, serves, and promotes the Nation's economic development and technological advancement. Within this framework and together with a policy of promoting the national interest through the encouragement of the competitive free enterprise system, the Department provides a wide variety of programs. It offers advice and information to domestic and international business; provides social and economic statistics and analyses for business and government planners; assists in the development and maintenance of the U.S. merchant marine; provides research for and promotes the increased use of science and technology in the development of the economy; provides assistance to speed the development of the economically underdeveloped areas of the Nation; seeks to improve understanding of the Earth's physical environment and oceanic life; promotes travel to the United States by residents of foreign countries; assists in the growth of minority businesses; and seeks to prevent the loss of life and property from fire.

The Department was designated as such by the act of March 4, 1913 (37 Stat. 736; 15 U.S.C. 1501), which reorganized the Department of Commerce and Labor, created by the act of February 14, 1903 (32 Stat. 825; 15 U.S.C. 1501), by transferring all labor activities into a new, separate Department of Labor. The Department of Commerce is composed of the Office of the Secretary and the operating units.

Department of Defense

The Department of Defense is responsible for providing the military forces needed to deter war and protect the security of our country.

The major elements of these forces are the Army, Navy, Marine Corps, and Air Force, consisting of about 2 million men and women on

The Department of Defense is the successor agency to the National Military Establishment created by the National Security

TABLE 3.27 ORIGIN AND PRIMARY RESPONSIBILITIES OF AGENCIES, COMMISSIONS, AND DEPARTMENTS (*continued*)

Title	Origin and Authority	Basic Responsibilities
Department of Defense	Act of 1947 (61 Stat. 495). It was established as an executive department of the Government by the National Security Act Amendments of 1949, with the Secretary of Defense as its head (63 Stat. 578; 5 U.S.C. 101):. Since that time, major amendments have been made to the act by Reorganization Plan 6 of 1953, effective June 30, 1953, and the Department of Defense Reorganization Act of 1958 (67 Stat. 638; 72 Stat. 514).	active duty. Of these, some 484,000—including about 50,000 on ships at sea—are serving outside the United States. They are backed, in case of emergency, by the 2½ million members of the reserve components. In addition, there are about 1 million civilian employees in the Defense Department. Under the President, who is also Commander in Chief, the Secretary of Defense exercises direction, authority, and control over the Department, which includes the separately organized military departments of Army, Navy, and Air Force, the Joint Chiefs of Staff providing military advice, the unified and specified combatant commands, and various Defense agencies established for specific purposes. Every State in the Union has some defense activities. Central headquarters of the Department is at the Pentagon, the "world's largest office building."
Department of Health, Education and Welfare (HEW)	The Department of Health, Education, and Welfare was created on April 11, 1953, under legislation proposed by President Eisenhower and approved by the Congress on April 1, 1953. That legislation abolished HEW's predecessor organization, the	The Department of Health, Education, and Welfare (HEW) is the Cabinet-level department of the Federal executive branch most concerned with people and most involved with the Nation's human concerns. In one way or another—whether it is mailing out social security checks, or improving the quality in American education, or making health services more widely available—HEW touches the lives of more Americans than any other Federal agency. It is literally a department of people serving people, from newborn infants to our most elderly citizens.

Federal Security Agency, and transferred all its functions to the new Department. In addition, it transferred all responsibilities of the Federal Security Administrator to the Secretary of Health, Education, and Welfare.

Department of the Interior

The Department of the Interior was created by act of March 3, 1849 (9 Stat. 395: 43 U.S.C. 1451) which transferred to it the General Land Office, the Office of Indian Affairs, the Pension Office, and the Patent Office. The Department also had responsibility for supervision of the Commissioner of Public Buildings, the Board of Inspectors and the Warden of the Penitentiary of the District of Columbia, the census of the United States, and the accounts of marshals and other officers of the United States courts, and of lead and other mines in the United States.

Over the 127 years of its existence, other functions have been added and removed, so that

As the Nation's principal conservation agency, the Department of the Interior has responsibility for most of our nationally owned public lands and natural resources. This includes fostering the wisest use of our land and water resources, protecting our fish and wildlife, preserving the environmental and cultural values of our national parks and historical places, and providing for the enjoyment of life through outdoor recreation. The Department assesses our energy and mineral resources and works to assure that their development is in the best interests of all our people. The Department also has a major responsibility for American Indian reservation communities and for people who live in Island Territories under United States administration.

73

TABLE 3.27 ORIGIN AND PRIMARY RESPONSIBILITIES OF AGENCIES, COMMISSIONS, AND DEPARTMENTS (*continued*)

Title	Origin and Authority	Basic Responsibilities
Department of the Interior	its role has changed from that of general housekeeper for the Federal Government to that of custodian of the Nation's natural resources. The Department of the Interior is composed of the Office of the Secretary, other department offices, and bureaus.	
Department of Labor	The Department of Labor, ninth executive department, was created by act approved March 4, 1913 (37 Stat. 736: 5 U.S.C. 611). A Bureau of Labor was first created by Congress in 1884 under the Interior Department. The Bureau of Labor later became independent as a Department of Labor without executive rank. It again returned to bureau status in the Department of Commerce and Labor which was created by act of February 14, 1903 (32 Stat. 827: 5 U.S.C. 591).	The purpose of the Department of Labor is to foster, promote, and develop the welfare of the wage earners of the United States, to improve their working conditions, and to advance their opportunities for profitable employment. In carrying out this mission, the Department administers more than 130 Federal labor laws guaranteeing workers rights to safe and healthful working conditions, a minimum hourly wage and overtime pay, freedom from employment discrimination, unemployment insurance, and workers' compensation. The Department also protects workers' pension rights; sponsors job training programs; helps workers find jobs; works to strengthen free collective bargaining; and keeps track of changes in employment, prices, and other national economic measurements. As the Department seeks to assist all Americans who need and want to work, special efforts are made to meet the unique job market problems of older workers, youths, minority group members, women, the handicapped, and other groups.

Department of Justice

The Department of Justice was established by the act of June 22, 1870 (16 Stat. 162: 28 U.S.C. 501, 503), with the Attorney General at its head. Prior to 1870 the Attorney General was a member of the President's Cabinet, but not the head of a department, the office having been created under authority of the act of September 24, 1789, as amended (1 Stat. 92.16 Stat 162: 28 U.S.C. 503).

The affairs and activities of the Department of Justice are generally directed by the Attorney General.

As the largest law firm in the Nation, the Department of Justice serves as counsel for its citizens. It represents them in enforcing the law in the public interest. Through its thousands of lawyers, investigators, and agents, the Department plays the key role in protection against criminals and subversion, in ensuring healthy competition of business in our free enterprise system, in safeguarding the consumer, and in enforcing drug, immigration, and naturalization laws. The Department also plays a significant role in protecting citizens through its efforts for effective law enforcement, crime prevention, crime detection, and prosecution and rehabilitation of offenders.

Moreover, the Department conducts all suits in the Supreme Court in which the United States is concerned. It represents the Government in legal matters generally, rendering legal advice and opinions, upon request, to the President and to the heads of the executive departments. The Attorney General supervises and directs these activities, as well as those of the United States Attorneys and U.S. Marshals in the various judicial districts around the country.

Department of Transportation (DOT)

The Department of Transportation was established by the act of October 15, 1966 (80 Stat. 931; 49 U.S.C. 1651 note) "to assure the coordinated, effective administration of the transportation programs of the Federal Government" and to develop "national transportation policies and programs conducive to the provision of fast, safe, efficient, and convenient

The U.S. Department of Transportation (DOT) establishes the Nation's overall transportation policy. Under its umbrella there are seven administrations and the Materials Transportation Bureau whose jurisdictions include highway planning, development, and construction: urban mass transit; railroads; aviation; and the safety of waterways, ports, highways, and oil and gas pipelines. Decisions made by DOT in conjunction with the appropriate State and local officials strongly affect other programs such as land planning, energy conservation, scarce resource utilization, and technology change.

TABLE 3.27   ORIGIN AND PRIMARY RESPONSIBILITIES OF AGENCIES, COMMISSIONS, AND DEPARTMENTS (*continued*)

Title	Origin and Authority	Basic Responsibilities
Department of Transportation (DOT)	transportation at the lowest cost consistent therewith.'' It became operational in April 1967 comprised of elements transferred from eight other major Departments and Agencies. It presently consists of the Office of the Secretary (OST), seven operating administrations, and the Materials Transportation Bureau whose heads report directly to the Secretary and who have highly decentralized authority.	
Federal Highway Administration	The Federal Highway Administration became a component of the Department of Transportation pursuant to the Department of Transportation Act (80 Stat. 932). It carries out the highway transportation	

programs of the Department of Transportation under pertinent legislation or provisions of law cited in section 6(a) of the act.

The Federal Highway Administration encompasses highway transportation in its broadest scope, seeking to coordinate highways with other modes of transportation to achieve the most effective balance of transportation systems and facilities under cohesive Federal transportation policies as contemplated by the act.

The Federal Highway Administration is concerned with the total operation and environment of the highway systems, with particular emphasis on improvement of highway-oriented aspects of highway safety.

Department of the Treasury

The Treasury Department was created by act of congress approved September 2, 1789 (1 Stat. 65: 31 U.S.C. 1001). Many

The Department of the Treasury performs four basic types of functions: formulating and recommending financial, tax, and fiscal policies; serving as financial agent for the U.S. Government; law enforcement; and manufacturing coins and currency.

TABLE 3.27 ORIGIN AND PRIMARY RESPONSIBILITIES OF AGENCIES, COMMISSIONS, AND DEPARTMENTS (*continued*)

Title	Origin and Authority	Basic Responsibilities
Department of the Treasury	subsequent acts have figured in the development of the Department delegating new duties to its charge and establishing the numerous bureaus and divisions which now compose the Treasury.	
Energy Research and Development (ERDA)	The Energy Research and Development Administration was established by the Energy Reorganization Act of 1974 (88 Stat. 1234; 4 U.S.C. 5811). The Energy Research and Development Administration was activated on January 19, 1975 by Executive Order 11834 of January 15, 1975. Additional responsibilities were assigned to ERDA by the Federal Nonnuclear Energy Research and	The purpose of the Energy Research and Development Administration (ERDA) is to reorganize and consolidate Federal activities relating to research and development on the various sources of energy in order to develop and increase the efficiency and reliability of the use of all energy sources to meet the needs of present and future generations, to increase the productivity of the national economy and strengthen its position in regard to international trade, to make the Nation self-sufficient in energy, to advance the goals of restoring, protecting, and enhancing environmental quality, and to assure public health and safety.

Development Act of 1974 (88 Stat. 1878); the Solar Heating and Cooling Demonstration Act of 1974 (88 Stat. 1069); the Solar Energy Research, Development, and Demonstration Act of 1974 (88 Stat. 1431);and the Geothermal Energy Research, Development, and Demonstration Act of 1974 (88 Stat. 1079). The Energy Reorganization Act brought together into ERDA functions of the Department of Interior related to coal research, energy research centers, and underground electric power transmission research; functions of the National Science Foundation related to solar heating and cooling development and geothermal power development; functions of the Environmental Protection Agency related to research, development, and demonstration of alternative automotive power systems; and the military and production activities and nuclear

TABLE 3.27 ORIGIN AND PRIMARY RESPONSIBILITIES OF AGENCIES, COMMISSIONS, AND DEPARTMENTS (*continued*)

Title	Origin and Authority	Basic Responsibilities
Energy Research and Development (ERDA)	research and development activities of the Atomic Energy Commission. Also transferred to ERDA were functions that under the Solar Energy Heating and Cooling Demonstration Act, the Solar Energy Research, Development, and Demonstration Act, and the Geothermal Energy Research, Demonstration, and Development Act, had temporarily been assigned to the National Science Foundation, the Department of Housing and Urban Development, the Federal Power Commission, the National Aeronautics and Space Administration, and the Federal Energy Administration.	

Environmental
Protection Agency
(EPA)

The Environmental Protection
Agency was established in the
executive branch as an
independent agency pursuant to
Reorganization Plan No.3 of
1970, effective December 2,
1970.

The Environmental Protection
Agency was created to permit
coordinated and effective
governmental action on behalf of
the environment, EPA endeavors
to abate and control pollution
systematically, by proper
integration of a variety of
research, monitoring, standard
setting, and enforcement
activities. As a complement to its
other activities, EPA coordinates
and supports research and
antipollution activities by State
and local governments, private
and public groups, individuals,
and educational institutions.
EPA also reinforces efforts
among other Federal agencies
with respect to the impact of their
operations on the environment,
and it is specifically charged with
making public its written

The purpose of the Environmental Protection Agency (EPA) is to protect
and enhance our environment today and for future generations to the
fullest extent possible under the laws enacted by Congress. The Agency's
mission is to control and abate pollution in the areas of air, water, solid
waste, pesticides, noise, and radiation. EPA's mandate is to mount an
integrated, coordinated attack on environmental pollution in cooperation
with State and local governments.

TABLE 3.27   ORIGIN AND PRIMARY RESPONSIBILITIES OF AGENCIES, COMMISSIONS, AND DEPARTMENTS (*continued*)

Title	Origin and Authority	Basic Responsibilities
Environmental Protection Agency (EPA)	comments on environmental impact statements and with publishing its determinations when those hold that a proposal is unsatisfactory from the standpoint of public health or welfare or environmental quality. In all, EPA is designed to serve as the public's advocate for a livable environment.	
Equal Employment Opportunity Commission (EEOC)	The Equal Employment Opportunity Commission was created by title VII of the Civil Rights Act of 1964 (78 Stat. 241: 42 U.S.C. 2000a), and became operational July 2, 1965. Title VII was amended by the Equal Employment Opportunity Act of 1972 (86 Stat. 103).	The purposes of the Equal Employment Opportunity Commission (EEOC) are to end discrimination based on race, color, religion, sex or national origin in hiring, promotion, firing, wages, testing, training, apprenticeship, and all other conditions of employment and to promote voluntary action programs by employers, unions, and community organizations to put equal employment opportunity into actual operation.
	The Commission's operations are decentralized to the five litigation centers, seven regional offices, and 32 district offices.	

Export-Import Bank	The Export-Import Bank of Washington was authorized in 1934 as a banking corporation organized under the laws of the District of Columbia (Executive Order 6581, February 2, 1934). The Bank was continued as an agency of the United States by acts of Congress in 1935, 1937, 1939, and 1940. It was made an independent agency of the Government by the Export-Import Bank Act of 1945 (59 Stat. 526; 12 U.S.C. 635), subsequently amended in 1947 to reincorporate the Bank under Federal charter. The name was changed to Export-Import Bank of the United States (Eximbank) by act of March 13, 1968 (82 Stat. 47).	The Export-Import Bank of the United States, known as Eximbank, facilitates and aids in financing exports of U.S. goods and services. Eximbank has implemented a variety of programs to meet the needs of the U.S. exporting community, according to the size of the transaction. These programs take the form of direct lending or the issuance of guarantees and insurance, so that exporters and private banks can extend appropriate financing without taking undue risks. Eximbank's direct lending program is limited to larger sales of U.S. products and services around the world. The guarantees, insurance, and discount programs have been designed to assist exporters in smaller sales of products and services.
Federal Communications Commission (FCC)	The Federal Communications Commission was created by the Communications Act of 1934 (48 Stat. 1064; 15 U.S.C. 21; 47 U.S.C. 35, 151–609) to regulate interstate and foreign communications by wire and	The Federal Communications Commission (FCC) regulates interstate and foreign communications by radio, television, wire, and cable. It is responsible for the orderly development and operation of broadcast services and the provision of rapid, efficient nationwide and worldwide telephone and telegraph services at reasonable rates. This also includes the promotion of safety of life and property through radio and the use of radio and television facilities to strengthen the national defense.

TABLE 3.27   ORIGIN AND PRIMARY RESPONSIBILITIES OF AGENCIES, COMMISSIONS, AND DEPARTMENTS (*continued*)

Title	Origin and Authority	Basic Responsibilities
Federal Communications Commission (FCC)	radio in the public interest. It was assigned additional regulatory jurisdiction under the provisions of the Communications Satellite Act of 1962 (76 Stat. 419; 47 U.S.C. 701–744). The scope of the regulation includes radio and television broadcasting; telephone, telegraph, and cable television operation; two-way radio and radio operators; and satellite communication.	
Federal Energy Administration (FEA)	The Federal Energy Administration was established by the Federal Energy Administration Act of 1974 (88 Stat. 96), effective June 28, 1974. The Federal Energy Office, which was established by Executive Order 11748 of	The purpose of the Federal Energy Administration (FEA) is to ensure that the supply of energy available to the United States will continue to be sufficient to meet our total energy demand. FEA also assures that in the case of energy shortages, priority needs for energy are met and the burden of the shortages borne with equity.

December 4, 1973, was abolished and its functions transferred to the Federal Energy Administration by Executive Order 11790 of June 25, 1974.

The Energy Policy and Conservation Act (89 Stat. 871; 42 U.S.C. 6201 note), effective December 1975, assigned many additional responsibilities to the FEA. Principal among them are the reevaluation of all existing allocation and pricing regulations; the development of conservation and rationing contingency plans; the development of product allocation and price decontrol plans; the administration of a petroleum storage program and a coal loan guarantee program; and the implementation of an appliance labeling program. In addition, the Energy Policy and Conservation Act prescribed that the FEA must identify major energy-conserving industries and establish industrial energy efficiency targets.

TABLE 3.27 ORIGIN AND PRIMARY RESPONSIBILITIES OF AGENCIES, COMMISSIONS, AND DEPARTMENTS (*continued*)

Title	Origin and Authority	Basic Responsibilities
Federal Maritime Commission	The Federal Maritime Commission was established by Reorganization Plan 7, effective August 12, 1961. It is an independent agency which administers the functions and discharges the regulatory authorities under the following statutes; Shipping Act, 1916; Merchant Marine Act, 1920; Intercoastal Shipping Act, 1933; Merchant Marine Act, 1936; and certain provisions of the act of November 6, 1966 (80 Stat. 1356; 46 u.s.c. 362) and the Federal Water Pollution Control Act Amendments of 1972 (86 Stat. 816; 33 U.S.C. 1151).	The Federal Maritime Commission regulates the waterborne foreign and domestic offshore commerce of the United States, assures that United States international trade is open to all nations on fair and equitable terms, and guards against unauthorized monopoly in the waterborne commerce of the United States. This is accomplished through maintaining surveillance over steamship conferences and common carriers by water; assuring that only the rates on file with the Commsission are charged; approving agreements between persons subject to the Shipping Act; guaranteeing equal treatment to shippers and carriers by terminal operators, freight forwarders, and other persons subject to the shipping statutes; and ensuring that adequate levels of financial responsibility are maintained for indemnification of passengers or oil spill cleanup.
	The Federal Power Commission regulates the interstate aspects of the electric power and natural gas industries.	

| Federal Power Commission (FPC) | The Federal Power Commission is an independent agency operating under the Federal Power Act (16 U.S.C. 791a–825r), as amended. This act was originally enacted as the Federal Water Power Act of June 10, 1920 (41 Stat. 1063), and subsequently amended by title II of the Public Utility Act of 1935 (49 Stat. 838), and the Natural Gas Act, enacted June 21, 1938 (52 Stat. 821–833, as amended; 15 U.S.C. 717N717w). Additional responsibilities have been assigned by subsequent legislation and by Executive orders. (*See Federal Power Commission Laws and Hydroelectric Power Development Laws*, Government Printing Office, 1966). | The Federal Power Commission (FPC) regulates the interstate aspects of the electric power and natural gas industries. FPC actions directly or indirectly affect the great majority of electric and natural gas consumers throughout the Nation. A principal concern of the FPC is that the Nation's consumers have adequate supplies of gas and electricity at the lowest reasonable rates. The continuing increase in demand for these commodities, accompanied by a growing concern for assuring a quality environment, have introduced new and complex challenges which the Commission is meeting with procedures designed to improve the regulatory process. |
| Federal Trade Commission | This basic purpose finds its primary expression in the Federal Trade Commission Act, cited below, and the Clayton Act (38 Stat. 730; 15 U.S.C. 12), both | The basic objective of the Federal Trade Commission is the maintenance of strongly competitive enterprise as the keystone of the American economic system. Although the duties of the Commission are many and varied under law, the foundation of public policy underlying all these duties is essentially the same: to prevent the free enterprise system from |

TABLE 3.27   ORIGIN AND PRIMARY RESPONSIBILITIES OF AGENCIES, COMMISSIONS, AND DEPARTMENTS (*continued*)

Title	Origin and Authority	Basic Responsibilities
Federal Trade Commission	passed in 1914 and both successively amended in the years that have followed. The Federal Trade Commission Act lays down a general prohibition against the use in commerce of "unfair methods of competition" and "unfair or deceptive act or practices." The Clayton Act outlaws specific practices recognized as instruments of monopoly. As an administrative agency, acting quasi-judicially and quasi-legislatively, the Commission was established to deal with trade practices on a continuing and corrective basis. It has no authority to punish; its function is to "prevent," through cease-and-desist orders and other means, those practices condemned by the law of Federal trade regulation; however, court	being stifled, substantially lessened or fettered by monopoly or restraints on trade, or corrupted by unfair or deceptive trade practices. In brief, the Commission is charged with keeping competition both free and fair.

ordered civil penalties up to $10,000 may be obtained for each violation of a Commission order.

The Federal Trade Commission was organized as an independent administrative agency in 1951, pursuant to the Federal Trade Commission Act of 1914 (38 Stat. 717; 15 U.S.C. 41–51). Related duties subsequently were delegated to the Commission by the Wheeler-Lea Act, the Trans-Alaska Pipeline Authorization Act, the Clayton Act, the Export Trade Act, the Wool Products Labeling Act, the Fur Products Labeling Act, the Textile Fiber Products Identification Act, the Fair Packaging and Labeling Act, the Lanham Trade-Mark Act of 1946, the Truth in Lending Act, the Fair Credit Reporting Act, the Robinson-Patman Act, the Hobby Protection Act, and the Magnuson-Moss Warranty-Federal Trade Commission Improvement Act.

TABLE 3.27 ORIGIN AND PRIMARY RESPONSIBILITIES OF AGENCIES, COMMISSIONS, AND DEPARTMENTS (*continued*)

Title	Origin and Authority	Basic Responsibilities
Food and Drug Administration (FDA)	The name "Food and Drug Administration" was first provided by the Agriculture Appropriation Act of 1931, approved May 27, 1930 (46 Stat. 392), although similar law-enforcement functions had been carried on under different organizational titles since January 1, 1907, when the Food and Drug Act of 1906 (34 Stat. 768; 21 U.S.C. 1–15) became effective.	The Food and Drug Administration's (FDA) activities are directed toward protecting the health of the Nation against impure and unsafe foods, drugs and cosmetics, and other potential hazards.
Interstate Commerce Commission (ICC)	The interstate Commerce Commission was created as an independent establishment by the act to regulate commerce of February 4, 1887 (24 Stat.	The Interstate Commerce Commission (ICC) regulates interstate surface transportation, including trains, trucks, buses, inland waterway and coastal shipping, freight forwarders, oil pipelines, and express companies. The regulatory laws vary with the type of transportation; however, they generally involve certification of carriers seeking to

provide transportation for the public, rates, adequacy of service, purchases, and mergers. The ICC assures that the carriers it regulates will provide the public with rates and services that are fair and reasonable.

379.383: 49 U.S.C. 1–22), now known as the Interstate Commerce Act. The Commission's authority has been strengthened and the scope of its jurisdiction has been broadened by subsequent legislation, such as the Hepburn Act, the Panama Canal Act, the Motor Carrier Act of 1935, and the Transportation Acts of 1920, 1940 and 1958.

The Commission was created by Congress to regulate, in the public interest, carriers subject to the Interstate Commerce Act which are engaged in transportation in interstate commerce and in foreign commerce to the extent that it takes place within the United States. Surface transportation under the Commission's jurisdiction includes railroads, trucking companies, bus lines, freight forwarders, water carriers, oil pipelines, transportation brokers, and express agencies.

TABLE 3.27 ORIGIN AND PRIMARY RESPONSIBILITIES OF AGENCIES, COMMISSIONS, AND DEPARTMENTS (*continued*)

Title	Origin and Authority	Basic Responsibilities
National Labor Relations Board (NLRB)	The National Labor Relations Board is an independent agency created by the National Labor Relations Act of 1935 (Wagner Act), as amended by the acts of 1947 (Taft-Hartley Act) and 1959 (Landrum-Griffin Act). The act affirms the right of employees to self-organization and to bargain collectively through representatives of their own choosing or to refrain from such activities. The act prohibits certain unfair labor practices by employers and labor organizations or their agents and authorizes the Board to designate appropriate units for collective bargaining and to conduct secret ballot elections to determine whether employees desire representation by a labor organization.	The National Labor Relations Board (NLRB) administers the Nation's law relating to labor relations. It is vested with the power to investigate and settle labor disputes, safeguard employee's rights to organize, and prevent unfair labor practices.

As of July 1, 1971, the Postal Reorganization Act (84 Stat. 719; 39 U.S.C. Prec. 101 note) conferred jurisdiction upon the Board over unfair labor practice charges and representation elections affecting U.S. Postal Service employees. As of July 26, 1974, jurisdiction over nonprofit Health Care Institutions was conferred on the NLRB by an amendment to the act (29 U.S.C. 152 et seq.).

National Transportation Safety Board (NTSB)

The National Transportation Safety Board was established as an independent agency of the Federal Government on April 1, 1975, by the Independent Safety Board Act of 1974 (88 Stat. 2156; 49 U.S.C. 1901).

The Safety Board consists of five Board members appointed by the President, by and with the advice and consent of the Senate, for 5-year terms. The President designates two of these members as Chairman and Vice Chairman

The National Transportation Safety Board (NTSB) seeks to assure that all types of transportation in the United States are conducted safely. The Board investigates accidents and makes recommendations to Government agencies, the transportation industry, and others on safety measures and practices. The Board also regulates the procedures for reporting accidents and promotes the safe transport of hazardous materials by Government and private industry.

93

TABLE 3.27 ORIGIN AND PRIMARY RESPONSIBILITIES OF AGENCIES, COMMISSIONS, AND DEPARTMENTS (*continued*)

Title	Origin and Authority	Basic Responsibilities
National Transportation Safety Board (NTSB)	of the Board for 2-year terms. The designation of the Chairman is made by and with the advice and consent of the Senate. The mission of the National Transportation Safety Board is to promote transportation safety by conducting independent accident investigations and by formulating safety improvement recommendations. In carrying out this mission, the Board also assesses techniques of accident investigation and publishes recommended procedures for accident investigations; establishes regulatory requirements for reporting accidents; evaluates the transportation safety consciousness and efficacy in preventing accidents of other Government agencies; evaluates the adequacy of safeguards and procedures concerning the	

transportation of hazardous materials, and the performance of other Government agencies charged with assuring the safe transportation of such materials; and reports annually to the Congress on its activities.

Occupational Safety and Health Review Commission (OSHRC)

The Occupational Safety and Health Review Commission (OSHRC) is concerned with providing safe and healthful working conditions for both the employer and the employee. It adjudicates cases forwarded to it by the Department of Labor when disagreements arise over the results of safety and health inspections performed by the Department.

The Occupational Safety and Health Review Commission is an independent adjudicatory agency established by the Occupational Safety and Health Act of 1970 (84 Stat. 1590; 29 U.S.C. 651).

The act, enforced by the Secretary of Labor, is an effort to reduce the incidence of personal injuries, illnesses, and deaths among working men and women in the United States which result from their employment. The Review Commission was created to adjudicate enforcement actions initiated under the act when they are contested by employers, employees, or representatives of employees.

The principal office of the Review Commission is in Washington, D.C. There are also

TABLE 3.27 ORIGIN AND PRIMARY RESPONSIBILITIES OF AGENCIES, COMMISSIONS, AND DEPARTMENTS (*continued*)

Title	Origin and Authority	Basic Responsibilities
Occupational Safety and Health Review Commission (OSHRC)	10 offices where Review Commission Judges are stationed.	
Pension Benefit Guaranty Corporation (PBGC)	Title IV of the Employee Retirement Income Security Act of 1974 (ERISA), approved September 2, 1974 (88 Stat. 1003 et seq.; 29 U.S.C. 1301 et seq.), established the Pension Benefit Guaranty Corporation to guarantee payment of insured benefits if covered plans terminate without sufficient assets to pay such benefits.	The Pension Benefit Guaranty Corporation (PBGC) guarantees basic pension benefits in covered private plans if they terminate with insufficient assets.
Securities and Exchange Commission (SEC)	The Securities and Exchange Commission was created under authority of the Securities Exchange Act of 1934 (48 Stat. 881; 15 U.S.C. 78a to 78jj) and was organized on July 2, 1934. The Commission also serves as adviser to United States district courts in connection with reorganization proceedings for	The Securities and Exchange Commission (SEC) provides the fullest possible disclosure to the investing public and protects the interests of the public and investors against malpractices in the securities and financial markets.

debtor corporations in which there is a substantial public interest. The Commission also has certain responsibilities under section 15 of the Bretton Woods Agreements Act of 1945 (59 Stat. 512; 22 U.S.C.A. 286–286k) and section 851(e) of the Internal Revenue Code of 1954 (68A Stat. 3; 26 U.S.C.A. 851(e)).

Small Business Administration (SEA)

The Small Business Administration was created by the Small Business Act of 1953 (67 Stat. 232), and derives its present existence and authority from the Small Business Act (72 Stat. 384; 15 U.S.C. 631 et seq.), as amended. It also derives its authority from the Small Business Investment Act of 1958 (72 Stat. 689; 15 U.S.C. 661), as amended, the Disaster Relief Act of 1970 (84 Stat. 1744; 42 U.S.C. 4401 et seq.), and section 9 of the act of April 20, 1973 (87 Stat. 24). The Secretary of Commerce has delegated to the Administration certain

The fundamental purposes of the Small Business Administration (SBA) are to aid, counsel, assist, and protect the interests of small business; ensure that small business concerns receive a fair proportion of Government purchases, contracts, and subcontracts, as well as of the sales of Government property; make loans to small business concerns, State and local development companies, and the victim of floods or other catastrophes, or of certain types of economic injury; license, regulate, and make loans to small business investment companies; improve the management skills of small business owners, potential owners, and managers; conduct studies of the economic environment; and guarantee leases entered into by small business concerns as well as surety bonds issued to them.

TABLE 3.27 ORIGIN AND PRIMARY RESPONSIBILITIES OF AGENCIES, COMMISSIONS, AND DEPARTMENTS (*continued*)

Title	Origin and Authority	Basic Responsibilities
Small Business Administration (SEA)	responsibilities and functions under section 202 of the Public Works and Economic Development Act of 1965 (79 Stat. 556; 42 U.S.C. 3142), as amended, and is further authorized to delegate to the Administration certain responsibilities and functions under chapter 3 of the Trade Act of 1974 (88 Stat. 1978; 19 U.S.C. 2101).	
United States General Accounting Office (GAO)		The General Accounting Office (GAO), created by the Budget and Accounting Act, 1921 (31 U.S.C. 41), was vested with all powers and duties of the six auditors and the Comptroller of the Treasury, as stated in the act of July 31, 1894, and other statutes extending back to the original Treasury Act of of 1789. The 1921 act broadened the Government's audit activities and established new responsibilities for reporting to the Congress. The scope of the activities of the General Accounting Office was further extended by the Government Corporation Control Act (31 U.S.C. 841), the Legislative Reorganization Act of 1946 (31 U.S.C. 60), the Accounting and Auditing Act of 1950 (31 U.S.C. 65), the Legislative Reorganization Act of 1970 (31 U.S.C. 1151), the Congressional Budget

and Impoundment Control Act of 1974 (88 Stat. 297), the General Accounting Office Act of 1974 (88 Stat. 1959), and other legislation.

The General Accounting Office is under the control and direction of the Comptroller General of the United States and the Deputy Comptroller General of the United States, appointed by the President with the advice and consent of the Senate for terms of 15 years.

The General Accounting Office has the following basic purposes: to assist the Congress, its committees, and its Members in carrying out their legislative and oversight responsibilities, consistent with its role as an independent nonpolitical agency in the legislative branch; to carry out legal, accounting, auditing, and claims settlement functions with respect to Federal Government programs and operations as assigned by the Congress; and to make recommendations designed to provide for more efficient and effective Government operations.

The United States International Trade Commission furnishes studies, reports, and recommendations involving international trade and tariffs to the President, the Congress, and other Government agencies. In this capacity, the Commission conducts a variety of investigations, public hearings, and research projects pertaining to the international policies of the United States.

United States International Trade Commission

The United States International Trade Commission is an independent agency created by an act of Congress approved September 8, 1916 (39 Stat. 795), as the United States Tariff Commission. The name was changed to the United States International Trade Commission by section 171 of the Trade Act of 1974 (88 Stat. 2009; 19 U.S.C. 2231). The Commission's present powers and duties are provided for largely by the Tariff Act of 1930;

TABLE 3.27 ORIGIN AND PRIMARY RESPONSIBILITIES OF AGENCIES, COMMISSIONS, AND DEPARTMENTS (*continued*)

Title	Origin and Authority	Basic Responsibilities
	the Antidumping Act, 1921; the Agricultural Adjustment Act; the Trade Expansion Act of 1962; and the Trade Act of 1974. Commissioners appointed after January 3, 1975, are appointed for a term of 9 years, unless appointed to fill an unexpired term, and are not elegible for reappointment. Prior to January 3, 1975, the Chairman and the Vice Chairman were designated annually by the President. Not more than three Commissioners may be members of the same political party. (Sec.330, Tariff Act of 1930; 19 U.S.C. 1330.)	

Adaptation from: U.S. Government Manual 1976 Edition, U.S. Government Printing Office

SOURCE: Adaptation of U.S. Government manual 1976 Edition U.S. Government Printing Office, Washington, D.C.

list of many but not all safety, health, and environmental statutes affecting the chemcial industry as shown in Table 3.28).

5. The authority of various statutes often overlap (e.g., some authority over the work place granted to both OSHA and EPA).

6. State and local laws also prevail. They add other requirements—usually more stringent because this is the thrust of new federal legislation (that is, the federal preempts the state unless the state is more restrictive)—and any or all of the problems of federal laws can also be seen in state and local laws.

7. The demands of contractors engaged in federal studies, surveys, and so on also add to the federal requirements; they are truly "hidden" cost, delay, and overall business effects.

8. While not regulatory in the direct sense, both the Office of Management and Budget and the General Accounting Office have their direct and indirect effects insofar as they review, analyze, and state opinions on both the government and the business community, and they pass on government actions within their areas of respective responsibility and authority.

9. The legislators themselves, which of course includes their staffs and those of various congressional committees, impose additional demands.

10. The courts that rule on various issues at litigation also affect the present and future in terms of the direct consequence of their decisions; the precedent value of their decisions in terms of case law; and more important

TABLE 3.28   MAJOR FEDERAL LEGISLATION THAT CONTROLS CHEMICALS

Occupational Safety and Health Act (OSHA)
River and Harbors Act of 1899
National Environmental Policy Act (NEPA)
Clean Air Act of 1970(CCA)
Federal Water Pollution Control Act (FWPCA)
Ocean Dumping Act
Solid Waste Disposal Act
Federal Food, Drug, and Cosmetic Act (FDA)
Consumer Product Safety Act (CPSA)
Federal Hazardous Substances Act
Federal Meat and Poultry Inspection Acts
Flammable Fabrics Act
Poison Prevention Packaging Act
Explosives and Combustibles Act
Toxic Substances Control Act
Federal Insecticide, Pesticide and Rodenticide Act
Resource Conservation and Recovery Act

insofar as decisions are tantamount to the establishment of national and agency policy implementation and congressional intent. The role of the courts is sure to be one of increasingly critical attention in years to come.

LEGISLATION AND REGULATION

There is a definite difference between the laws or the enabling legislation and the rules and regulations that derive from them. In terms of numbers alone no true comparisons can be made. New laws enacted by the president or the Congress have numbered around 200 per year for the past few years, while regulations number in the thousands (approximately 25,000 in 1974 alone). For us even to try to summarize the regulatory labrynth would be impossible. From the statutory viewpoint, however, we can identify and highlight some of the major acts. Most of the legislation we will describe is from the post-1970 period. Because custom seems to be to deal with the top anything in units of 10 Table 3.29 follows this convention and summarizes the legislative "hit parade"—the top 10 most significant laws affecting business. The selection here is, of course, open to question depending on the point of view others could and would be selected. The attempt was to select those that have the broadest actual and potential implications, applications, and effects on most businesses.

MAJOR EFFECTS OF AGENCIES, LEGISLATION, AND REGULATIONS

The debate over the effects of agencies, legislation, and regulations rages. Those who are strong advocates of business control for social benefit contend that the pluses are essentially all on the side of the public. This is, of course, the major intention. Business is not alone in maintaining that while there is a need for some regulation and there are some undenied benefits, they are often not demonstrated, are excessively costly, or even illusory. In some instances the objective may be achieved but the result can be counterproductive and possibly even counter to the public interest. Obviously, we are not going to be able to put these arguments to rest. Much remains to be done to prove the contentions—whether they be favorable, whether they demonstrate reasonableness or unreasonableness, and whether the public has been served or swindled. Our purpose here is not to take sides; it is to examine the issue as objectively as possible and to highlight some of the effects. As the lawyers say, *Res ipso loquitor* (Let the facts speak for themselves). Table 3.30 is an attempt to do so by illustrating the gamut of macro-to-micro effects that range from cost of goods to money supply without attempting to draw any conclusion or inference. The effects are real and demonstrable. Some may be positive and some negative, or there may be varying

TABLE 3.29 A CONCISE SUMMARY OF THE TOP 10 STATUTES EFFECTING BUSINESS

Act	Year Enacted	Respon- sible	Concise Summary of Major Intention and Provisions
Federal Food, Drug, and Cosmetic Act Amendments	1962	FDA	Substantial expansion of the authorities and requirements of the original Pure Food and Drug Act of 1906 and later amendments. It requires pretesting of drug efficiency and safety in addition to generic labeling.
Civil Rights Act	1964	EEOC	A socially oriented act, it was the basis for establishing the Equal Employment Opportunity Commission. The objective is to end discrimination in employment and pest employment job practices and opportunities based on color, race, religion, sex, or nationality. Many voluntary and involuntary programs are involved, along with complex compliance requirements.
Occupational Safety and Health Act	1970	OSHA	The object is to provide a safe work place for all employees. The agency has the authority to issue standards for work place practices and conditions and has to date promulgated several hundred of these. Each employer is required to comply with these standards. The government is granted extensive enforcement rights, and employees have the right to request OSHA Inspections.
Clean Air Act of 1970	1970	EPA	This act is directed towards the control of air pollution from all sources, both mobile and stationary. Air quality standards are to be established by authority granted to the agency. Mandatory compliance and severe penalty provisions are included.

TABLE 3.29 A CONCISE SUMMARY OF THE TOP 10 STATUTES EFFECTING BUSINESS (*continued*)

Act	Year Enacted	Responsible	Concise Summary of Major Intention and Provisions
Consumer Product Safety Act	1972	CPSC	This act created the 5-person Consumer Product Safety Commission which has broad regulatory authority over consumer products which are in turn broadly defined. In addition, authority for enforcement of several other statutes was consolidated under this act (e.g., Flammable Fabrics Act, Hazardous Substances Act). In addition to regulation, the commission can ban consumer products and require recall. Both civil and criminality penalties are established.
Equal Employment Opportunity Act	1972	EEOC	Related to the earlier Civil Rights Act, this provides further authority to EEOC, including the right to sue employers over EEO activities.
Federal Water Pollution Control Act	1972	EPA	This law established goals for the control of pollution discharges into our waters according to a predetermined schedule, with a national goal of total elimination by 1985. It grants EPA authority to establish standards and to issue discharge permits. Citizens' suits against polluters and the EPA are permitted, and severe civil and criminal penalties are established.
Employee Retirement Income Security Act	1974	ERISA	The aim of this law is to provide for pension programs where they do not exist or for certain modification of those that do within the preview of the legislation. It also established guarantees of payments, vestment, and other employee rights and protections.

Toxic Substances Control Act	1976	EPA	A new law that requires premarket notification of all new chemicals and premarket testing of selected ones. It grants broad regulatory powers to EPA, including banning, limited production, uses, and many other requirements. Existing chemicals are also covered, as are substantial new uses for existing chemicals. Extensive record-keeping and reporting requirements and civil and criminal penalties are established. Both citizens' suits and petitions are provided for.
Resource Conservation and Recovery Act	1976	EPA	Another new act with many provisions that relate to solid waste disposal, recovery, and therefore to energy. Additional very broad authority over "hazardous" waste regardless of physical form is granted to EPA. This will include authority for permits; standards of performance and disposal manifest systems. Both civil and criminal penalties are established.

Note: While not mentioned specifically because we have deliberately avoided extensive review of tax and tax-related matters because this is such a highly specialized area, we cannot fail to mention the passage of the new (1976) Tax Reform Act. Many of the requirements of this act will apply to the marketing executive as they relate to deductions, travel and expenses, entertainment, etc. It may yet make the "top 10."

TABLE 3.30 EFFECTS OF GOVERNMENT LEGISLATION AND REGULATION ON BUSINESS, MARKET, AND BUYER

Macro	Micro	Micro
Limitations of choice	Competitive status	Recall
Restriction of options	Labeling	Plant location/expansion
Growth in service sector (support, nonproductive jobs)	Cost	Employment
Disposable income	Packaging	Personnel practice policies
Restrictions on market entry and withdrawal	Delay	Accounting
Productivity declines	Paperwork	Labor relations
Technology transfer	Prices	Production
Inflation	Bans	Processes
Market structure	Restrictions	Work places and practices
Rate and route determination	Limitations	Patents
Communications	Allocations	Copyrights
Transportation	Standardization	Representation
Taxation	Testing	Advertising
Capital formation	Planning	Promotion
Investment	Image	Repurchase
Disclosure (confidentiality)	Organization	Return of investment

International trade	Liability	Profit
Balance of payments	Insurance	Opportunity costs
Fiscal position	Grants	Divestitures
Interest rates	Contracts (government business)	
Money supply	Subsidies	
	Literature	
	Sales	
	Credit	

Notes

1. This list is not intended as a "laundry list" but to capture the basic "real" elements of concern. For this reason, it also does not attempt to list any of the many other conceptual philosophical aspects that might be included.

2. *Macro* in this context equals gross, cross-cutting and more prevasive effects, including those of basic socioeconomic consequence. Many if not all, are difficult to quantify precisely.

3. *Micro* in this context equals more specific, limited, and essentially quantifiable effects.

4. Benefits, while not tabulated as mentioned before, would include improvements in health, safety, environment, equality, security, conservation, responsible action, social effects.

5. The entire tabulation is one of mixed composition—that is, inclusive of not only economic but scientific, technical, and motivational effects.

degrees of positivity and negativity. At this point no judgments are being passed. Later we look at some of these in far greater detail, both qualitatively and quantitatively, and draw some conclusions. Ultimate analysis will no doubt reveal that some are positive, some negative, and some fall into the "we don't know yet" category. All of this is helpful if openly admitted, for if there are to be any changes in the overall approach and attitude towards business regulation, changes will have to be made not only by the government and the public interest groups, but by industry itself. We do not mean always to be pointing only towards the negative; we acknowledge that there are positive effects in many cases. But not all actions are beneficial, and many are taken without really knowing if the intended benefit will in fact occur, and mechanisms are not provided to make this determination either before or after the legislative or regulatory fact.

THE MATRIX

What we are confronted with is not a simple set of agencies versus a set of acts or regulations. That would be complicated enough, but it is a vast and intricate matrix. A matrix that combines act, regulation, agency, and business in a network of intertwined requirements, which are serious enough in themselves but take on an awesome dimension when considered in their totality. The totality must be considered by the recipients of this kind of attention. How lucky we are to be so well attended!

WHO PAYS?

The vital question of who pays can be answered by the adage, which tells us, quite truly, it is always both you and I. The free lunch stand is an illusion. Obviously, legislation and regulation result in cost increases. These are ultimately borne by the buyer. But there is yet another cost, one that is not so apparent—that is the cost of creating, sustaining, and administering all of this, a cost that you and I pay through our taxes. Federal expenditures for business regulation in the years 1974, 1975, and 1976, as shown in Table 3.31. are very revealing.

A steady increase is evident, and we are safe to observe that the pattern in the years following 1976 will show no reversals. As a case in point, the basic budget of the Consumer Safety Commission (CSPC) for FY 1977 is $39 million (890 positions) and the FY 1978 request is $40 million (928 positions), or an overall increase in excess of $1 million (actual request is $40,152; 000) and 38 positions. These compare to $19 million in 1974, $43 million in 1975 and $37 million in 1976. Somebody is paying. Guess who!

TABLE 3.31 FEDERAL EXPENDITURES FOR BUSINESS REGULATION (Fiscal years, in millions of dollars)

Agency	1974	1975	1976
Agriculture	330	376	381
Health, Education and Welfare	145	171	189
Interior	59	74	79
Justice	270	345	383
Labor	231	343	397
Transportation	178	212	234
Treasury	246	306	320
Civil Aeronautics Board	89	85	85
Commodity Future Trading Commission	–	–	11
Consumer Product Safety Commission	19	43	37
Equal Employment Opportunity Commission	42	54	60
Federal Communications Commission	33	127	208
Federal Energy Administration	38	49	50
Federal Power Commission	27	37	36
Federal Trade Commission	32	41	45
International Trade Commission	7	9	10
Interstate Commerce Commission	38	47	50
National Labor Relations Board	55	63	70
National Transportation Safety Board	8	10	10
Nuclear Regulatory Commission	80	139	198
Securities and Exchange Commission	35	45	49
All other	17	21	23
Total	1079	2599	2925

Source: The New Wave of Government Regulation of Business (Murray L. Weidenbaum), *Business and Society Review,* Fall 1975. Used by permission.

The true cost to the public must be fully and completely determined. It has to be measured in terms of both elements—the price in the market and the amounts shown in the withholding column. These are quantifiable; that there are less measureable quantitative effects such as employment and real purchasing power we will not even discuss. If all of this is justified in the public interest, as in some cases it was and is, then no contest. But where it is excessive, where it reflects an indiscriminate bureaucratic preoccuaption with minutiae, costly but unessential and therefore detrimental or excessive, the question of public benefits remains—only now accentuated.

FOUR

WHAT THIS MEANS TO
Marketing

Certainly the aspects of the regulatory environment are of great interest to the marketing executive; but many of the elements of social concern, concepts of entitlement, and attitudinal shifts towards government and the business community at large are distant to the short- and intermediate-term interests and responsibilities of marketing.

When we talk of alterations in preceptions regarding government, business and the public interest, the concerns over free enterprise and the effect of the media in creating or fostering such changes, we do have to admit that to a large degree these fall more within the realm of senior management responsibility. The basic changes in the corporations' perception and attainment of social responsibility will have to be undertaken and implemented from and through them. This does not deny, however, that there are many actions that marketing people can undertake in these areas; they are important in developing marketing strategies, tactics, and plans. After all, marketing is and has to be concerned with and involved in such external affairs. Marketing actually operates in the external world, and therefore any changes there have to be considered in terms of marketing actions.

ENERGY, MATERIALS, AND MARKETING

Our examination of concerns over energy, raw materials, and shortfalls hits much closer to the marketing home. What marketing manager has not already felt both the direct and indirect effects of these crises? Who at one time or another in recent years has not been confronted with either outright shortages or cost increases, or both? Therefore, when we speak of the oil, gas, electric

110

problems or cost increases and possible curtailments, we are coming to the heart of practical marketing issues. Problems related to raw materials and the need for conservation, substitution, and product modification are not of the same urgency because they have not been felt so drastically by so many. However, this does not detract from their existence. Were the economy running at full capacity, were production units manufacturing to 100 percent rather than an average of 80 percent, many of these and the underlying energy shortfalls would not be valid threats but hard realities. The problems that these create represent areas of far more immediate concern for the marketing manager. Moreover, they are elements in the actions and reactions of the market and as such are a double threat to marketing. To the marketing manager there is the two-fold spectre of effect on availability and cost and reaction in the marketplace as these conditions reduce purchasing power and as they alter consumer attitudes. For example, allegations of profiteering or resentment over use of critical materials for nonessential purposes results in changing consumer attitudes. For these reasons we have devoted considerable attention to these aspects and discuss them in greater detail later, because marketing must learn how to contend with and respond to both. How to anticipate such conditions and consumer response must also be considered in order to provide for them in marketing plans and activities.

THE EFFECTS OF ECONOMICS AND ECONOMIC THEORY

The interdependency of economic well-being, prosperity, and growth, or stultification, retrenchment, and depression are obvious. The problems of inflation, stagflation, recession, or whatever other economic phenomena that ensue are part of the complex of economic and socioeconomic effects that are too commonplace to warrant elaboration. Yet they cannot be ignored. That they affect purchasing power is beyond doubt. That they are a vital element in the destruction of confidence in both government and business may not be so apparent. After the Great Depression of the 1930s the government contended that it knew not only the cause but the cure. It could not happen again. Recent past and still painful present conditions—high prices, high unemployment, and low demand—have shown us that the government was wrong. While the public gives fair measure of blame to government, they also blame business. In fact, one has difficulty judging whom they blame more for the problems. Certainly they blame government for failing to prevent, but they resent business for increasing prices and reducing services. That classical economics have failed us is more than clear. Economists were not able to predict or prevent, and they have not yet been able to correct the condition. Business economists were no better than government in this instance. Regardless of who were the ''rights'' and who the ''wrongs,'' the truth is that both business and government economists missed the mark. Now we both share the resentment and the consequences that affect the marketplace in many overt and subtle ways.

Because this is not a book on economic theory, it is unfair to unduly criticize. We are not in a position to recommend solutions, either pragmatic or theoretical, although we can make the observation that a new economics is necessary—one that is more egalitarian in its approach and is far more sensitive to energy and material effects in its general construct than has been true in the past. It will also have to be more attuned to the market and to the reactions of the public if it is to assess behavior and response. Economists have been so preoccupied with numbers and their relationships that perhaps they have lost sight of the fact that they are actually trying to make determinations that are ultimately the result not of the interactions of abstractions but of the animate interactions of people. Putting humanistics back into statistics will help.

UNPRECEDENTED DEMANDS

Business is generally unprepared to respond to the unprecedented demands on marketing. Many of us are still trying to understand so that we can respond. Business has been trapped in an identity crisis. In trying to make adjustments it is caught in the conflict of trying to determine which role it should play. Should we continue in the traditional role and proceed essentially on a "business as usual" approach, or should we convert to a visible, vocal, and highly social institution? Neither of these seem to be right, and in fact, they are not. While marketing cannot proceed with a business as usual approach, it cannot be a purely social entity. How we can strike a balance that allows business to have purpose while considering and responding to the social need is one of the subjects that we shall be examining. Needless to say this too is the problem of the corporation and of business in general. Insofar as these elements are inseparable as they interrelate to the total business organization and action, and that of marketing, they too are considered here. However, no detailed expostulation of corporate action and adjustment is planned. Our purpose is to consider marketing and only insofar as it is necessary for this purpose will we extend beyond this functional boundary and delve into the rarified atmosphere of corporate conduct.

WHERE THEN MARKETING?

Where are we insofar as marketing is concerned? Because by its very nature marketing is a central and complex activity, reaching far and wide both within and without the company, it must be concerned with both the internal and external aspects of these multifaceted problems. Here we attempt to relate them

TABLE 4.1 EIGHT GENERIC MARKETING-ORIENTED CONCERNS

Concern	Characteristics to Examine for Change
Marketing mix	Price, promotion, place, and product to be reassessed against the background of the overall conditions that are being described and discussed. Restrictions and opportunities.
Internal operations	Relations to other departments and functions within the company, including responsibilities, authorities, integrations, and coordination.
Economics	Supply/demand, price/demand, and spending/borrowing/savings relations. ROI, investment, restrictions, opportunities, costs, capital formation and international inter-relations.
Buyer/seller relations	Attitude alterations, preception, wants, appeal, response, loyalty, and purchasing habits. Alterations in relations between customer—either consumer or industrial—and between seller and supplier. (Our focus is on the former, but most of what is discussed does relate to your relationships to your supplier and the new demands that you will place on him, and he on you, either by option as you deem necessary or as a result of legislation and regulation.
Market	Restriction on marketing activities; customer relationships; company activities in the overall; relationships between companies and industries; direct effects on the market; structural alterations; and more specifically demographics, attitude changes, income distribution, expectation, response, ethnic changes, cultural changes, satisfaction, debt assumption, income, and expenditures.
Risk	Product and other liability insurance, transportation, business, safety, health and environment, economic limitations and restrictions, and statutes and regulations.

113

TABLE 4.1   EIGHT GENERIC MARKETING-ORIENTED CONCERNS (*continued*)

Concern	Characteristics to Examine for Change
Legal	Specific requirements in statutes and regulations, altered latitude and autonomy, liability, expense, litigation, conduct in marketplace between companies and with government, lending, credit, advertising, promotion, guarantees, literature, labeling, representations, civil and criminal penalties.
Planning	All phases of the planning process will have to include consideration of legislative requirements, rules and regulations, liability, risk, and contingencies; including voluntary and mandatory compliance programs and social concerns. Additionally, revisions in existing planning approaches, assumptions, elements, outlook, definitions of short and long term, level of planning, strategies, objectives, and flexibility are required. These will not only improve the planning process and the resulting plans but help reduce planning costs (which are high) and free personnel for more productive activities. Raw material and energy costs and availability will have to be factored in.
Product	Opportunities, limitations, compliance, needs, durability, safety, labeling, packaging, advertising, promotion, competition, restrictions, recalls, repurchase, design, research and development, commercialization, guarantees, liability, health and environmental effects, insurance, costs, raw material and energy.

to marketing and to relate marketing to them. Thus we can best provide solutions for many of the most pressing marketing problems of today and tomorrow.

Now is the time to examine some of these more specifically in marketing effect terms. We limit our initial examination in Table 4.1 to nine generic marketing concerns: marketing mix, internal operations, economics, buyer/seller relations, market, product, risk, legal, and planning. Later we look at many more and at subelements of these generics.

The objective in examining them now is not to treat them exhaustively but to raise an awareness of these elements so that in reading later you will have these concerns in the background in order to place some of the subsequent discussions and recommendations in better perspective.

THE NEW SELLER/BUYER DYNAMIC

One of the first new relationships that we must understand is that we are now confronted with a new buyer/seller dynamic. Of course there has always been a relationship between the buyer and the seller, which will continue into the future. However, we must recognize that the old relationships no longer pertain.

There was a time, very early in the history of business, when the buyer was to a major extent at the mercy of the seller. This was reflected legally ("let the buyer beware") as well as in the general conduct and attitude of the company. As we all know, this was so fundamentally entrenched in company philosophy that the approach until the early 1900s was characterized as one in which the company sold what it could make. In effect it ignored the market and the customer. This changed radically shortly thereafter and was in fact among the earliest events in development of marketing theory that proceeded on the premise that the company should make what it could sell, which was related to what the customer and the market wanted. Obviously this represented a major transition. The legal aspect of the issue has changed also, and many new demands and obligations have been placed on the seller. More will come. Already they are such that the old "buyer beware" situation is more aptly a "seller beware" situation. The alteration is not only a legal one, but a common-sense marketing one, for concomitant with these legal changes have been significant alterations in buyer attitudes. Consumerism, environmentalism, concern over safety and health are all influences and criteria by which our companies and our products are now judged. This has led to a new relationship between the buyer and seller. The buyer is now not only suspicious and sometimes even cynical, but skeptical and resentful. He often now buys not because he wants to, but because he has to. But having to buy goes only so far. He still feels, and rightly, that the choice ought to be his and insofar as there are many suppliers of any product or service, he will exercise his options within whatever may be the limitations of product or service package availability. He wants and will demand a choice.

The old attitude, "we don't need him, he needs us," is dead. Even highly service-oriented institutions such as banks, hospitals, colleges, universities, and insurance companies are no longer starting with this premise. The accent is on customer service, and the shift is clearly to a recognition that we need them. Marketing has long had this basic attitude. It has been one of its basic tenets. Yet there is still within marketing the attitude that what the company does or does not do does not relate to marketing or the buyer. There is still the misconception that company environmental and social effects do not influence buyer decision or that the customer will accept the products of the creative corporate imagination: The public will be satisfied not through quality and service but through advertising and promotion. These are all false and misleading notions. The new buyer/seller dynamic will require that these company perceptions are altered and that our task will be to determine more accurately and reliably what the public wants, not only in product terms but in social terms, and we will have to provide it not only in product terms. It will be a totally new way not only of doing, but of looking at business.

To do this effectively we are going to have to understand our customers and our markets far better than we do now. Questions of market research, advertising and promotion, research and development, and so on all relate to these determinations and our subsequent actions. As background Table 4.2: General Attitudinal Alterations of Importance to Marketing should help in focusing our attention to this opportunity. (The word *opportunity* is deliberately chosen, for if marketing is to survive we had better recognize that this is an opportunity, not a problem.)

THE CONCEPT OF ENTITLEMENT AND ITS IMPORTANCE

One of the elements that is listed in this table is a switch from the old work ethic to that of entitlement. Although this may seem to be somewhat recondite and too theoretical for our consideration, it is not. This idea is related to the attitude that there are certain things in life—for our purposes physical goods and services—to which one is entitled by virtue of existence (theirs and the objects) with no relationship to earnings or effort. Clearly depending on what these are-—subsistence or luxury, for example—there can be valid pro and con arguments. Consistent with our attempt at not taking sides prematurely, no judgments are implied. The concept, which clearly goes beyond only marketing interests, is important to marketing, however, because it can have both positive and negative effects in terms of customer buying patterns.

Looked at from the government and public interest viewpoints, in terms of social benefits and programs, the reason we should be interested in this hypothesis should be apparent.

TABLE 4.2 GENERAL ATTITUDINAL ALTERATIONS OF IMPORTANCE TO MARKETING

Old Attitude	New Attitude
Trust in business	Lack of trust in business
Trust in government	Lack of trust in government
"Spend today; let tomorrow take care of itself" attitude	"Save; who knows what tomorrow may bring" attitude
Confidence in the economy	Lack of confidence in the economy
Confidence in the "American way"	Lack of confidence in the "American way"
Expectation of unending growth	Pessimism about growth potential
Enthusiasm for new products	Apathy for new products
Faith in institutions	Suspicion of institutions
Shift towards ego-need satisfaction (Maslow Triangle)	Shift back to physiological needs (Maslow Triangle)
Confidence in inherent stability of the family unit	Disintegration of the family unit
Basic feeling of security	Basic feeling of insecurity
Basic confidence in self	Basic lack of self-confidence
Dedication to the work ethic	Rejection of the work ethic—switch to entitlement
Willingness to work and wait for rewards	Desire for immediate gratification
Desire for quality and durability	Acceptance of the temporary, emergence of the disposable/replaceable society

WHAT OUGHT WE TO DO?

Many changes will have to be made by and in the company and the marketing function. In the next several chapters we examine in detail the causes and conditions and some suggested solutions. After discussing overview questions regarding general company organizational and implementation requirements, we proceed with the primary discussion of marketing effects and alterations. The reason we discuss the total company first is that many general management concerns have to be considered to put recommendations for marketing into better perspective. Both marketing and management must understand them all. This will assure better operations and will assist the marketing manager in "selling" his organizational and operational recommendations. By looking first at the broader companywide aspects and options he will be in a better position to make more specific marketing-oriented recommendations and thus to obtain management endorsement.

FIVE

HOW TO FUNCTION IN A
Regulated Environment

Some new business challenges, obligations and responsibilities are imposed upon us by legislation; others derive from social, political, and economic evolutions. Whatever the cause and whatever the impetus, the results are apparent: To survive in the current and future environment business must find new ways of doing new things. This is a double challenge: Not only must changes in methods of operation and conduct evolve (we must find new ways of doing old things), but simultaneously—and this is probably the more important aspect—we must find new activities for the corporation to undertake to meet mandatory and voluntary obligations. Furthermore, we will have to develop new forms of organizations, assign new responsibilities, establish new objectives, and alter our outlook and conduct.

While we do all of these, we must also not lose sight of the fact that business has an a priori purpose—namely, to provide goods and services, optimize productivity, make a profit for employees and shareholders, and provide employment. These are no mean objectives in themselves. However, we and the public and the government must be made to realize that they are not only objectives but obligations. This does not imply that these obligations cannot be altered as can other objectives, but such alterations proceed from a different point of departure and move only so far in a social dynamic which recognizes that they are in fact valid, essential, and obligatory. In essence they do serve such a priori social purposes. What needs alteration is not so much kind as degree, not so much exclusion of action but inclusion of consideration.

We cannot delve too deeply into the concern of overall business conduct; the social role of the corporation; and those revisions of action, intent, and purpose that the corporation and the community would agree are necessary, meaningful, and beneficial to both. We cannot address the question of revising the basic role of business in society; or alternative forms of business, such as the substitution of the corporate form; or inclusion of the public on the private board by virtue of representation instead of election. Cogent as these are, we must limit ourselves to the aspects of the problem that more clearly fall within the realm of marketing and its activities. Actually, these are so numerous and pervasive that we will still be addressing many of the issues that do involve total corporate concern and commitment.

WHAT ARE THE BASIC FACTORS TO CONSIDER?

As marketing executives we should be considering some of the essentials that are needed to satisfy attitudinal, operational, and functional aspects. Having identified and considered them, we will be in a position to explore in detail some of the basic effects of legislation and regulation on the marketing activity and evolve some specific answers to the organizational and other questions that are inherent in our present review. We will also then be in a more advantageous position to arrive at some definite conclusions regarding selection of approaches and solutions for application in our own organizations. What we will be examining now are some of the activities, functions,and organizational considerations that closely relate to marketing.

The elements that should be considered in this context are:

Basic business philosophy and conduct
Organizational additions or modifications
    The job of government relations
    The job of public relations
    The job of safety, health, and environment
    Counsel environmental concerns
Corporate involvement in the legislative and regulatory process, including
    Determination of activity
    Advocacy
    Representation
Methods of relating to the government and the public
    Voluntary compliance
    Mandatory requirements
    Voluntary standards
    Voluntary codes of conduct

Working with agencies, departments, and commissions
Working with the public
Working with contractors
Voluntary disclosure
Media considerations
Working with trade, professional, and technical associations
Use of consultants
Public education
Business planning and government effects

This is a formidable list by any standard. We can only touch upon some, while giving more detailed attention to others. In making the selection for those to treat at greater length, the basis has been one of concern for its relationship to marketing and of its potential application by or usefulness to the marketing manager. Those that are more in the general management sphere have received comparatively light treatment.

BASIC BUSINESS PHILOSOPHY AND CONDUCT

The essential topic of basic business philosophy and conduct would require more than one book to do it justice. From our viewpoint, however, there are several elements that can be tabulated as areas that warrant conscious concern and decision. They are elements that closely involve marketing and decisions here, as its other key management areas, should not be made by default but after considered judgment. Among the more prominent questions (with implicit resulting activities) that management should be posing and resolving for itself are:

What should be the role of marketing in overall corporate management?
What should its role be in relationship to representing the company to:

(a) the consumer?
(b) the supplier?
(c) the public?
(d) the media?
(e) the government?
(f) trade, professional and technical associations?

What profit objectives should be established and by whom?
What personnel objectives should be established and by whom?
What safety and health objectives should be established and by whom?
What environmental objectives should be established and by whom?
What should be the nature of the products sold?
How should sales activities be undertaken?
What R&D programs and policies should be established?

How can ethical standards be developed and included in all activities?

To what degree should there be participation in trade, professional, and technical associations?

What should be the relationship to government?

How can the corporation and marketing best work with the government?

What should be the relationship to the community?

How can the corporation and marketing best work with the community?

What should be the corporate and marketing relationship to the employee?

How should advertising and promotion campaigns be designed?

What quality and performance standards should be established?

How should customer complaints be responded to?

How can the corporation and marketing change their image?

What positive contributions, outside of employment and product or service, if any, should the corporation or marketing make to society?

In posing these questions we are obviously not satisfied with traditional answers. What we should be seeking is a new way of examining these questions and the underlying issues that they represent as well as new solutions. In dealing with the specifics and other nonpolicy issues later, we should not lose sight of the fact that unless we come to grips with these, which are the underguardings of all that follow, we will accomplish little. Basic philosophical and policy decisions must be made if marketing and the company are to remain effective and successful. Those that do not seek and find these answers, which well may differ from company to company because there are no universally right or wrong solutions, will probably not have to worry about them for long. This is not to imply that those companies will fail, although some will, but rather that the people and the government will find answers for them. Because we are already less than enraptured by some of the "solutions," we had better seek and apply our own while the few choices that remain can be made.

ORGANIZATIONAL ADDITIONS OR MODIFICATIONS

Having a new philosophy or new objectives is useful insofar as there are organizations and mechanisms by which they can be effectuated. This means that in finding new ways we must also look to new organizational approaches, which may involve several options:

Reassignment of responsibilities within existing functions
Establishment of new reporting relationships
Establishment of new objectives for functions
Establishment of new priorities for functions
Elimination of functions
Addition of new functions

In evaluating these we should be mindful of our underlying objective: We start with a marketing orientation and the intention of surviving in a new environment, which requires new ways of doing new things. While recognizing that all of these might work and the selection of one or more is extremely variable, we will not attempt to dissect them all but elaborate only on the addition of new functions. Adding new personnel may not be necessary to provide for new responsibilities; rather, two approaches may be combined by reassignment of responsibilities. Clearly, marketing is one of the functions to which such reassignments may be very appropriate. A brief description of these new functions should be beneficial in determining if they should be added, how they might best be included, scope of activity if adopted, and relationship to existing functions and management:

Government Relations

Because the effects of government are so basic and far-reaching, many companies have added a function—government relations—to their organizations. Reporting to upper management, or in some instances actually a part of such management, government relations people are basically responsible for working with the government in all areas and at all echelons. The object is to represent accurately and fully the company's interests, while keeping the company informed on the latest developments and government activities, including legislative, regulatory, congressional, and others, that might affect business operations and conduct. The duties are many and varied, and the staff may range from a single individual in the company offices to a large permanent staff in Washington. In some instances, depending on the nature of the activity, some of the personnel involved may have to register as lobbyists to comply with the Federal Lobbying Act.* Company representation in trade associates is often effected through this department or the public relations department.

Public Relations

The opinion and position of the public relative to business and marketing is a key determinant both in terms of buying decisions and in legislative and regulatory development that is responsive to actual or perceived public opinion and sentiment. Therefore, although some confuse the two, there are substantial differences between public relations and government relations. The confusion no doubt stems from the fact that there are some overlaps. Obviously, the relationships between the two, if they coexist, must be close; or in some companies the

---

*There are instances in which, instead of having your own full-time representatives, or in addition to them, you may want to employ a lobbyist. There are many available and their services may be very desirable in certain situations. This represents another variation on the government relations recommendation.

responsibilities of both are combined as one function. The basic job of public relations people is to represent the company in the community, which may be local or include the state or the nation. Public relations people do not only attend functions, issue releases to the media, and perform similar "relations" duties; they act as the official vehicle by which the corporation expresses itself to the public. This takes many forms from contacting and working with the media to acting as the fulcrum for employee participation in public affairs. Here, as in government relations, the alternatives are many.

Safety and Health

A great deal of the post-1970 legislation and regulation is concerned with matters of safety and health. To deal effectively with the many and highly technical issues, which require experts in a number of disciplines such as medicine, toxicology, chemistry, biology, many companies have established a separate department to monitor federal, state, or local requirements in these fields and to undertake and implement compliance programs, surveys, studies, training, and assure worker security and safety. To assure impartiality and to avoid any internal conflicts of interests, such departments have no profit or other commercial responsibilities and are in the best position to make recommendations and implement approved policies and programs in this sensitive area. In addition to the internal operations aspects responsibilities include monitoring developments in the field and representing the company when and where necessary. Often such representation is in professional associations or as part of a team that may be dealing with public, legislative, or regulatory issues. This function should not be consolidated under marketing, although health and safety personnel should work closely with marketing personnel because many of the activities do have a bearing on marketing operations—for example, representing the company marketing aspects when safety or health questions arise from customers. Therefore, there is written, oral, and personal customer contact. Complying with OSHA is naturally one of the major responsibilities.

Counsel

Because most of what we are dealing with in this book derives directly from legislation and regulations which involve legal issues and procedures, subsequent interpretations, recommendations, and potential litigation, counsel is required. Because of the number of legal specialties, we now find in the larger corporations lawyers who are solely responsible for areas such as product liability, insurance, safety and health, the environment, antitrust, and so on. If a corporation cannot afford legal specialists or even one lawyer, outside counsel will be needed. Again depending on the requirement, a generalist or a specialist

may be in order. In some cases both may be needed. This is another area in
which there are a number of available options that include the possibility of using
both—that is, in-house and out-of-house counsel on the same or different issues
as circumstance and resource warrant. Whatever the limitations of resources,
however, a business can no longer operate effectively without some provision for
legal advice. This area cannot be assigned to marketing, but it requires close
coordination with marketing. This is true not only of activities that might in any
way involve potential antitrust or related questions, but in areas such as product
liability, insurance, compliance with Comsumer Product Safety Commission
requirements, labeling, or a myriad of other concerns. Legal counsel must also
be ready to respond to or initiate litigation.

Environmental Concerns

The subject of much of the post-1970 legislation, and the object of high visibility
in the media and high priority with the public, is environment and pollution.
From kindergarden to Congress, everyone now knows all about the problems of
pollution (real or imagined) and the need for legislation, regulation, control, and
sanction. The public outcry is loud, and the federal response is correspondingly
dramatic with the creation of another household word, the EPA. From control of
polluters to certifying the mileage on new automobiles, we are all constantly
reminded of EPA. Clearly, there is a need for specialists in this field. To provide
a focus for needs, such as effluent analysis, compliance, permits, treatment
technology, review and discussion with agencies, several disciplines, such as
engineering, sanitation, physics, chemistry, biology, have to be called upon.
Many companies have now established an environmental department, under one
designation or another, within the company. While concerned primarily with
manufacturing operations (usually the origin of the most significant pollution
problems), environmental personnel do not necessarily have any profit, production, or commercial responsibilities per se. They are responsible for compliance
in the most efficient and cost-effective manner. For obvious reasons, this function cannot be combined with marketing, although it could be combined with
some other technical operations such as manufacturing. However, because many
of the actions and decisions affect cost of goods, availability, production
scheduling, and other market-related interests, close coordination is vital.

CORPORATE INVOLVEMENT IN THE LEGISLATIVE AND
REGULATORY PROCESS

Legislation and regulation do not just occur without initiative. This can come
from the public; our elected representatives; the agencies, commissions, and
departments in government; or even from industry itself. The inception, while

variable, is a public process that is open to comment, review, and participation. Any consideration of the involvement of the company in the total process must include the fundamental aspect of participation before legislation or regulation is proposed or in its earliest formative stages. To some extent this could involve lobbying as well as contact with legislators, agencies, media and the public. Participation techniques are highly specialized and to some measure beyond our scope, which is the level of corporate participation that relates to marketing. We must limit our discussion to areas that involve marketing or relate to activities that marketing can initiate and techniques that are at the disposal of the average marketing manager. Within these limitations there are a host of activities that can be undertaken beneficially both before and after the legislation or regulation has been proposed and even after it has been enacted or promulgated (see Table 5.1).

A few underlying principles deserve mention.

1. Try to cultivate relationships with your senators or congressmen before you have a problem.

TABLE 5.1   POSSIBLE BUSINESS ACTIONS RELATIVE TO LEGISLATION AND REGULATION

Before Enactment or Promulgation

Initiate congressional visits and discussions.
Initiate visits and discussions with members of committees or agencies.
Submit business position papers.
Undertake and present studies.
Make constructive legislative or regulatory proposals.
Analysize and present alternatives.
Testify at hearings or proceedings.
Submit written positions at hearings, post-hearing comments, committee meetings.
Participate in trade, technical, or professional association activities.
Lobby.

After Enactment or Promulgation

Participate in trade, technical, or professional association activities.
Exhaust all remedies, administrative or other.
Undertake litigation.
Submit positions and documentation of effects.
Participate in rule-making procedures.
Lobby.
Participate in amendment procedures.

2. Invite senators or congressmen to visit your facilities so that they can have a firsthand appreciation of what the company does and how it is done. This exposure should encompass all aspects of the business, including community and social activities.
3. Support your senator or congressman (not only financially) when his or her actions are in concert with your company positions.
4. Make parallel efforts with appropriate contacts in agencies, commissions, and departments.
5. Communicate. There is no purpose in business communicating only to business; the message must be taken to the Congress, the agencies, and the people.

None of this can occur however unless a positive determination for involvement is made. Such determination can be made both on an overall as well as case-by-case basis. There is nothing inconsistent with a general commitment to participation which then proceeds on a more or less detailed basis as specific legislative, regulatory, or other issues arise. Once the commitment is made, be sure that all of your approaches are well coordinated. If marketing is to take the initative in a particular instance, be sure that all involved persons in the company know that and are fully informed about what position is being taken and why, what is to be done, how it is to be done, and who is going to do it. This can avoid duplications and possible embarrassments.

Methods of Relating to the Government and the Public

Because the requirements of the government derive from the expression of the wants of the people, the question of relating to the government must also encompass relating to the public. If one looks solely to satisfying business perceptions of what the government wants or will require, a very important factor in the equation is completely ignored. To relate to the public is as important if not more important. Establishing a public relations department is not enough. We must also support it with other corporate policies, alterations, and actions.

Voluntary Compliance. Compliance with informal standards such as are now being proposed by NIOSH is important. By the agencies own admission these standards do not have the force of law, but compliance with them may go a long way in developing relations with both government and public.

Mandatory Requirements. Although one has to comply with mandatory requirements, certain aspects of implementation (e.g., employee training, equipment availability) can lead to better relations between management and employees and hence the public.

Voluntary Standards. Many of the standards that have been adopted by the government have been essentially those that were developed by consensus (so-called consensus standards). Various trade, professional, and technical associations have been very instrumental in developing these. This is certainly an effort that must be continued and actively supported by industry. Some government agencies initially frowned upon these standards and others gladly adopted them, but even those who were skeptical now seem to be endorsing their need and development.

Voluntary Codes of Conduct. Although it is far from new, the idea of voluntary codes of conduct has not been universally adopted. Because it could include any aspect from technical to corporate ethics, we can mention it only in the sense of a basic philosophy, a voluntary system of determining standards of behavior that are then adopted by subscribing companies. Such codes have usually been developed through some form of external cooperative efforts such as in a trade association. They have been effective for establishing an industry's position in regard to important issues and aspects of its business with the government and equally effective in relation to the community. They also make good business sense because some commonality of responsible position is good business.

Working with Agencies, Departments and Commissions. Because we discuss working with agencies, departments, and commissions in subsequent chapters, at this point we want to mention only that it is one of the elements that must be provided for. The experienced marketing man knows the importance of direct contact, the ultimate one-to-one, face-to-face contact that is so analogous to the sales situation. Here, if nowhere else, we should be selective in choosing our people, our approach, and the seriousness with which we take this responsibility and opportunity.

Working with the Public. The *public* here is a broad and undefined term. It is meant to be, for we must be prepared to work with the public under any circumstances, in any forum, and on its own terms. One of our failings is our reluctance to recognize this when we proceed with active involvement. We considered this question to some extent when we discussed public relations. When we deal with the public or the government in any capacity we are always "salesmen," for our companies and for business. This also includes our private activities, because even in our private lives we still carry the mantle of our corporate representation. This goes beyond the realm of a functional responsibility, regardless of what that function might be.

Working with Contractors. One area that can easily be overlooked, but which warrants a few words, is that of relationships with contractors. In addition to their direct requests of information, access, samples, survey data, and so on, the government often hires contractors to do this or more for them. Questions of both logic and law are involved in our relationship to the contractor. Although in some instances the contractors' requests are equivalent to the agencies' requests and although for all practical purposes their authority is the same, there are instances in which this equivalency and authority are not clear. In working with contractors, then, we should examine not only the business aspects and public relations dimensions but the legal ones as well. In this context we must mention that some of the marketing concerns that have been expressed relate to confidentially—that is, the establishment and protection of trade secrets. This is obviously important for many business reasons, and the concept of trade secrecy is well established in both statutory and case law. When dealing directly with agencies there are certain safeguards and protections for the corporation. Although they also apply to contractors, for practical reasons we must be aware that the safeguards and the remedies are attenuated.

Voluntary Disclosures. Business must be credible. Too many opinion polls point only too clearly to a decline in faith in business, a lack of respect for the once revered and venerated businessman. Therefore, we start any discussion with the public or government from a point of disadvantage. In many cases there is an air of mistrust and a lack of confidence in the reliability of anything that is said even before it is said. As responsible members of the business community, each of us must make changes in public relations, government relations, the corporation. If we want to be believed, we must be believable and willing to admit where we have been wrong. One of the ways that this can be accomplished is by coming forward where problems are known or suspected in areas where this is not strictly mandatory. By making such voluntary disclosures we cannot hope to complete a task that will require much time and effort—that is, the restoration of confidence in the fidelity and basic honesty of business. However, combining this with some of the other suggestions that have been made, we can take ourselves several steps further. Sometimes this decision may be difficult, particularly where the situation may go beyond the operations or activities of the individual company and involve some more widely applicable operation or activity. But business had better face up to this, as to other painful decisions, lest even this decison is wrested from it through broad and indiscriminant compulsory disclosure requirements.

TRADE, PROFESSIONAL, AND TECHNICAL ASSOCIATIONS

There are approximately 5000 trade, professional, and technical associations in the United States. This may seem to be an inordinately large number. However, because there is no legislative or regulatory obligation for their creation, substance, or existence and because they depend upon individual and corporate funds for their continuation, there must be a reason for them all.

Although they play a significant part in establishing contact among professionals with common expertise and interests and provide opportunities of exchange and dialogue that goes towards advancing the state of the particular art, they have a rather more basic and important meaning to business. They can and do provide an effective instrument for the presentation of a consolidated industry position on many issues. This is particularly true of the so-called trade associations as well as the professional and technical ones. In fact, one of the interesting facets of associations is not only the changing composition of their membership but of their roles.

The list of what these associations can and cannot do for business and marketing is long. In examining it there are certain factors to keep in mind:

1. A trade, professional, or technical association is only so strong as is the support of its membership.
2. Such support is not only financial—that is, dues, assessments, and so on—but psychological and physiological—minds and bodies are needed.
3. We cannot look to the association, whatever its nature, to do everything for us. There is a time and place of collective representation. But by its very nature this means that not all issues will be addressed, not all will be considered to have the same importance and hence the same priority or emphasis, and many positions will be arrived at by consensus, which often means concession. Therefore, there are many instances where individual company efforts are required, despite participation in the activities of the association. That such may be the case should not be allowed to detract from the need to belong to, and participate in, the associations' activities. Labor, the public, and the government act in a concerted and coordinated manner. So too must industry. If nothing else, these associations allow a legal, and effective mechanism by which to do this.
4. These associations, conducted within the confines of existing statutes, present a legal vehicle by which industry can come together within the association and review its concerns and act in a concerted manner to voice its position for or against. With our complex and extensive body of law, which imposes many restrictions and proscriptions on industry, this aspect of the instrumentality of the associations cannot be ignored. It is a very essential ingredient in membership justification.

With these thoughts in mind, an examination of the specifics things such associations can and cannot do for business should be helpful (Table 5.2). No differentiation is made between the general activities of the trade, professional, or technical association, although certainly differences exist. For our purposes, however, the distinctions are not extremely pertinent. Our perspective is that of the importance of these in relationship to working with the government and the public, not the other aspects of their activities.

TABLE 5.2 WHAT TRADE, PROFESSIONAL, AND TECHNICAL ASSOCIATIONS CAN AND CAN NOT DO FOR BUSINESS

Can Do	Can not Do
Provide a legal forum in which to meet	Substitute for individual participation on specific issues
Provide for concerted coordinated industry action	Make industry's decisions for it
Develop industry positions	Exist without support—money and company manpower and resources
Initiate litigation	Address all issues and concerns
Express industry positions at	Substitute for individual contacts with government or the public
Hearings	Address highly specific company issues on its behalf
Meetings	Replace the company's efforts with respect to public relations, government relations, agency or congressional contacts
Seminars	Provide the benefits of "firsthand" involvement
Association meetings	Provide legal services
Media functions	Afford the opportunity for first hand exposure, by staff or government officials to business, including not only personnel but office and plants
Provide a legal forum by which to collect and distribute industry data	
Act as an "amicus" in some proceedings	
Develop relationships to government and the public	
Act as a vehicle by which to effect introductions	
Engage in educational programs	
For the public	
For the industry	
Develop position papers, press statements, public statements	
Issue publications, reports, summaries, etc.	
Appear on behalf of industry at proceedings	
Undertake industry public relations campaigns	
Provide analysis, intpretations, and guidance on legislation, regulation, issues	
Collect and disseminate information that is of interest and concern to the industry, trade, or profession	
Undertake cost shared studies or evaluations	

131

EXERCISING OUR OPTIONS

From the rather lengthy list of options that have been presented, we can see that business is not totally impotent, despite all of the limitations and restrictions that exist. There are many problems, obstacles, and trying times. However, we must find some common ground, and the position of business in furthering common societal goals must be recognized and enhanced. In the final analysis what is required is the establishment of mutual goals, objectives, and the strategies by which we will attain them, not in terms of parochial interests, but through common accord. We need a partnership of the public interest, the government, and the business community, which will lead eventually to the identification of priorities, direction, intention, and needs that not only relate to each but allows such interrelation. In selecting our options, then, in pursuing our objectives, in establishing our relationships, we must keep these criteria clearly in mind. Marketing and business are going to have to change, but so is the environment that is the subject of our concern. It is not a unilateral or even bilateral question; it is a multilateral one. Because it is the most visible and externalized element of corporate outreach, marketing has a unique opportunity to accomplish much not only for itself but for the corporation and for "business."

This is an opportunity that can also be considered an obligation. If "business" is to be successful in dealing with issues of its own and society's interests, we had all better come to realize that they are the same and must be addressed together.

SIX

Marketing:
FUNCTIONAL ANALYSIS
OF REGULATORY EFFECTS

The preceding chapters of this book have attempted to cover a broad spectrum of concerns. These ranged all the way from basic legislative intent and purpose to a comprehensive review of individual agencies and departments with specific descriptions of their regulatory intent and purpose as well as their authority. Naturally, we have extended such consideration into some of the paramount effects on the nature and conduct of the total business activity.

When presenting this broader picture we have endeavored to establish a foundation, a basis upon which the full effect of federal statutory authority and resultant regulatory authority can be grasped by those who have not had the opportunity to devote as much time and attention to this vastly important subject as they may well should have.

Federal intervention does affect corporate conduct from the broadest perspective of general policy determination to the most finite and specific instances of product and process control.

Now we want to focus our attention on the effects of such government action as they relate to the marketing function. Clearly, marketing is a central element of business concern, a perspective that has been constantly validated in recent years. There is little need to review completely basic marketing theory or the central role that the marketing function has come to play in the contemporary corporation. Most of you are knowledgeable about its basic theory and do not need to be convinced either of the need for or the centrality of marketing.

Yet most marketing managers do not have a full sense or appreciation of the effect of federal law and regulation although many of these laws and regulations directly and indirectly affect the marketing function. Because the marketing manager has a wide area of responsibility, the actions of diverse entities such as the Department of Transportation (DOT) and the Occupational Safety and Health Administration (OSHA) cannot be uppermost in his or her mind. In Chapters 6, 7, and 8 we review in the broadest terms the contemporary and traditional responsibilities of the marketing function to the degree necessary to contrast them effectively to marketing in the future—that is, marketing that takes into full account the effects of legislative and regulatory action. Again, however, we cannot deal with state and local legislation in depth, and hence our primary examples and recommendations are predicated on federal legislative and regulatory activity. The effects and the action/reaction patterns and strategies that we will be exploring are generally applicable on the state level. In developing informational systems and in making various other determinations, the marketing manager should keep clearly in mind the individual organizational needs as they might be related to state and local legislation. Some companies will be primarily involved with and affected by federal activities; others may be sensitive to state and local actions. This is an individual determination. Obviously, it will be dependent upon the specific circumstances attendant to the geographical location of an organization and the degree of intervention through legislation and regulatory activity prevailing in a particular state or community. The balance between state and federal effects is a matter that must be left to the discretion of the individual corporation because this is a highly variable circumstance. However, the philosophical considerations examined here and the pragmatic recommendations that are provided are as applicable to state and local conditions as to those that are based on federal activities.

The marketing manager must fully recognize and appreciate the need for his involvement in the area of regulatory activity. Despite the broad ranging direct and indirect effects of federal activity on the marketing function, most marketing managers remain somewhat uninformed or at least insensitive to the realities of regulatory effects; therefore, they have not created an atmosphere within their own operations that is conducive to including consideration of these factors. More specifically, they have, by and large, failed to include specific mechanisms (including planning and regulatory involvement) in their formal operating procedures.

Traditionally, marketing has been extremely farsighted and a focal point of immediate and effective response to the external environment. Currently- —when, for example, a decision by DOT can affect the size and volume of goods that might be shipped and a decision by the Consumer product Safety Commission (CPSC) regarding packaging can result in radical package redesign—we have somehow failed to perceive the full implications of legislative and regulatory activity and to provide the focus within the corporation for responding to these activities.

Our intention here is to review traditional marketing functions and contrast them to future needs and, in addition, to assist the marketing manager in recognizing some of the effects of government intervention, particularly those of an indirect nature that may not be readily apparent. We also examine various specific actions that he and his organization can undertake to ensure growth and survival in a regulated environment.

THE NEED FOR COMPLETE REALIZATION OF EFFECT

The effects of legislation and regulation are extremely broad-based and pervasive; they range across the full sweep of all business activities. Many of these effects ultimately affect and influence the marketing operation both internally and externally (the latter, in terms of how they affect the marketplace). The following list of effects (Table 6.1) should help to emphasize the need for marketing and organizational consideration of these influences. Only by such full understanding of their importance can we hope that the necessary realignment of marketing responsibilities and the new organizational considerations will receive the attention and implementation that is urgently required. This list appears to be somewhat one-sided: Tabulated on a numerical basis, there are more depressing and negative effects than stimulating or beneficial effects. On either a quantitative or a qualitative basis, this may not be the case. In fact, this is one of the very real problems that faces business, the government, and the public interest activists. Any side can make the assertion that the benefits are there, or conversely, that they are not. Many of the pertinent decisions are ultimately social—what the public is willing to expend or forego for a particular benefit. Here we are taking no particular position either in general or in specific. We are merely pointing out actual and potential effects and posing the rhetorical question, which is too ofen neither asked nor answered: Is it worth it? That answer may well be yes. Alternatively, it may just as well be no. In too many cases we simply do not know, nor has anyone really objectively and quantitatively tried to find out. Much of what we are advocating will either help in finding this out or at least point in directions that will enable honest, objective, and impartial cost/benefit analysis to be undertaken. We return to this point later when considering cost effect in more detail.

WHAT CAN BE ACCOMPLISHED?

One of the psychological and organizational problems we must overcome is the somewhat cynical defeatist attitude that seems to prevail in some companies. Recognizing the influences and effects of government and recognizing some of the difficulties in dealing in the legislative arena, many companies have gravi-

TABLE 6.1   PRACTICAL EFFECTS OF LEGISLATION AND REGULATION

Depressing Effects	Stimulating or Beneficial Effects	Depressing? Stimulating? Beneficial?
Increased paperwork	Creation of new opportunities	International trade
More complex marketing	Substitution possibilities	Balance of payments
More limitations and restrictions	Social benefits	Capital formation
Increased costs	Reduced accident and injury	Investment
Increased prices	Reduced adverse health and environmental effects	Employment
Decreased number of options	Increased consumer protection	
Increased risk	Technology transfer	
Increased liability	Conservation	
Reduced R&D		
Reduction in new products		
Reduction in new uses		
Reduction in productivity		
Reduction in innovation		
Transfer to service employment		
Increased litigation		
Technological stultification		
Reduced expansion		
Reduced business incentive		
Increased lead times		
Demise of free market		

tated toward a position of resolute acceptance—the rather fatalistic percept that there is nothing they can accomplish in terms of altering or even affecting the legislative or regulatory process. Therefore, they tend to a position of making the best of whatever comes along. This, unfortunately, is somewhat analogous to the "dropout" mentality.

Although we cannot contend that affecting government programs and activities will be easy, by no stretch of the imagination is it a hopeless or futile task. One of the great problems that government has identified, in developing legislation and regulation, is the failure in many instances of many industries or at least specific industrial sectors to represent themselves adequately in the various proceedings that transpire before legislation is enacted. The records of public hearings and proceedings on legislative and regulatory issues show this to be true. It is perhaps even more evident in the development of rules and regulations subsequent to any particular act and department or agency implementation. If industry is to be effective, it must, first, recognize the need and, second, develop a position that is not merely negative or in opposition to a particular piece of legislation or rule or regulation (unless, of course, this is the only basic and justified position), but one that can take the form of positive suggestion or contribution of alternatives. The posture taken in any given instance is not for the moment important. What is important is that industry recognizes that it can be instrumental and effective before the fact in dealing with government legislation as well as with rule and regulation. In addition, it can also be effective after the fact in terms of amendments or post-rulemaking hearing procedures.

The focal point of many of these influences is clearly within the marketing function, and the marketing manager should be fully appreciative of these effects and take upon himself the initiative of organization change. Naturally, securing top management support is not only important but essential. However, if the initiative is not forthcoming from upper-management echelons, such initiative should be undertaken by marketing management because the main effects such as cost increases, market alterations, availability, profit, and so forth, are felt in marketing.

WHAT DO WE HOPE TO ACCOMPLISH?

At this time a rather specific question as to just what we think we can and would like to accomplish in and through the marketing discipline is in order. Perhaps one of the best ways to do this is merely to pose several questions to be the subject of discussion, review, and for which any number of optional recommended solutions are proposed. In this way we can refocus on some of the specific objectives that as marketing managers we should bring to our review of the entire legislative and regulatory effect. From this, too, we should gain a new insight and a sharper perspective with regard to some of the specific actions that we should and can be undertaking. Some of the major questions to be addressed from this viewpoint are:

What are marketing's present responsibilities?
What should future marketing responsibilities include?
What are the specific effects of legislative and regulatory activity on marketing functions?
How can these be anticipated, planned for, and responded to?
What response options are available to the marketing manager?
How can the marketing manager himself and the marketing function adapt to this changed regulated environment?

How can new marketing opportunities (many created by this legislation and regulation) be identified and utilized?

What organizational and attitudinal changes are needed to function effectively in a regulated environment?

What redirections of effort, if any, are needed?

What new relationships, if any, should be created between functions?

How can marketing be most effective?

What of the legislative and regulatory future?

What new marketing theories and approaches are needed?

Are there any strategies for marketing success in a regulated environment and if so what are they?

As the active marketing manager reads through this list of questions, no doubt many others, some highly specific, will occur to him. This is good because the object now is to increase the degree of sensitivity to the legislative/regulatory arena and to provide a little thoughtful background and a preconditioned attitude in reading and considering the following review, theories, and recommendations. We strongly urge that as you read through these next few chapters, you do so with a very practical objective: not only to secure answers to the questions we have posed here, as illustrative of the kind that should be examined, but to find answers to your own more specific questions that will enable you to translate our assessments and recommendations into practical marketing activities within your organization.

THE CONTEMPORARY ROLE OF MARKETING

Marketing has evolved into a key, if not dominant, business function, and there is little reason to deny the validity of this evolution or to challenge a continuation in this direction. What we will see, however, are some shifts in marketing responsibilities as well as in marketing relationships. This should not be either surprising or necessarily problematical because one of the major responsibilities of marketing has been overall internal organizational coordination and optimization of corporate resources.

All of the major marketing responsibilities that are generally traditionally assigned in the contemporary business organization are derived from active implementation of present marketing theory. Fundamentally, marketing theory evolved around the basic premise that the organization does not exist in a vacuum and that the company must be attuned and responsive to the needs of the marketplace. This perception is perhaps an oversimplification but is certainly correct. It evolved out of an earlier organizational premise that essentially was based on the assumption that the company would sell what it could make, a rather internal or introspective approach that failed to recognize the realities and dynamics of the external environment—that environment in which the corporation survives or fails, namely, the marketplace.

Conversely, contemporary marketing theory starts with the premise that the company will make what it can sell, clearly a reflection of the realities of the demands and dynamics of the marketplace and the adaptability of the corporation to satisfy and meet those needs and demands. Using this as a rather brief synopsis of marketing theory, clearly the inclusion of legislative and regulatory events in terms of their effect on the marketplace is a logical extension of the normal broad-based responsibilities of marketing. In addition to the consideration of the traditional factors in terms of market research and market assessment and the influences thereof on needs, demands, and corporate success or failure, we must now include in this complex of considerations the mandated requirements of existing and anticipated legislation and regulation as they apply to the company and the marketplace. Unfortunately, we must also add to this complex of factors some additional ones: overall concerns with social values, social evolution, economics, energy, resources, and a far more highly informed, sensitive, and concerned public.

Marketing will broaden its responsibilities further to encompass these new factors in terms of evaluations and assessment of the external environment—the marketplace. However, there is yet another dimension to the problem: These legislative and regulatory effects apply not only to the marketplace but to the internal operation of the company and, of course, somewhat to the external operations of the company. Effects that would be experienced internally through the Federal Water Pollution Control Act (FWPCA), for example, are control of effluents, which in turn can effect processes and production costs. Some external marketing effects beyond the traditional price and competitive restraint of trade determinations are exemplified through, for example, the Truth in Lending Law, which imposes new arrangements between the buyer and the seller when the seller is buying under any form of credit agreement.

The marketing function is now being subjected to new demands that are external to the corporation as created by legislation and regulation. These new demands are going to have at least two influences: the influence on the marketplace in terms of various direct and indirect effects and the direct and indirect effects within the organization. There seems to be little doubt that the responsibility for assessment of the external effects and for inclusion of their consideration in the corporation's activities in the marketplace should fall within the marketing organization. Inclusion and corrdination of the effects on the internal operations, unfortunately, is an area of far greater discord and disagrrement. In fact, herein lies one of the major problems of the contemporary business: the failure to integrate fully the totality of the legislative/regulatory effect on the internal operation of the company. Most companies have not paid sufficient attention to this problem, they have not even attempted serious internal structuring to optimize internal operations in the context of legislative and regulatory compliance.

This is not so illogical as it might seem because, obviously, the enactment of legislation and regulation is a gradual process. What has occurred is that companies have responded on a rather piecemeal basis to one piece of legislation or one rule or regulation after another, with little thought to the full influences and effects on the corporation or on the interrelationship of each of the pieces and their subsequent effect on the corporation. What we have seen is that certain responsibilities are assigned to the Legal Department as they might relate, for example, to compliance with EEOC; others, for example, compliance with Clean Air Act (CCA) or Federal Water Pollution Control Act (FWPCA); go to the Engineering Department; others, for example, compliance with Occupational Safety and Health Act (OSHA) go to the Department of Industrial Medicine or the Plant Manager; others, for example, compliance with Department of Transportation (DOT) labeling requirements, go to the Transportation Department; still others yet would fall into Marketing. These, of course, would be the more traditional concerns with price, restraint of trade, and unfair competitive trade practices. All of this makes for a rather diffused, certainly inefficient, and often a contradictory set of internal requirements.

Although this may sound highly critical and unsympathetic, it is not meant to be. It merely is meant to reflect the reality of the contemporary situation, which is not too surprising when we consider that the response mechanism within the organization was created as a response to specific legislation or regulation. However, the time now has come to recognize that the host of compliance requirements and the complexity of them does necessitate a reassessment within the corporation and obviously needs internal coordination. Within marketing product management evolved to focus attention on the product and to provide for internal coordination from a product perspective. Similarly, the time has come to provide internal review and assessment for coordination and optimization of corporate resources in terms of compliance with legislation and regulation. Obviously, this is needed for existing requirements and for pending, developing, and future legislation and regulation.

Strong arguments can be made that marketing may not be the right locale for such a new responsibility. However, many of the effects do directly impinge upon the marketing function, and marketing already has a foundation for internal coordination and optimization. Therefore the primary responsibility and focus for such integration in the small to medium-sized company might well be assigned to marketing.

Strategies for dealing with the problems must follow recognition of the problems and call for the creation of internal coordination mechanisms to assure compliance and optimum internal coordination to minimize cost, duplication of effort, and to raise compliance to the highest degree of efficiency possible. Because many of the actions that would be required to accomplish these objectives are related to marketing concerns, the force of logic moves us in the direction of integration of many of these requirements within the marketing function.

Before we can examine the various alternatives that might be entertained and the various alterations that might be needed either within marketing or the corporation to accomplish these rather fundamental changes, let us first review the major responsibilities of the marketing function and then contrast them with the specific effects that we have seen resulting from various legislative and regulatory actions as they relate to practical experiences of the recent past. In this way we will have a far more pragmatic insight into the need for organizational revision.

MAJOR MARKETING RESPONSIBILITIES

The following list represents existing major responsibilities assigned by most companies to the marketing function. The perspective is obviously that of the traditional concerns of marketing—for example, successful new product introduction, market share, profit, cost control, market expansion, product life.

Marketing Management	Forecasting	Cost/Profit
Market Research	Sales	Risk
Product Management	Advertising and Promotion	Customer Service
Market Planning	Distribution	

FUTURE ROLE OF MARKETING

Revisions within the marketing operation will be needed regardless of whether all responsibility for legislative and regulatory monitoring and integration within the business occurs through marketing or not. This is a basic decision that sooner or later must be faced. Obviously, more than one approach to this problem exists. The decisions that will have to be made in this regard go to the very core of senior management decision-making. At least three approaches can be postulated (leaving aside a very unsatisfactory fourth—namely, doing nothing and allowing things to continue as they are):

1. Organize and centralize through the marketing function.
2. Organize and centralize through the legal function.
3. Establish a corporate staff function with overall organizational and integration responsibility with appropriate key coordinating individuals assigned within other functions—marketing clearly being one of the most important.

Depending upon the size of the firm and the nature of the business plus existing personnel and organizational factors, any of these might be suitable. Because this is a complex question, probably no two organizations will eventually end with the same conclusion or the same organization. Clearly even within what would appear to be comparable organizations there could exist the widest possible differences in assignment of responsibilities and delegation of authority.

While my own leaning is towards the third option—and for the larger corporation, at least, this would appear to be the most appropriate long-term solution—the main concern at this time is less with the specifics of organization than it is with the need for examination and assignment of responsibility. The time to consider and provide for this new business requirement is now, even if only provisional structures and assignments can be made. We can look to more formal and permanent arrangements later.

With this in mind, however, we can look to certain immediate and long-term marketing requirements that will pertain regardless of which of these options, or others, are selected. While clearly marketing will retain its traditional assigned responsibilities at least two new factors must be provided for:

1. There must be a new perspective given to examination and execution of traditional marketing responsibilities—that is, the effect of government legislation and regulation.
2. A series of new relationships must be developed outside of those that now exist—for example, marketing management must communicate directly with manufacturing and engineering.

Taking these two new elements as a point of departure leads to examination of new needs and new relationships, both of which are summarized in Table 6.2.

In a later chapter we present some recommendations as to how this coordination, communication, and integration can be accomplished regardless of whether marketing is given a leading and central role or is merely part of a larger organizational team. For now, and in summary, the marketing executive should recognize that all legislation and regulation has some effect on marketing. True, the buyer ultimately always pays the bill, but this is only true so long as the bill can be identified, or even more basically if the product or service can be offered. There is no bill to be paid if the company collapses or if the product or service is discontinued, whatever the reason. To survive and prosper in a regulated environment is to have the capability to recognize, address, and resolve these issues.

LIABILITY

Much attention has recently been focused on the subject of liability. It is an area that must receive both substantial and careful consideration in all stages of decision-making. Although the question of liability has been with us in one form or

TABLE 6.2 NEW MARKETING NEEDS AND RELATIONSHIPS

Needs	Relationships	
	Internal	*External*
Informational	Manufacturing and	Agencies (federal, state)
Laws	engineering	Departments (federal,
Rules	Planning	state)
Regulations	Legal	Legislators (federal,
Interpretational	Finance	state)
Laws	Research and development	Trade associations
Rules	Government relations	Professional associa-
Regulations	Public relations	tions
Compliance programs	Personnel	Technical associations
Cost accounting	Systems	Study groups
Reporting	Health	Surveys and assessments
Records	Safety	Consultants
Staff	Environmental services	Contractors
Planning	General management	Media
Education (training)	Purchasing	Public-interest groups
Responsibility	Transportation	
Market research		
Consumer attitudes		
Budget		
Communication		

another since any formalization of business, only the events of the recent past have placed it in a position of such prominence. These events can be classified into legal effects—those specific laws, rules, or regulations and subsequent court decisions that build the body of case law which can be so important in this area—and the aspects of public opinion and public action that result in increased litigation (which one in the interest of impartiality must accede can be as spurious or opportunistic as it can be valid and genuine).

While either or both of these can be considered problematic, we have to look to the effects which are also manifested in different ways. The effect of recent laws has been to increase specific liability and penalty; the effect of the public action has been to increase cost of insurance, where it can be obtained, and risk in the marketplace. Although comparisons to medical malpractice cases—in terms of number of suits, settlements, or insurance premiums—may seem farfetched, those who have had any exposure to product liability recently know it is not so improbable. Will the day of "no fault" product liability come? This too is not far from the realm of reality. If we are prepared to accept this as true, the obvious question is: What can be done? Again we must first start with an awareness of the problem before we can even attempt a solution; and second, we must look to the motivation—that basic mistrust of industry within the public and some industry misconduct—to gain some insights and hints at possible solutions. Before we do that however, examination of the present nature and structure of liability is required.

Although we cannot go into the history of product liability, one of the most recent and important pieces of legislation in this area, the Magnesson-Moss Warrantee Act, provides an excellent example of where things have gone and specifies a number of new business requirements. This legislation is far too complicated and far too long to treat adequately here, but we urge readers who are involved with consumer products to obtain a copy of this act and study it carefully.

Another closely related aspect of product liability is that of the courts and their recent interpretations and decisions. All who have followed this area even superficially have noted large awards by the courts, a drifting away from classical liability to one of strict liability (liability for defective products irrespective of fault). This has led not only to soaring insurance rates but in some instances to serious limitations on product introduction or consideration. This has become such a pressing problem that the President of the United States has ordered a special task force under the Department of Commerce to examine the situation and make recommendations relative to possible federal action which might even include availability of federal insurance.

What we do want to accomplish in this area is awareness of the changes that have occurred in actual and potential liability and the real problems this presents in terms of risk, insurance, and indemnification. Equally important are the numerous specific provisions of relevant statutes that must be followed to obtain whatever protection they afford to the marketing executive.

Inherent in consideration of this subject is risk, which has also been altered considerably from the traditional perspective. A good way of examining this changed world of risk and liability may be by examination of a tabulation that contrasts both traditional and new elements (Table 6.3).

Once more marketing must expand its horizons of immediate and long-term concern. While preparations for short-term coverage—for example, insurance——are difficult enough, the far more difficult question is protection from potential liability and litigation 20 or even 30 yerars into the future. This is not an unrealistic expectation when considering, for example, the long latency of such chemically induced health effects as possible occupational cancer. Fortunately, these are rare instances and are the present object of many comprehensive control, prevention, and correction practices within any of those industries actually or potentially effected. This and other long-term potential liability, however, does exist and must be acknowledged. Both this type of liability and liability for short-term effects must be incorporated into any marketing decision-making.

Since we have made a consistent attempt to place some of these seemingly

TABLE 6.3 TRADITIONAL AND NEW ASPECTS OF RISK AND LIABILITY

	Traditional	New
Risk	Business	Product
	Legal	Process
	Civil	Health
	Criminal	Environment
	Economic	
Liability	Product	Health (SOHA, TSCA)
	Trade practices	Safety (OSHA, CPSC)
		Environment (EPA)
		Social (EEOC, ERISA)

theoretical and some of the seemingly nonmarketing oriented concerns into practical perspective, the following list of direct and indirect effects may help place this problem into the realm of real concern where it belongs.

DIRECT EFFECTS

- Increased insurance rates
- Refusal to insure
- Delays in obtaining insurance
- Delays in shipping
- High penalties
- Disportionate liability
- Nonworkmen's compensation costs
- Class action suits
- Cost increases
- Revenue and profit reduction

INDIRECT EFFECTS

- Adverse publicity
- Loss in consumer and employee confidence
- Aura effect on product and company
- Capital problems

Examining these problems and effects is to no avail without some indication of what the marketing manager might do to minimize existing risk and liability, while also attempting to reduce costs, assure obtaining available insurance and protections, and obviating new legislation or regulation. The last question is in many respects the most difficult, for once more we are dealing with projections as to probabilities of occurrence—and in the arena of government affairs, politics, and the public interest.

Some suggestions for approaching the more immediate and less tenuous problems of reducing risk and obtaining maximum protection follow:

1. Review the entirety of the problem with the legal department (or external counsel if none in house) to be sure you understand the requirements, risk, compliance aspects, penalties, and potential protection available.
2. Make a similar review with your insurance company regarding the immediate and long-term aspects.
3. Examine the possibility of self-insurance, as an economy or as a necessity.
4. Examine revisions in deductible increases to reduce premiums.
5. Develop an industry or sector organization to obtain group insurance.
6. Carefully examine risk/liability plans to reduce both wherever possible—for example, in packaging, labeling, literature, notices, product design.
7. Develop positive review programs—history of complaints, litigation, settlements, and so on—to apply this knowledge in future decision-making.

EFFECTS ON INNOVATION

One of the most hotly debated aspects of government legislation and regulation is its effect on innovation. No matter how we define or approach innovation, whether in terms of pure R&D, applied R&D, technological development, product or process, or innovation in the nonphysical sciences such as marketing and A&P, there are those who argue that there is no effect and those who argue that the effect ranges from stimulating to minimal in some industries to stultifying and devastating in others. As is so often the case, the truth probably lies somewhere in the middle (but depending on the industry that middle, which can include any of the effects we have been or will be considering, can be a very negative one). One of the most important points to realize, however, is that even though this battle rages, those who have studied it the most concede that: (1) the science of determining the effects is far from perfected and in all too many cases no one clearly knows what they are; and (2) there are effects even if it is not certain that they are salutary or stultifying.

One recent study conducted by Washington University, funded by the National Science Foundation, R&D Assistance Program, verified these conclusions. After a nine-month intensive study of 15 years of the open literature, the object of which was to determine how government regulations affect technological innovation, both product and process, the results were at best inconclusive as to specifics.

With the exception of negative effects on the pharmaceutical industry, which we examine more closely on the premise that it is a valid example for analogy and extrapolation, the multidisciplinary team decided that the problem of effect was so elusive as to defy documentation. They found that "there is no substantial body of theoretical or empirical literature" that could clarify the matter. Although many will not agree with this conclusion, even allowing for the norms of descent, the fact that this prestigious group came to this conclusion tells us that there is confusion, uncertainty, and—considering the arguments that industry has made to the point of negative effects—disbelief, incredibility, or we are simply not getting our message out and across to the right people. These latter aspects are important because they are valid. We do have credibility problems, communication problems, and a reluctance even to convey our message, regardless of the terms in which it is couched.

One specific conclusion of this study was that there were negative effects in the pharmaceutical industry. This industry has long been regulated by the Food and Drug Administration and has been the subject of much careful study—both public and private—especially after the famous amendments of 1962. In an interesting and succinct article, which appeared in the January 1975 issue of *Chemtech*, "Impact of FDA on industrial R&D," Dr. Lewis H. Sarett, President of Merck, Sharp and Dome Research Laboratories, provided some telling documentation on this issue. He concluded that the first and most direct effect of regulation on R&D was in fact on the, as he put it, D, rather than the R. On the D side he mentioned that the average development time for human health products increased from two years in 1958–1962 to four years in 1963–1967 and later to 5 1/2–8 years in the period 1968–1972. These figures tell a clear story of the tripling of development time within a 10-year period. After this development still comes the time required for regulatory approval, and the tremendous increase in the average times required reveals an equally alarming set of statistics and pattern. Of even more interest is the comparison of the United States to overseas temporal requirements, as revealed in the following table from Sarett's article.

TIME FOR REGULATORY APPROVAL AVERAGE (AND RANGE) IN MONTHS

	1962	1969	1972
United States	6	40	Variable
	1961	1967	1972
Overseas (UK, Holland, Sweden, France, Germany)	6(0-24)	9(2-24)	16(6-24)

Source: Impact of FDA on Industrial R&D (L. H. Sarett), *Chemtech,* January 1975. Used by permission.

Although the word *variable* appears in the table, the realities are that the 40 months required in the United States in 1969 now seem alacritous. Adding the two factors of development time and regulatory approval gives a total of 7 1/2 to 10 years between innovation and marketing. In this framework one also has to consider the cost dimension and the effect was calculated in Sarett's article.

AVERAGE DEVELOPMENT COSTS FOR A SINGLE DRUG
(Millions of Actual Dollars)

	1962	1967	1972
United States	1.2	3.0	11.5
Overseas	0.9	2.1	7.5

Source: Impact of FDA on Industrial R&D (L. H. Sarett), *Chemtech,* January 1975. Used by permission.

There is nothing to indicate that either the rate of increase or the absolute effect has declined. When looking to the question of effect on R, there are equally depressing aspects. In this case we have both Sarett's conclusion that R has changed—the changes ranging from shift in allocations of moneys from R to D to a decrease in the actual number of research projects. The ultimate effect of all of this has been referred to in the literature as the "drug lag." To demonstrate this we can examine two graphs (Fig. 6.1) from an article by Dr. Alfred Burger, University of Virginia, "Behind the Decline in New Drugs," *Chemical and Engineering News,* September 22, 1976.

Although the intent of the legislation and regulation that gave rise to all this was not to be detrimental to business or to the public, serious questions as to the ultimate benefit have been raised by persons who are well qualified to do so. For our discussion we need not determine if the pro regulators are proven right or wrong in any given case. The fact remains that there are time and cost effects as well as reductions in effort, product, and market.

Other examples exist from highly regulated industries—for example, the pesticide manufacturing industry. Rather than elaborate on them, let it suffice to say that these instances also demonstrate such negative effects and are a valid basis to predict with some certainty the cost, time, product, and marketing effects. As a matter of fact a recent study on a new piece of major safety and health legislation was undertaken to demonstrate predictively what would be the probable effects--in ranges—on the industry that would come under this new legislation. The industry was the chemical industry, and the legislation was the recently enacted (November 12, 1976) Toxic Substances Control Act (TSCA). Based on an industry survey impartially conducted by Foster D. Snell, Division of Booz, Allen and Hamilton, the conclusion insofar as R&D effects were concerned reflected an

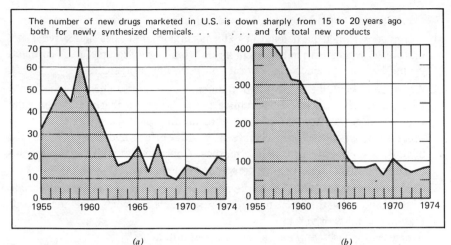

The number of new drugs marketed in U.S. is down sharply from 15 to 20 years ago both for newly synthesized chemicals. . .   . . . and for total new products

(a)   *(b)*

Figure 6.1   The number of new drugs marketed in the United States is down sharply from 15 to 20 years ago both for (a) newly synthesized chemicals and (b) total new products. "Behind the Decline in New Drugs" (Dr. A. Burger) Chemical & Engineering News, September 22, 1966. Used by permission.

estimated 30%) reduction in the total number of new products that would be developed and marketed by the industry as a consequence of the legislation, unless some offsetting increases in R&D expenditures were undertaken.

One additional point to remember in even attempting analysis is that none of these laws or regulations can or should be evaluated singly. One also has to examine the additive or cumulative effects as they proliferate and come to bear on a particular industry or business sector. This aspect of analysis is often neglected by all concerned—business, government, and public. Industry is the focus and will eventually feel all effects that apply.

Having explored this question of effect on innovation, we can conclude that, at the very least, there is a need to document effects and, at the most, to convey them to the legislators, regulators, and public in understandable terms.

To do this effectively, convincingly, and credibly there are several factors to consider.

1. All effects—cost, delay, reduction in R&D effort, reduction in new products, markets, and so on—should be documented. Few corporations make any serious effort to identify, quantify, or capture these elements. Systems must be devised to do so.

2. All such assertions, whether based on individual company efforts or as part of larger trade or professional association studies, should be conducted with the utmost concern for conservative estimates to assure maximum credibility.

3. Consideration should be given to external impartial studies and surveys.
4. Companies should participate in external impartial studies and surveys not originated by their own industries or associations—for example, those initiated by the National Science Foundation and government agencies.
5. Arguments should be in clear and understandable terms. There is too often a tendency to advance only self-serving arguments or those that consider only the negative effects without any attempt to be rational and logical by also attempting, insofar as possible, to determine the positive effects and then to look to cost benefit, cost effectiveness, or alternatives. Consulttation with the public relations department could help in presenting statements.
6. The message should be taken to the appropriate parties and in the appropriate forums, including the legislature, agencies, and departments. Specific consideration should be given to
   Senate and House committees and subcommittees
   Regulatory agencies
   Departments
   Office of Management and Budget
   Council on Wage and Price Stability
   Official hearings
   General Accounting Office
7. Such documentation can be employed in litigation if and when necessary. The data will be useful as either plantiff or defendant.
8. The information will be of prospective value in internal planning—particularly when one is confronted with newly proposed or recently enacted or promulgated legislation or regulation.

CONFIDENTIALITY

Another area of business concern is confidentiality, the preservation of trade secrets, and the balance between the public's right to know and the legitimate concern about valuable business information. This is an area that affects everyone and also applies in instances where government is seeking information through other sources that may not be subject to even the normal controls and review—for example, contractors' studies. Marketing personnel must be knowledgeable about rights regarding the claiming of confidential information, trade secrecy and must clearly claim all that is realistically in this category when filing or reporting. There are mechanisms by which this can be done to prevent or limit disclosure. Although a claim may be challenged, at least one has the initial protection and then due process when challenged and before public disclosure.

EFFECTS ON PRODUCTIVITY

There are many advocates of the theory that one of the ways to "beat inflation" is to increase productivity. If the effects of legislation and regulation are difficult to quantify precisely and determine with respect to innovation, they are even more difficult with respect to productivity. While common sense, logic, and intuition indicate that there is a negative effect, proving it is something else. From our earlier discussion of macroeconomic versus microeconomic effects, this is probably not so surprising.

Rather than try to cite the many studies that have been made to illuminate this thorny issue, it may be better to pause and reflect on what is purported to be a true story. The House of Representatives was considering a new census. One of the questions that arose was whether college students would be qualified to take the census. Determining that this was a valid issue, the representatives duly decided to have a study undertaken—for a very substantial sum of money we might add—to decide this issue. After having taken the vote which approved the study and funding, a member of the Congress arose and is reported to have said, "Ladies and gentlemen, since we have already voted on this, I will now undertake to give you here and now, and for free, the results. The study will show that some can and some can't." Lest the appropriateness of this story, apocryphal or not, escape you, the sum and substance of the studies that have been made in this area tend to leave one with the same conclusion: Some show that they do and some show that they do not—effect productivity that is.

As with innovation, our major concern for the moment is not really taking sides on this issue—although many undoubtedly will—but rather in calling attention to this other and most important aspect of legislative and regulatory effect. Despite what has been said about some studies, this aspect is essentially neglected. Therefore, as with the question of innovation, industry should pursue similar efforts. If we do not objectively build our own case—whichever way it comes out—there is little doubt that it will either not be built; be built upon foundations with which we do not agree; arrive at conclusions with which we also disagree; or at the best leave us in a position of uncertainty, vulnerability, and with no basis upon which to put forth our own position.

PAPERWORK

Some have called it a snowfall; others describe it as a blizzard; and others term it an avalanche. Whatever it is called, few of us—to mix metaphors—ever even get to come up for the second time, so voluminous and omnipresent is the paperwork burden. The paperwork proliferation is preponderously prodigious! Here, at last, we come to a common ground: citizen, bureaucrat, businessman—we all agree there is plainly and simply too much paperwork. What to do about it? How to curtail it? How to reduce it? How to manage it? Ironically, these questions seem to be beyond the ken of man. For a change, everyone seems to recognize the problem, laments it, and tries in one way or another to propose solutions. That these solutions never seem to come to much is yet another problem.

To place the paperwork burden into some perspective, let us remember that, in addition to tax forms, some 5146 different feudal report forms are issued annually. (Dont't take this figure too literally; it is probably even larger. No one seems to know acurately just how many there are, and that includes the Commission on Federal Paperwork. However, this is not their fault because not all forms have to have federal clearance—another problem.) The man hours and costs associated with these forms, their execution by those who must fill them out, and their analyses (we hope they are analyzed and used) by those who receive them are not really known. Perhaps not knowing is best, for truly the facts must boggle the mind and might just push some over the brink.

We must not make too light of this situation, for in fact it is serious. We must give it the attention and creative thinking that is obviously needed to come to some solution. Because the problem cuts both ways and has a clear sympathy and empathy within the government, it should be approachable with a certainty of solution—provided that there can be a meeting of the minds and common interests can be explored to resolution. One extremely encouraging sign in this area is the creation of the aforementioned Commission of Federal Paperwork. This body, whose basic job is to review, analyze, and determine the effects of the federal paperwork burden and to recommend changes is doing yeomen's work and is seemingly not yet fully recognized or appreciated. Unfortunately, the Commission is not a permanent one and is to be discontinued in 1977. However, it does expect to complete its basic charge and report to Congress on schedule.

Just as no one yet knows precisely how many federal reports there are(not to mention state and local reports), no one yet knows precisely how much this is costing. Once more the cost is double-edged—cost to business, cost to government—but both eventually cost the consumer. Original estimates of $40 billion a year are already assessed as being outdated by the Commission, and the number will probably be more like $60 billion annually (although this is not to be considered as a final figure at the time of this writing). Whether $40 billion or $60 billion doesn't seem to matter. Clearly it is too much. For the marketing and business executive, another way of expressing this is that the estimated range of costs to business are from 0.25 to 1% of net sales. The average appears to be somewhere in the area of 0.5%, with small companies tending to incur the higher than average costs.

There are a number of reasons why the burden is so great and the costs are so high. Some of the more obvious ones are:

1. Duplication of reporting.
2. Underassessment by government of the expenses and time involved in completing reports. In one instance an agency estimated that a one-time survey would require only 15 to 100 hours per respondent. Industry response indicated that it would in fact require 1000 to 3600 hours. In another case the General Accounting Office (GAO) hired a consultant to estimate something on which they had what they considered to be a ridiculously low estimate from an agency. In general the consultants confirmed the industry estimate, which was much higher.
3. Lack of sensitivity and accountability. Agencies just do not seem to realize or recognize what is involved. At the same time they have no accountability for the additional effort or cost they impose. Related to another case in which GAO was questioning an agency estimate, the agency involved said, "If an agency states that it needs the information, the issue of burden becomes moot." An interesting attitude, to say the least.
4. Failure of Congress or its staff to predetermine what the paperwork burden will be for proposed or new legislation. This is a similar problem with regard to regulations in general promulgated after enactment of enabling legislation. This factor is clearly appreciated by the Commission. One of their recommendations will be that such prior assessment be made. There is expectation that the Congressional Rules Committee will accept this.
5. Failure to consider fully existing reports and reporting requirements to avoid duplication. This also includes the aforementioned aspect of state and local requirements.

On the other side of the question—what is being done to overcome this—we can refer again to the Commission who has active impact studies based on cooperative effort now underway with some 125 major business and 140 trade associations. From this they will be reporting on several areas (in fact some of the reports—e.g.; Occupational Safety and Health Act—have already been issued).

IMPACT STUDIES

Large corporation
Small business
Labor
Agriculture
State and local governments
Regulated industries
Individual beneficiaries
Consumers

PROCESS STUDIES

>   Information value and burden assessment
>   Information management
>   Federal/state/local cooperation
>   Confidentiality and privacy
>   Role of Congress

PROGRAM STUDIES

>   Tax
>   Energy
>   Education
>   Health
>   Procurement
>   Income Security
>   Statistics
>   Housing
>   Environment impact
>   Statements, public works

RESEARCH/SPECIAL STUDIES

>   Occupational safety and health
>   Equal employment opportunity
>   Financial reporting for pension (ERISA)
>   Title XX

Most marketing managers probably do not fully realize the company work load in the area of paperwork and hence do not fully appreciate the indirect costs associated with these efforts. Table 6.4 is an example of a summary of a cost study for a typical large company, prepared using Commission on Federal Paperwork guidelines and definitions. It was obtained from the Commission and is revealing not only from its "bottom line" but as it illustrates the scope of involvement. After looking at this, one has to be convinced that analysis and understanding are needed. However, industry has failed to cost account these reporting and informational requirements fully and accurately. If done at all, cost accounting is at best a piecemeal effort, scattered throughout the company. Few, if any, people in the organization know how many forms the company actually executes and what this costs in time, money, and misdirected effort. Realizing that this is probably true and that only with accurate information can the case against excess paperwork be built, the Commission has designed the following form (Table 6.5), which is being used by the various companies mentioned in the previous impact and related studies. It is an excellent approach and is reproduced here as a working, practical guide for marketing use in determining both direct and indirect costs.

TABLE 6.4 COST OF COMPLYING WITH FEDERAL INFORMATION
REQUESTS-1975 (In Thousands)

Department of Labor		
Occupational Safety and Health Administration	$1,384.5	
Office of Workman's Compensation	1,066.5	
Wage and Hour Division	507.9	
Pension Benefit Guaranty Corporation		
(ERISA)	182.3	
Miscellaneous Department of Labor Reports	24.7	
Total		$ 3,165.9
Environmental Protection Agency Reports		1,837.5
Department of the Treasury		
Internal Revenue Services		1,719.3
Equal Employment Opportunity Commission		
Equal Employment Opportunity Reports	$1,153.5	
Affirmative Action Programs	485.7	
Total		$ 1,639.2
Securities and Exchange Commission		791.5
Interstate Commerce Commission		618.5
Energy Research and Development		
Administration		327.9
Department of Health, Education and Welfare		
Food and Drug Administration	$ 241.0	
Social Security Administration	67.6	
Total		$ 308.6
Consumer Product Safety Commission		307.1
Federal Trade Commission		198.3
Veterans Administration		55.2
Department of Transportation		
Federal Aviation Administration	$ 25.0	
Federal Railroad Association	17.9	
Total		$ 42.9
Department of Commerce		
Bureau of Census		41.6
Commission on Civil Rights		27.9
Federal Communications Commission		7.0
Cost Accounting Standard Board		2.8
All other agencies (such as NASA,		
Department of Defense, and		
Renegotiation Board)		55.0
TOTAL		$11,146.2

Source: Commission on Federal Paperwork, Washington, D.C.

TABLE 6.5 ANALYSIS OF FEDERAL PAPERWORK COSTS-
AN APPROACH SUGGESTED BY THE COMMISSION ON FEDERAL PAPERWORK

1. Name of information request (IR)	2. Originating agency and agency's IR number	3. OMB or GAO clearance number	4. Is the IR mandatory or voluntary (M or V)?	5. Times completed per year	6. Times submitted per year	Time Required to Respond —in hours per year			10. Total time to respond
						7. Administrative/management	8. Clerical	9. Other— specify	

Source: Commission on Federal Paperwork, Washington, D.C.

When examining the effects of paperwork, just as the Commission is doing, marketing personnel should look at all informational requirements, including nonreport form responses, data system (manual or automated), microfilm, data banks, and so on. All or any of these can be the result of federal, state, and local requirements and therefore should be included in assessments. From a marketing viewpoint, there are others that have at least two dimensions—cost and marketing impact. These considerations involve labeling requirements, notice and notifications, literature and disclosure. For example, some labels are specifically required, as is the information that they must contain—for example, nutritional information, ingredients, and so on for food products or, in the case of some invoices, notice of the Federal Fair Credit Billing Act and summary of its provisions and procedures. These requirements are definitely beneficial in some instances, but they are costly in all instances and should be included in the assessment of the true and complete cost of regulatory compliance.

In addition, the actions suggested below can be useful in taking finite information into the amphitheater and taming the paper tiger.

Direct Costs Required to Respond —Annually					16. Total costs to respond per year	17. What % of the costs would be avoided if the IR is eliminated
11. Labor (direct wage plus fringe)	12. EDP	13. *External* costs (e.g., CPA, legal, etc.)	14. Other— specify	15. Over- head		

1. Know which forms are mandatory and which are not—not all federal forms have to be completed and if you know which ones are not mandatory you can exercise judgment as to which you will or will not complete.

2. Document and demonstrate duplication and waste so that this can be brought out.

3. Do cost analysis to
   (a) Document effects in government, public, or other representation
   (b) Identify and apply costs correctly.

4. Bring your experiences and your message out to government with recommendations for change. By the time this book is published the Commission of Federal Paperwork will no doubt have been decommissioned. However, if this is not the case, certainly they are a vehicle; if they have been, there will be other avenues.

5. Use the data developed projectively to determine future paperwork impact.

6. Use data in legislative and regulatory proceedings involving either pending legislation/regulation or in review or amendment situations.

7. Use official forms as internal forms wherever possible to reduce in-house duplication.

8. Many state and local governments are requesting duplicative data or data which are so similar as to warrant review. Bring this to their attention and determine if single forms can be devised.

9. Remember the ''hidden'' aspects of labeling, literature, notices, data banks, productivity losses. These should be calculated and included in your allocations and representations.

EFFECTS ON COSTS, PRICES, AND PROFITS

That federal legislation and regulation affects corporate costs, prices, and profits is not even debated. Even the most conservative person admits that all can be increased. The debate centers around the questions of amount, benefit versus cost, and the issue of internalization of these costs versus their distribution over the public at large. These are important aspects of the overall issue. However, our discussion is centered on the identification of these costs, their control (if that is possible), and their accurate measurement for purposes of passing on those that are justifiable and to be able to answer some of the more fundamental societal questions posed before. There are additional equally important questions, such as the contribution of (as Dr. M. L. Weidenbaum has called them in his book of the same title) *Government Mandated Price Increases* (American Enterprisse Institute for Public Policy Research, Washington, D. C., February 1975) to inflation, the ultimate public benefit, business survival and growth, monetary policy, international trade, economic and political security. Before we can address these questions, however, we must know more about how these costs accrue and how to both identify and analyze them. In addition, we must better understand the role of business in society, the need and nature of profit, and the role of the business institution in the economic and political world. After understanding all of these, we must learn to better utilize and better communicate the results (a recurrent theme throughout this book).

Let us first examine the broad question of the role of business in society, economics, and politics: essentially a free market system in a democracy. Business provides employment, employment provides income, and income provides the revenue with which can be purchased wanted goods and services at perceived values. This then is the cycle that defines (admittedly materialistically) the role of business in society. Without the employment, without the income, without the purchasing power, there would have to be a number of obvious but relevant questions asked about how society, at least as we know it, could or would function.

True, there are other nonmaterial aspects of the system, and their importance is not being denied; however, when we reduce it to essentials, this is what it is all about. To provide employment and income there must need be an incentive. That incentive, again examined on the most simplistic level, is for the corporation exactly what it is for the indivdual—profit. The individual sells his service either physical or intellectual for a price. The price of such service, minus basic survival expenses, is his profit. Just as the individual will seek employment to obtain and maximize his profits so will the corporation. Putting aside for the moment the relative bargaining power of the individual and the corporation and the measure of what such profit should be, the fact that the corporation seeks to do just what the individual does should come as no surprise, nor should it be repugnent.

This is a rather crass materialistic analysis, but it seems to capture the essense of the capitalistic system. (Thank heavens, that there is truly far more to life than that, but we are not looking to questions of self-actualization, art, religion, or the humanities—essential and desirable as these aspects of life are.) Allowing that this is the sequence of events and the motivation, what then? We are left with the perhaps surprising conclusion that business has an intrinsic social value and social purpose. This is more fundamental than mere social programs deliberately constructed or the effects that derive from its disportionate influence on the social structure and the economy (areas of legitimate public and government concern and control). We are also left with the conclusion that profit is a good thing, although the word and concept are often disparaged. Business should not be ashamed of profits; it should take pride in them (assuming now that they are reasonable and just—an issue of possible disproportion mentioned before).

Once this is understood and demonstrated, we come to the question of public education. Despite what was said in the earlier quotation from the *U.S. News and World Report* survey—that the public did not perceive that corporate profits were too high—other studies, the media, and general observation tend to the contrary. The public does in fact think that profits are too high. Furthermore, the public is uninformed as to what actual company profits are. Although individual estimates vary from industry to industry, the public seems to believe that corporate profits in general range from 25 to 50%. Some interesting facts on this matter are presented in a booklet "prepared in the public interest" by the Advertising Council and the U.S. Department of Commerce in cooperation with the U.S. Department of Labor—"The American Economic System and Your Part in It" (1976). The section of interest here is as follows:

BUSINESS INCOME

Now let's look at business income, also called *gross profit*. This is the money that is left from sales and other revenues after all costs of doing business (*not* including income taxes) have been paid.

If you lump all American manufacturing corporations together, the average gross profit over the period 1965–1974 was 8.2 cents on each dollar of sales. Of this sum, 3.6 cents went for corporate income taxes, 2.1 cents were distributed as dividends to stockholders, and 2.5 cents were retained by the corporation.

Retained profits are typically used for business expansion, for new plants and equipment, or to repay loans. It is from retained profits that producers can create new jobs and improve their competitiveness by increasing their productivity.

Net profit is the term used to describe what is left from gross profit after business income taxes have been paid. For the period 1965–1974, corporate net profits were less than five cents on a dollar of sales, or about a 12 percent return on stockholder investments.

When a corporation, or other business, does not earn profits, at best only operating costs are covered. The company must then rely more heavily on sales of new stock or borrowed money to expand or bring its production processes up to date. But this is difficult, because investors' confidence in the business declines when profits evaporate—and this makes investment money hard to obtain.*

Obviously, we are not alone in our concern that the public does not understand business, the economy, or the interrelationship of consumer, producers and governments. This booklet, which is a free government publication succinctly and effectively presents a lesson in basic economics in a balanced way for general public consumption and education. When we talk of the need for public education in this field, we are obviously in good and happily active company.

An a priori assumption is that legislators and regulators do not set out with adverse business or economic intent. That this occurs is often the by-product of a process set in motion to achieve an intended public benefit. Normally it is begun on an assumption that any costs incurred are more than offset by the benefits derived and that the internalization of the costs—that is, making them applicable to the manufacturer and then, through normal marketing and economic forces, to the buyer—redistributes the costs to the beneficiaries of the product or service rather than to the public at large. Similar logic obtains with regard to environmental protection, resources conservation, and general social and economic well-being when considering other socially oriented legislation. There is, however, a serious question on the opposite side—that is, that the costs in fact may exceed the benefits. This leads us to the overall recommendation that benefits should be calculated, demonstrated, and ultimately proven to exist. There must be quantitative and qualitative assurance that the intended benefit will occur. It is too easy to raise the emotional flag of public interest and public benefit without the corresponding quantitative justification. When we were dealing with relatively limited or less impactive legislation or regulation, or when there were fewer rules and regulations with which to comply, perhaps this need was not so acute. However, when each piece of major legislation and each new series of regulations seems to become more complex—paralleling the irresistible force of an overall more complex structure—each does warrant this careful and considered documentation. The additive burdens of all legislation and reglations must also be considered. The facts and figures on statistical government in Chapter 2 put this argument into context. It is far from an academic point.

Government must fully and carefully analyze the cost effect, cost benefit, and cost effectiveness of its legislation and regulation before the fact, during the fact, and after the fact, so that the most beneficial necessary legislation and regulations are enacted or promulgated. The need must be justified. Industry too must make similar analyses and evaluations so as to present its "case" to both government and the public. However, we must be even more careful to be accurate, realistic, and objective in our analysis and assertions. Public confidence is essential if our arguments are to be heard and believed.

We now turn our attention to the specifics of cost, prices, and economic effects as they most directly concern the marketing executive. Because we have been describing direct and indirect effects in general, there is no surprise to the fact that we have both direct and indirect costs associated with legislation and regulation. The direct cost effects, for example, might be specific testing requirements pursuant to the Toxic Substances Control Act (TSCA); an indirect cost effect might be the control of interstate freight rates as per the ICC. Either can be taken individually and applied to the product or equally well applied collectively to all products via some form of allocation. Whether direct or indirect, however, these costs ultimately are really applied in one form or another to the product or service. They are then transferred to the market.

Other sets of cost effects that affect the general market and sale of the product are derived from legislation such as the Truth in Lending Act, or the labeling requirements of the Consumer Product Safety Act, or from other more directly socially oriented legislatiion such as the Equal Employment Opportunity Act. In addition, although they are not cost effects per se, other influences result in economic effects on the market—the product and the buyer. These may be clearer if we examine them through examples as indicated in Table 6.6.

As we look at this table, the individual and cumulative effects are apparent even if we are not yet able to attach dollar signs to any of the elements either collectively or to any individual service or product. This in fact should be one of our objectives—that is, the finite determination of such costs on product/process and on overall operations. These should eventually be identified on a product-by-product basis where this is feasible and desirable (there are cases where it may be infeasible or unnecessary). Such specific product-by-product cost-effect knowledge is important in many decisions and can be a valuable tool by which to

TABLE 6.6 EXAMPLES OF DIRECT AND INDIRECT EFFECTS OF
LEGISLATION AND REGUALTION ON COST, PRICE, AND THE GENERAL
ECONOMY THROUGH EFFECTS ON SELLER, BUYER, AND THE
MARKET

Effect on	Seller	Buyer	Market
Direct	Economic*	Taxation (increase)	Capital formation Interest rates
	Product costs	Cost of living (increase)	(increase)
	Social†	▲	
		+	+
	Testing costs		
		Disposable income	Inflation
	+	(decrease)	Availability of
		Expenditure for	goods and services
Indirect	Economic*	goods and services	
		(decrease)	
	Insurance		
	Social†		
	Benefits programs	Reduced demand	Limited market
	Higher costs ⟶ Higher prices ⟵		Distorted GNP Higher inflation

*Economic orientation (antitrust, unfair trade practices, restraint of trade, taxation, etc.)
†Social orientation (Health, safety, environment, employment, security, equality, etc.)

make determinations regarding markets, products, or process, and—lest we
forget—profits. (We leave other quantification, analysis, or uses such as long-
term capital formation, investment, divestment, etc. to others in general management.)

In Table 6.6 we have identified only illustrative examples of generic effects on
the seller. To see in more detail how these occur specifically by statute or agency
we can again borrow from the excellent work of Weidenbaum. Table 6.7 shows
the start-up costs for FTC Line-of-Business reports—an example of economically oriented legislation with indirect operational cost effects. In Tables 6.8 and
6.9 we have examples of socially oriented legislation and regulation as imposed
by OHSA.

TABLE 6.7 ESTIMATED START-UP COSTS FOR FTC
LINE-OF-BUSINESS REPORTS

($ thousands)

Company	Estimated Mean Start-Up Costs
American Metal Climax	75
Anaconda	1,000
Combustion Engineering	100
Crown Zellerbach	100
Deere	1,000
Dow Chemical	400
DuPont	500
Ex-cell-o	350
Exxon	1,000
General Instrument	100
Inland Steel	100
Lear Siegler	400
McGraw-Hill	45
Mobil	500
Nabisco	100
Northrop	300
Outboard Marine	100
R. J. Reynolds	1,000
Singer	500
Standard Oil, California	800
Union Carbide	1,100
U.S. Steel	2,000
Varian Associates	63
Westinghouse	2,000
Westvaco	75
Total	13,708
Mean	548

Source: Government Mandated Price Increases—A Neglected Aspect of Inflation (Murray L. Weidenbaum), American Enterprise Institute for Public Policy Research, Washington, D.C., 1975. Used by permission.

TABLE 6.8 ESTIMATED COMPLIANCE COSTS OF OSHA SAFETY
STANDARDS, BY INDUSTRY

($ in millions)

	Investment in Employee Safety and Health		
Industry	*1972*	*1973*	*Percent change*
Manufacturing:			
Stone, clay, and glass	30	87	+ 190
Miscellaneous transportation equipment	6	15	+ 150
Rubber	15	35	+ 133
Aerospace	14	26	+ 86
Miscellaneous durables	37	66	+ 78
Instruments	12	21	+ 75
Machinery	86	131	+ 52
Petroleum	68	99	+ 46
Fabricated metals	20	29	+ 45
Food and beverages	71	95	+ 34
Chemicals	72	96	+ 33
Paper	50	66	+ 32
Nonferrous metals	37	46	+ 24
Textiles	58	67	+ 16
Electrical machinery	57	64	+ 12
Iron and steel	193	215	+ 11
Miscellaneous nondurables	24	25	+ 4
Autos and trucks	88	74	− 16
Nonmanufacturing:			
Electric utilities	203	370	+ 82
Communications	404	569	+ 41
Mining	84	116	+ 38
Gas utilities	23	26	+ 13
Railroads	31	34	+ 10
Airlines	54	55	+ 2
Miscellaneous transportation	70	66	− 6
Trade	702	663	− 6
Total	2,509	3,156	+ 26

Source: Government Mandated Price Increases—A Neglected Aspect of Inflation (Murray L. Weidenbaum), American Enterprise Institute for Public Policy Research, Washington, D.C., 1975. Used by permission.

TABLE 6.9 ESTIMATED COMPLIANCE COSTS OF OSHA NOISE
STANDARDS, BY INDUSTRY
($ millions)

Industry	85 dbA (proposed)	90 dbA (existing)
Utilities	$ 6,300	$ 3,200
Nonelectrical machinery	4,200	1,400
Fabricated metal products	3,200	1,100
Transportation equipment	2,900	1,100
Textile mill products	2,700	1,100
Food and kindred products	2,600	590
Electrical machinery	2,300	780
Primary metals	1,900	900
Chemicals and allied products	1,400	1,100
Printing and publishing	1,000	870
Lumber and wood products	650	150
Furniture and fixtures	580	190
Stone, clay and glass	520	290
Paper and allied products	500	140
Rubber and plastic products	500	302
Petroleum and coal products	260	210
Tobacco	90	48
Apparel and related products	10	0
Leather and leather products	8	0
Total	$31,618	$13,470

Source: Government Mandated Price Increases—A Neglected Aspect of Inflation (Murray L. Weidenbaum), American Enterprise Institute for Public Policy Research, Washington, D.C., 1975. Used by permission.

Although all this is valuable, the marketing manager's direct concern is how this relates to his product. Therefore another, and to him more helpful way of examining and analyzing these influences, is to look more precisely at the agencies and acts that at one time or another throughout the life of a product will come to bear upon it. This enables not only better visualization of the complexities and when and where the effects take place, but also better focused cost analysis. Such an example is provided in Table 6.10, which represents the various stages of a product's life and the various agencies or departments that will affect it in this case a consumer product. When looking at this, keep in mind that several actual acts or regulations may apply—for example, within the authority of the cited agency or department—and that there are also indirect effects to account for when attempting to determine the total.

TABLE 6.10 PRIMARY FEDERAL AGENCIES AND DEPARTMENTS THAT AFFECT PRODUCT COST THROUGH RULE OR REGULATION AT VARIOUS STAGES FROM R&D TO CUSTOMER SERVICE*

			Consumer Product			
Stage						
R&D‡ $\longrightarrow$	M&E $\longrightarrow$	Commercial development $\longrightarrow$	A&P $\longrightarrow$	Distribution $\longrightarrow$	Sales $\longrightarrow$	Customer service
Agency or department†						
OSHA	OSHA	EPA	FCC	DOT	DOC	FTC
EPA	EPA	NIOSH	DOC	ICC	FTC	CPSC
NIOSH	NIOSH	CSPC	CPSC	FTC	EPA	
CPSC						
DOC						
FTC						

*This is for a typical consumer product not involving food, drugs, or other special legislation or regulation that would add considerably to the list.
†Does not include agencies or departments that affect "cost of doing business;" infrastructure effects including costs associated with specific acts indicated—ERISA, EEOA, IRS, workmens compensation, potential product liability, corporate liability, personal liability, old age survivors and disability insurance, hospital insurance, unemployment compensation—or tenuous effects of CAB, FMC, DOJ; or multiple statutory effects within an agency or department (e.g., EPA-FWPCA, CAA, SDWA, TSCA, RCRA.)

‡Glossary: Because there are so many acronyms employed in the previous chart, the following glossary may be helpful in identifying the agencies, department, and acts referred to.

OSHA. Occupational Safety and Health Administration

EPA. Environmental Protection Agency

NIOSH. National Institute of Occupational Safety and Health

CPSC. Consumer Product Safety Commission

DOC. Department of Commerce

FTC. Federal Trade Commission

FCC. Federal Communication Commission

ICC. Interstate Commerce Commission

IRS. Internal Revenue Service

CAB. Civil Aeronautics Board

FMC. Federal Maritime Commission

DOJ. Department of Justice

DOT. Department of Transportation

ERISA. Employee Retirement and Income Security Act

EEOA. Equal Employment Opportunity Act

FWPCA. Federal Water Pollution Control Act

CAA. Clean Air Act

SDWA. Safe Drinking Water Act

TSCA. Toxic Substance Control Act

RERA. Resource Conservatory and Recovery Act

What we have is a series of individual actions taken by government, as a reaction to the forces of business (we must blame ourselves in fact for some legislation and regulation), those of the public interest activists, and those that are politically self-initiated. This generally results in cost increases that we can consider to be either direct and indirect; it also sets into motion a dynamic that affects the buyer individually and the market and the economy collectively. This dynamic is, of course, not all one-sided but is actually the result of the effects of all three elements. Our concern, however, is that the equilibrium that should prevail may well become unbalanced. Later we offer recommendations to reestablish this balance so that the best interests of all three elements are not only represented but accomplished without relinquishing either our essentially free market, democracy, or individual rights and freedoms.

From this analysis of cost and economic effects we can proceed to some concrete actions. Among the many are:

1. Education of the public and, where necessary, the government about the realities of profit—need, nature, and amount.
2. Education of the public and, where necessary, the government about the role of business in society.
3. Establishment of product-by-product cost effects.
4. Establishment of product-by-product profit objectives—that is, each product must be made to stand on its own or have some other clearly understood and demonstrated reason for continuation.
5. Establishment of account-by-account profit objectives—that is, like products, each account must be made to stand on its own or have some other clearly understood and demonstrated reason for continuation.
6. Cost, price, and profit should be fully and carefully preplaned.
7. Allocated costs for government-mandated effects should be carefully analyzed. These costs can be even more deceptive than traditional cost allocations, and "loosers" can easily slip by.
8. Establishment of cost-accounting procedures and practices for effects on key products that capture legislative and regulatory cost on a product-by-product basis if at all possible or at least to the degree and extent consistent with reasonable judgments (the old 80/20 rule in action).

SEVEN

TOWARD A NEW

Theory of Marketing and Product Development

Conventional approaches to business in general and to marketing in particular no longer suffice. Numerous events affecting the general social and economic climate have resulted not only in changes in consumer response, buyer attitudes, disposable income, and other obviously directly related factors, but also in alterations in markets. Certain extrinsic economic alterations beyond the control of the buyer or seller (e.g., the consequences of the oil embargo, inflationary trends, material shortages) have led to alterations in the overall marketing environment that influence marketing decisions and thus affect both the buyer and seller.

In practical terms what do these changes or trends mean? Clearly, any astute marketing manager is sensitive to them and, in many cases, already fully recognizes them. The problem that confronts us is not so much one of acknowledging alterations in economics and markets. We must find some new approaches to take these alterations into consideration and to construct a new marketing dynamic that will also provide for more responsive marketing programs, product research and development, product introduction, or in short, provide a better foundation for the entirety of the marketing process.

It is in this sense that classical approaches to economics, business theory and marketing have failed. Although at first this may seem to be a rather harsh judgement, if not an irresponsible statement, closer examination will indicate that in fact it is not only supportable but valid. The present economic conditions, the inflationary recessionary economy; the failure of present tax and financial programs; the dwindling availability of critical resources; failure to establish international, national, or even local energy policies and programs, all reflect the basic inability for contemporary macroeconomic theory to contend with prevailing conditions. Examining this on a more limited basis—namely, from the business perspective—we can see analogous circumstances prevailing. Admittedly, many of these are not necessarily derived from a lack of recognition or consideration within the business community but, when examining these particular factors, from the lack of position or posture in the government sector. This, however, does not completely negate the fact that in many instances business itself has not been fully responsive to, nor has it given full recognition to, these factors.

MARKETING AND THE FREE ENTERPRISE SYSTEM

Looking at other general economic questions, one can hardly avoid discussion of the free enterprise system. Of course, historically, most Americans avowed a free enterprise system and still advocate its retention as the most effective system in a democratic society. On a practical level, however, with the present degree of federal, state, and local intervention in business, we hardly need to point out that the free market system as traditionally understood no longer prevails. Many have said that the free enterprise in the United States is more a myth than a reality and that free enterprise has long since died. Clearly, there are many externally imposed controls that so limit the marketing function as to severely restrict activities and, therefore, the free enterprise system, as historically perceived, no longer exists. However, to say that there is no free enterprise is extremist.

What really has evolved is a modification of the free enterprise system that allows for some conventional free market activity (e.g., entrance to and withdrawal from the marketplace, product modification to meet consumer demand, and various channels of distribution) that at the same time is more restricted in that legislation (e.g., fair trade practices, truth in lending, truth in advertising, rate establishment, and various antitrust statutes) prevents abuses. Although we do have severe limitations on the free market system, at the same time we do not have a totally artificial, controlled or restricted market without any of the flexibilities or market safeguards inherent in the free enterprise system. Although we can argue the merits and the degree to which free enterprise has been modified and the necessity for such modification, the fact remains that we do not have the totally free enterprise system that classical economics and classical democratic political theory visualized. Moreover, we are drifting further in the direction of additional regulatory control with further constraint on the free enterprise activity, and this radically changed market/marketing condition must be recognized by the business community with appropriate response—particularly learining to optimize performance within such constraints.

Turning now to the broader question of overall business conduct, some difference between historical and contemporary events should be examined. In the main business perceived of itself as an independent entity, dependent upon sales and hence the ultimate consumer but, nevertheless, business has historically tended to visualize itself as an autonomous self-directed activity. It pursued its own course and conduct based essentially on its own self-perception, aims, objectives, and purposes. Today this concept and construct of business must be seriously challenged. Contemporary society, of course, places far different demands on business than in the past. The consumer—not only as a buyer but, as expressed in collective activities, through public interest groups—forces reconsideration. One need only reflect briefly on the events of the consumer movements of recent years to validate this assumption. Simultaneously, government intervention has placed its imprint on the nature of business character and conduct.

What has ensued is, quite obviously, a need to reassess and redetermine the position, aims, and purposes of the business. The business manager must recognize this tripartite determinism—that is, the effects of business, government, and the public interest as they relate and interrelate.

From this discussion, we can reach several practical and important conclusions:

1. Business has historically perceived itself to be an independent autonomous entity, self-directed and moving toward the accomplishment of self-generated and self-imposed aims, objectives, and purposes.

2. This approach has been more and more limited as a consequence of legislative and regulatory intervention and constraints leading to the present extent and degree of federal, state, and local control.

3. Simultaneously restrictions have been those imposed by consumer response and attitudes as reflected in the consumer movement. These have resulted in two rather distinct and important manifestations: (a) individual buyer reaction and (b) formation of consumer groups and the vocal and visual efforts by such public interest groups in terms of modification of business practices and as a major factor in the government's enactment and implementation of legislation and rule and regulation.

4. Business constraints, therefore, involve two separate extrinsic elements—those deriving from the government and those from the public interest. The

public interest effect, moreover, is bifunctional in that there is a direct influence in terms of buying decisions as well as in terms of affecting business conduct either directly through advocacy or indirectly through initiation of government restriction.

5. The general trend and direction of government intervention and consumer reaction will continue, by and large, in its present course. Many people have recognized the limitations placed upon business, and from a governmental viewpoint some action has already been taken toward reassessment of the degree, extent, and effect of government action on general business operation. However, so far there seems to be little serious consideration of such effects by consumerrs and little indication of actual slowing of intervention by the government. These trends will probably continue, although we hope, at a slower pace and based on far more realistic assessment of need and potential negative economic and social effects than we have experienced in the past.

6. Even acknowledging a slowing in the general trend of "ism" movements and government intervention, there is still a vast basic repository of legislation, rule, regulation, and consumer attitude. This warrants a reexamination of business philosophy, conduct, and practice and necessitates a new theory of business operation, marketing, product development, and product introduction in order to optimize performance and to provide an operational foundation.

7. These factors are important, and should be understood and should permeate the entirety of the business activity not only the areas of concern to general management and the marketing manager. It is just as important for the front-line salesman to recognize these factors and their implications so that he can better operate in the real world of his sales contacts as it is for these ideas to be recognized and applied as general business philosophy and theory. For any theoretical determination of business to have meaning, it must be translatable into practical operating line-level activities.

BUSINESS, GOVERNMENT, AND THE PUBLIC INTEREST

We must now recognize the triatic nature of social determination. This can be visualized as an equilibrium between three dominant dynamic forces.

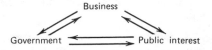

Recognizing that these three forces have a variable degree of influence on each other, decision at any particular time will be a consequence of the relative merits, needs, and position of each.

Future business and personal decision will, by and large, not only be influenced and constrained but will be created and determined through this byplay of forces. This is not an abdication of the role of business in the total social framework, nor is it a denial of the importance or the need for business. Rather, it is an advancement of the position that, in terms of practical marketing viability, one must recognize the triatic nature of social evolution and optimize the performance of business within such a dynamic.

This should not be one-sided. The government and public interest sectors must have a similar recognition of the role and responsibility of business within the total structure of society. There are some indications that the government has already begun to reexamine its role and the consequences of its actions on the business community. The main area requiring futher education is the public sector. This is indeed, one of the many problems that must be addressed by marketing. Ultimately, we sell to a consumer and the consumer's attitudes, as they relate to an individual company or to business in general, are going to influence and affect buying decisions as well as the position taken with regard to legislative/regulatory activity and business control. The force created by business, government, and the public interest provides the foundation for action in any given instance. What is eventually needed, of course, is a balancing of these interests in order to make decisions that affect policies that have as their ultimate purpose, objective, and (most important) accomplishment the actual improvement of the public situation and society as a whole. This will require the businessman and the marketing manager to provide an on-going educational effort, both within the organization and for the public.Because of the lack of credibility of the business community and the detriment it has in terms of effective business operation and representation, we must educate both the businessman and the customer. This is something that has been lacking and is needed if we are going to restore the business image and position as well as reestablish a rapport with both the customer and the government.

On a much broader strategy scale, however, we must reexamine business and marketing theory and endeavor to provide a new basis upon which to operate in this changed and changing climate.

TRADITIONAL MARKETING THEORY

Reduced to its utmost simplicity, present marketing theory is predicated on certain rather basic precepts: We should make what we can sell. The business does not operate in a vacuum, and therefore, we must take into consideration the market and marketplace, the so-called extrinsic environment. A precise organizational operating unit should be responsible for the successful operation of the marketing activity; its discrete and specific responsibilities include sales, advertising, promotion, distribution, and product management. Added to this is the clear responsibility for integration of internal business functions to accomplish the ultimate objective and purpose of the corporation, which is the successful introduction of new products and the continued successful sales of existing products. The ultimate purpose is to derive revenue and profit.

This extremely succinct summary represents only the essentials of the present marketing theory and practice. None of the precepts are incorrect, but they are based on a rather lengthy evolutionary process. Certainly business, historically, was at a disadvantage in that the original introspective posture taken by most companies failed to reflect adequately the realities of the external market environment. The prior philosophy of selling what could be produced was totally disdainful of and completely ignored external realities. The transition to make what can be sold was a natural progression and reflects a more adequate and realistic assessment of market influences. Similar progress was made with the recognition that the business does not exist in a vacuum and must be market sensitive and more knowledgeable of the marketplace. A better appreciation of consumer needs and an understanding of consumers and how to appeal to them helped in identifying new product and market opportunities. Thus business could ensure successful introduction of a product. The evolution of marketing theory to the more sophisticated levels including market research, commercial development, and similar efforts is also a logical outgrowth. The role of marketing in the total business enterprise is an extension of recognition of the need for and the centrality of the product and, of course, of successful marketing to accomplish the corporate objective of revenue and profit. Centralization of related functions such as sales and advertising and promotion within one particular organizational unit is not only sensible but allows for optimization and coordination around this central purpose. The assignment of these responsibilities within the marketing organization is a step in the direction of improving corporate operating efficiencies and ensuring more successful products. The specialization of functions within the marketing discipline such as sales management, product management, advertising and promotion management are, again, only logical extensions of the basic precept that such centralization and coordination of function is not only desirable but necessary. Over the course of years, as competition has increased the sensitivity of the marketing operation has correspondingly increased, and of course, its value to the organization has received additional recognition.

There is no attempt here to deny the validity of any of these concepts and the subsequent practices they have generated. The question that has to be asked, however, is whether these efforts are, in fact, sufficient, based upon the new concerns and constraints that we have explored. The need to produce what we can sell must still be recognized. The question, however, is now what is it that we can make and sell? Clearly, what we could make at one time without major environmental or ecological or regulatory constraints was very different from what we can make today considering these influences and controls. Therefore, a series of new assessments has to be made in terms of exactly what product can be made. Similar questions arise with regard to the continued manufacture or production of existing products. We clearly do not have the flexibility or virtually limitless freedom of choice in this area that we once had. Therefore, the conventional approach to assessment of product must be critically reexamined, and the classical approach of rather simplistic first-level analysis must be modified to the extent that these external constraints apply to product identification selection and ultimate availability. In these specifics lies the challenge to the traditional perception of making what we can sell, and because of these specific modification of marketing theory is necessary.

No business operates independent of its market. This is true whether the market is consumer goods or an industrial product or process. In the final analysis the product, regardless of what it is or where it is being marketed, does have to meet certain requirements—specifications, performance criteria, or merely perceived performances or needs satisfaction. Total sensitivity to the realities of the marketplace is even more necessary now than it was in the past. The difference is that the level and degree of sophistication necessary to determine marketing reactions has altered. Moreover, demands have changed. The perception of the corporation, for example, is clearly different today—the business community is highly suspect—and of course the aura effect attached to the product from such attitudinal responses must be taken into account. Products themselves are being challenged as to their need and performance. Competitive practices in the marketplace have also changed—for instance, naming a specific competitor's product for comparative purposes in advertising and promotion campaigns is no longer uncommon. This means a shift in advertising and promotion. Marketing management must have an understanding of what is taking place in this instance to gear up his own advertising promotion program both active and reactive.

Assessment of the marketplace is no less significant today than it was historically; however, perhaps the most salient difference is that the market is no longer essentially "free." The degree of legislative regulatory intervention has placed a number of significant constraints in terms of marketing activities and of course in market response. Here again, we see a two-fold multifacet effect: (1) direct effect on the company via specific controls and limitations and (2) an indirect effect on the consumer in that his attitude and actions and reactions are influenced and a direct effect on the consumer because he, too, is subject to many specific laws and regulations that either limit or control his activity in the marketplace.

Other indirect effects also occur, of course—namely, that as federal policy taxation affects disposable income, purchasing power is correspondingly affected. Other indirect influences include international trade agreements that affect goods and services available in the domestic marketplace, financial policies and programs that affect capital formation which relates to the availability of capital for business development, modification, improvement, or expansion. There are a number of additional examples that could be provided, but these should be sufficient to make us realize that the effects in the marketplace are now far more complex than they were when the original role of marketing and the original perception of the extrinsic factors first evolved. This means that a modification in terms of marketing theory is necessary to include consideration of these many new and complex factors.

Clearly, integration of responsibility within the marketing operations is as necessary as it ever was. The closely related efforts that comprise the total marketing activity—that is, sales, advertising, promotion, market research, commercial development, product management, project management, distribution, and planning elements—are also as necessary today and in the future as they ever have been. The ultimate purpose of these responsibilities, which are centered around the product, is clearly market success, corporate revenue, and corporate profit.

This system was predicated upon historical perception of business responsibility, product, and market; but since these have changed, we must determine how the specific responsibilities of the marketing discipline must change. One of the many questions that businesses will have to address is the basic one of how it will deal with federal, state, or local legislation and regulatory activity. From our marketing orientation here and recognizing that our approach is severely limited, we can take into account here only how to include consideration of legislative regulatory effects and impact specifically on and in the marketing area. Within the marketing discipline provision must be made for assessing these effects and for determining what response should be made and what active programs should be undertaken. Marketing can and should play a prominent role both from the viewpoint of determining limitations and constraints and learning to "live with" and optimize operation in such a regulated environment and from the viewpoint of how to take a more active position so that the balanced legislation and regulation is enacted.

A NEW THEORY OF MARKETING

There is a need not only for reexamination of contemporary marketing theory but to put forward some new thoughts with regard to the marketplace, the marketer, and our general conceptual foundation of the interrelationship between the buyer and the seller. In referring to the buyer and the seller we describe the dynamics that transpire between any corporation or company and the ultimate consumer of its product regardless of the nature of that product.* The new theory that we examine, therefore, can be applied equally well to industrial goods that go into processes or products not in the direct consumer chain as well as those that are produced and manufactured for direct sale to the ultimate consumer. By and large the same sets of conditions and judgments are involved in market dynamics whether sales are directed to the ultimate consumer or through some indirect intermediary.

By adhering to the rather simplistic buyer/seller structure, all of these dynamics can be more adequately and less confusingly described. More importantly, such perception is necessary because some theories have tended to be restricted to: (1) industrial marketing, (2) consumer goods marketing, or (3) government marketing. Some valid modifications are necessary in dealing with the government sector—for example, as a buyer—as contrasted to direct consumer sales because there are many more objective quantifiable factors involved. Nevertheless, the base line conceptual foundations we explore apply equally as the basis for establishing the fundamentals of any buyer/seller relationship.

The Product Myth

The first impediment we must overcome in the construction and understanding of a new marketing theory is that of the product. Most of us are convinced that our basic business is the selling of some specific product or service. Operating under this constraint, we have visualized an interrelationship between the buyer and seller that is essentially dominated by a preoccupation with the specifics of the product or service offered. Many of the existing constraints have developed from this fundamental misperception of the true interrelationship between the buyer and seller.

Our first premise, therefore, is to recognize that, heretical as it may sound, *no one is actually engaged in selling a product or service; conversely, no one is actually buying a product or service.*

What is taking place is that we are actually selling *the means by which to accomplish a particular function or effect.* The seller is engaged in the manufacture, distribution, and marketing of some specific entity—whether it be a physical product or service—that satisfies the need for the acceptable accomplishment of this function or the attainment of this effect. The buyer is looking only to the accomplishment of this function or effect, and the product or service per se is completely incidental to this basic fundamental exchange. The product or service

---

*The word *product* here and throughout the book is to be construed in its broader sense to include all services ancillary to the product as well as service as a product.

is merely the means by which function or effect satisfaction is accomplished. If this is recognized, it is equally clear that the physical properties of the product or the specifics of the service as conceived by the seller or the buyer are to a major degree incidental to the actual ultimate purpose, which is function or effect attainment.

The theory, then, should be based upon the identification of a particular function or effect to be achieved and the molding of the marketing activity ultimately to satisfy the function or effect. This recognition enables us to construct a new perception of the marketplace and of the interrelationship between the seller and the buyer. It is also extremely important not only from the marketing research viewpoint but in terms of product development, research development, innovation, advertising, promotion, and sales activity. All of these should now be examined from the viewpoint of the buyer and, equally important, from that of the seller in order to identify function and effect needs which the buyer perceives as necessary to satisfy his function effect demand and which the seller can provide.

We are going to say a great deal more about this particular concept as it relates to other aspects of the entire theory. Obviously, one of the most significant factors that people constantly identify in regard to selling of a product/service (visualized now from a traditional perspective) is that of price. All too long have they regarded price as being the dominant, if not the only, determinant in effecting the transaction between the buyer and seller. Although price clearly is an important factor, the premise that the price is either the primary or sole determinant is definitely a misconception. In fact, price is an artificial construction, one established by the seller based on his conception of what a buyer will accept and, conversely, one accepted by the buyer not because of its imposition by the seller but because the buyer can accomplish some function or effect at a particular cost.

Inherent in the cost is obviously a value judgment, which leads to the next perception—that is, that *price is in fact nothing more than the sum that any particular buyer is willing to spend for the satisfaction or accomplishment of a specific function or effect at a perceived value*. Looked upon in this manner, we have a different approach to a price and its establishment because we now have included a significant new element—that is, accomplishment of function or effect at perceived value. The question then that must be addressed in some depth is the identification of perceived value. We must examine the elements employed by the buyer, by which he makes his determination of perceived value. Therefore, price becomes the relationship between that sum the seller can afford to apply to his particular product or service that is correspondingly acceptable to the buyer in terms of accomplishment of function or effect at perceived value. This is a clear example of the dynamic interrelationship that must take place between the buyer and the seller in terms of the establishment of realistic marketing practices in the future.

We discuss the concept of perceived value and the elements that are included in perceived value judgement in far greater detail later. At this point we need merely to recognize that price is not necessarily *the primary* or sole determinant in this exchange but merely *one of the representations* by which a perceived value determination can be effected and upon which a buying decision can be made.

Exactly the same conditions prevail on behalf of the seller—that is, the seller too is merely looking to the satisfaction of the particular function or effect in terms of the corporate objective. Certainly the seller function or effect may be far more limited in terms of the variables which are incorporated into this particular complex; nevertheless, in establishing its price the corporation is merely making a value judgment as to what is optimal in terms of the accomplishment of the corporate function/effect. This may be corporate short-term high-profit oriented, or it may be on a longer-term orientation. Looked at from the marketing perspective, it may be a new product introduction to gain market penetration, and in that context the value may not be in direct terms of profit and revenue but may be more in terms of "establishment" and "position" in a particular marketplace with visualization of longer-term profit based on sequential introduction of the new products and market expansion. The point remains, however, that in the establishment of price, the seller is himself effecting the same perceptual value judgement within the context of function/effect in terms of satisfying the corporate objective.

The Perceptual Value Cluster

A central feature of the function and effect theory revolves around the aspect of the individual value associated with the product and the influence of this perceptual value on the ultimate buying decision. In this sense the approach is highly individual and reflects a substantial difference from conventional theory, which is based on a tendency to look to a market or at least an aggregate of purchasers rather than endeavoring to reduce this to the lowest possible denominator—that of the specific individual effects on and decisions by the ultimate buyer.

This is not altogether true, because of course, in the consumer's goods area consideration of the individual purchaser has been a basic tenet for some time. However, when considering industrial goods, the government sector, and even some of the consumer goods markets, we have fallen far short of the analysis and the evaluation of the individual purchaser.

Even in the government and industrial sectors, regardless of whether complex decision models are employed, and even in the light of highly advanced techniques employing computerized systems, the ultimate decision always comes dowen to choices by individuals. In this sense we are always dealing with at least some concerns and considerations imposed by the judgement of an individual or a group of individuals.

To give proper cognizance to this aspect in the entirety of the marketing dynamic advanced here, several questions should always be asked by the seller, regardless of the nature of the product or the market. These questions should be answered as specifically as possible even though they may seem to be extremely simplistic.

1. Who purchases my product? (identification of the specific buyer when and whereever this is possible).
2. Who makes the purchasing decision? The ultimate buyer may indeed not be the person or group of persons who makes the actual purchasing decision, so it is important to ascertain who individually or which group of individuals actually affect the choices and ultimately make the buying decision.
3. Why does the buyer buy my product? The seller often does not know why he is successful, and ascertaining the specific reasons why any particular product is successful with any particular customer or group of customers can be useful.

The answers to these simple questions can be very important not only in market research and identification or potential or new markets but also from the viewpoint of continued success with existing products. As we explore further the function/effect theory, combined with other elements that form the basis for the new marketing concept, the reasoning behind this will become apparent; and the application of detailed answers to such questions will be more than obvious.

The perceptual value cluster itself can be visualized as consisting of several elements which can be divided into two major categories: quantitative and qualitative. These are listed in Table 7.1 under the appropriate headings. In some instances the same factor is listed under both the qualitative and quantitative headings. This is because such elements do have overtones of both a qualitative and a quantative nature and, therefore, can be determinatives within the context of either.

In reviewing these factors no effort has been made to be include all, but rather to reflect the primary determinants in each category. Moreover, no buying decision is made in a vacuum and similarly, no perceptual value judgement is made in a vacuum. In fact, the word *judgement* clearly implies some relative or comparative assessment. A noncompetitive market is a fallacy, and, when visualized in the broader context of function and effect, the rare exception is to be dealing with a totally noncompetitive situation. In this sense, therefore, the buyer is always either consciously or unconsciously making a comparison and his decision is relativistic. In instances where there is a clear definite equivalent product or service, the comparison is, of course, relatively simple and quite obvious. In other cases where we are dealing with comparable function or effect achieved through other products or services, the comparison may be less apparent and more difficult and, in fact, may be virtually totally subjective on the part

TABLE 7.1   PERCEPTUAL VALUE CLUSTER

Quantitative Factors	Qualitative Factors
Performance	Color
Specifications	Texture
Repair and maintenance	Physical satisfaction
Replacement (or replacement from original or secondary supplier)	Psychological satisfaction
	Availability*
Service	Convenience
Durability	Aura effect (influence of other goods
Availability*	and services, reputation, etc. of
Reliability	supplier)
Packaging	Taste
Disposal	Anticipation/expectation
Recycling/recovery	Packaging
Cost/price	Disposal
	Cost/price*

*Some factors are both quantitative and qualitative where judgements are involved.

of the buyer. We examine this concept of functional and performance equivalency in some greater detail later. Even in instances where we cannot perceive of such a comparison, there will still be some conscious or unconscious comparison made by the buyer. The comparison may be even more tenuous in that he is making a value judgement against some perception or anticipation that is an idealization of the product in the sense of a function/effect accomplishment which he has determined for himself. Therefore, even in those instances, a relativistic situation prevails, and the value judgement, although against a theoretical construct, is nevertheless taking place.

All of these points are being made because they are quite significant in terms of determining why the buyer buys and what factors influence or affect his buying decision. Of course these are primary dictates in virtually every facet of marketing decision-making. These interrelationships will be clarified as we proceed through the subsequent discussion of the total concept.

Only in consumer marketing have we seen any extensive application of a thorough going assessment of the decision-making and appeal process as it relates to the individual buyer. This is by and large a reflection of our own perception of what the major market segments consider important and, conversely, what we consider important in terms of analyzing and servicing these markets. In terms of extending the perceptual value judgement system beyond the consumer market, Table 7.2 provides a synopsis of the relative importance of the perceptual value judgement quantitative and qualitative factors related to the three traditionally identified major market sectors, (industrial, government and

TABLE 7.2   RELATIVE IMPORTANCE OF PERCEPTUAL VALUE CLUSTER IN VARIOUS
MARKET CATEGORIES

	Industrial	Government	Consumer
Quantitative Factors	Very important	Primary importance	Relatively unimportant
Qualitative Factors	Relatively unimportant	Relatively unimportant	Primary importance

*Reflects judgment that the significance of quantitative factors in the industrial market is not as clear or absolute as most believe.

consumer). Again, we are making a comparative statement—that is, the perceptual value judgement is important in all three categories, and both the quantitative and qualitative determinants are also important. What we are endeavoring to do is to put them on some basis of comparative reference to provide some insights in terms of ultimate application in these markets.

Z Factor Marketing Theory

Any new theory of marketing, to be pertinent and viable, must take into consideration all of the forces that have been described so far. Moreover, it must have sufficient adaptability to ensure ability to comply with and respond to future changes. Marketing as a dynamic discipline is concerned with the reaction mode. From a business viewpoint, it also has been concerned with the active mode-—that is, initiating action or affecting actions external to the organization. This should be the case, both in terms of marketing activities and general business conduct, in this broader context of societal evolution. Therefore, this theory should also enable the expostulation of marketing and industry position to influence the eventual environment in which the business will be conducted. This is the essence of the triatic nature of the general social value judgement/social advancement system that was mentioned before. Therefore, business must have the ability to provide its input into this dynamic so that a balanced reasoned ultimate position ensues.

Most analyses proceed on a monodimensional basis, comparing any of two parameters in a conventional ordinate abscissa, or X and Y framework.

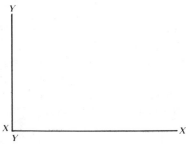

In marketing analysis the X, Y approach is used to capture for example information regarding sales and profit of an individual product by appropriate plotting, or measuring, of units as a function of price or cost. The examples are virtually endless. The points are, however, that only two dimensions are being studied and the analysis is essentially confined to the assessment of a particular single relationship such as product or market share.

In Z factor analysis we introduce a third dimension. Visualizing it within the context of the same analysis technique, for comparative purposes, we would add the Z axis to the X and Y axes.

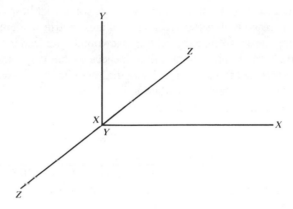

On the Z axis we now introduce the additional element of temporal analysis —that is the ability to compare the two parameters contrasted to a third, time, enabling us to direct our thinking toward present and future events in a discontinuous mode as well as looking at past, present, and future as a continuum. This is extremely important because, obviously, the history of the market or product has a definite relationship to its present and future.

In addition to inclusion of the Z dimension, we also now wish to superimpose analysis and evaluation of four other elements in Z factor markeing theory—the GEEM Factors.

GEEM Elements

There are four major areas that will either control, constrain, or direct future marketing efforts. To a large degree they already are a significant influence in most markets and in reality do control some, albeit rather few at this point. The premise we have explored throughout this book is that government effects will be on the increase and that they become the operative limitations within which the business must function. Our objective has been to ascertain what they are and determine how best to modify our marketing activities to optimize performance within these constraints. The entire Z factor marketing theory is based on this intention but, moreover, concludes that in addition to the effects of government will also be the operative constraints arising from a series of other factors. Some of these are directly related to government action; some are the indirect consequences of government action so that there is a definite interrelationship between the legislative/regulatory activity, including, of course, the political action in these areas as well. Moreover, there are also certain constraints, such as energy and materials, that are extrinsic and, to a large measure, beyond the control of government.

Whether we are talking about a clearly government-created and controllable situation or one that is only modified, affected, and influenced by government intervention and action is, for the moment at least, somewhat beyond our point. What we are concerned with is ascertaining what these extrinsic elements are and then determining how, from a marketing viewpoint, we can best evaluate, analyze, and understand their effects and influences so that they can be incorporated into any theoretical foundation for marketing activity that has as its ultimate purpose translation into practical marketing activities.

The primary elements we can identify are:

G. Government activity including legislation, rules regulations, controls, import/export, political activities, and so on.

E. Energy. Here, obviously, we are talking about the availability as well as the cost of energy sources. One need think back only a few years to the famous Arab oil embargo and the ensuing energy crisis and the spiraling inflation that this touched off to appreciate the implications of the energy dimension.

E. Environment. Once again recent events have clearly demonstrated the importance of environmental considerations. In this category we include all of the aspects of ecology and environmental health effects.

M. Materials. Although the question of materials shortages as such have not in recent times loomed on the horizon with anywhere near the importance that has been attached to energy and environmental concerns, clearly, there are underlying materials shortage questions. Availability of materials will become one of the paramount constraints of future years.

These four factors must be superimposed over the *Z* factor marketing theory (see Figure 7.1).

The way that one can most realistically visualize the effect of these factors is that they will become clear determinants in all marketing considerations in the future from R&D and market research through ultimate pricing, packaging, distribution, product modification. They will also be considered in decision-making related to advertising and promotion. They will be the most pervasive factors in analysis and evaluation in all marketing activities. (Practical examples of representative factors in GEEM are tabulated in Table 7.3.) Conceptually we can construct three clear periods in the history of product develop-

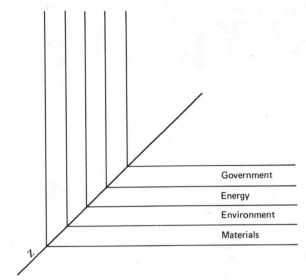

Figure 7.1   Z-Factor theory plus GEEM considerations.

ment, market research, process development and materials selection from the before the marketing fact situation and to sales, advertising, promotion and distribution as representative of after the fact marketing events as follows:

The GEEM Independent Period

This is a period which prevailed into only the most recent past. During this time manufacturers and processors, marketing managers, market researchers, general business managers, all, by and large, were essentially unconcerned with the GEEM factors. Products were identified, manufactured and distributed without any major attention to most if, in fact, any of these factors, (with the exception of a few clearly regulated marketing areas such as pharmaceuticals, pesticides, food, food additives where, of course, legislation and regulations controlling activities in these fields have been extant for some time). The generalization, however, is still true that, with the exception of the specific regulated areas and then even within those attention was only paid to the aspects that were regulated, business was not preoccupied with the GEEM concerns nor, in fact, in most instances even identified, conceived of them or allowed them to be major determinants in the business decision or marketing decision making process.

Transition Period

By the transition period, we are referring to what is, in effect, the contemporaneous situation. That is, while there is an increasing awareness of the validity of

TABLE 7.3   REPRESENTATIVE FACTORS IN GEEM CONSIDERATION

Government	Environment	Energy	Materials
Federal legislation	Legal constraints based on legislation/regulation	Availability	Availability
State legislation	Public opinion	Cost	Utilization
Municipal legislation	Future trends	Recovery	Allocation
Federal regulation	Existing and future limitations	Substitution	Substitution
State regularion	Effect on growth and expansion	Allocation	Limitations
Municipal regulation	Retro-fit effects	Conservation	Cost
Pending/legislation/ regulation	Land-use constraints	Emergency Supply	Recovery
Anticipated legislation/ regulation	Voluntary programs	Sources	Alternative uses
Policies	Liability*	Alternatives	Energy (use, alternatives)
Programs	Energy (use, alternatives)		Process factors
Agencies	Air, water, occupational health effects		Recycling
Departments	Intermedia effects		
Regulators	Solid waste		
Legislators			
Indirect effects (public opinion, action/reaction)			
Cumulative effects			
International trade			
Energy*			
Material			
Environment			

*Several factors, such as liability and energy, appear in more than one category because although the basic factor is the same, the perspective or consideration varies whether examined from an environmental, energy, materials, or government viewpoint.

GEEM considerations on the part of many, there is yet to be a universal acceptance of this proposition and there is only a gradual awakening of the influences of all. For the moment, again, attention is focussed primarily on the one or two which take immediate effect rather than attempting to visualize this on any kind of a totally integrated basis nor to recognize that it must become an integral part of the entire business, marketing activity.

GEEM Dependent Period

In the GEEM dependent period we are predicting future events in which the GEEM factors will become the major and dominant elements that will control and constrain the entire business marketing activity. In such a situation one will be looking from the viewpoint of measuring marketing activities, including product identification, market research and all of the before and after marketing events, not in terms of what the manufacturer can do in the marketplace, but in terms of what the manufacturer will be allowed to do. This is a significant movement away from contemporary marketing theory, which proceeds on the basis of manufacturing what we can sell. It is, in fact, as significant a departure from the older sales approach (we will sell what we can make) as was the transition to contemporary marketing theory (we make what we can sell). The future marketing imperative will be we will make what we will be allowed to sell and we will make and market this in a manner that will appeal to the new perceptions of our customers.

Figure 7.2 shows the superimposition of GEEM factors on the Z axis, with a delineation of the GEEM independent transitional and dependent phases. We must bear in mind that, in the main, we are still in the transitional phase, with all of the psychological and intellectual problems this imposes in regard to either acknowledging or accepting or proceeding on the basis of such a theoretical construct.

Visualization of GEEM Factors Regarding Marketing Decision-Making

The GEEM factors will be central to all marketing decision-making. This means that from a practical viewpoint one can take any of the classically assigned marketing responsibilities and measure activities in terms of GEEM criteria. Consequently, marketing decision-making in these areas will proceed as a function of interpretation of the GEEM factors either as being mandatory constraints, such as might be imposed by specific legislation and regulation, or as voluntary application, such as might occur versus the determination of potential customer reaction in regard to, for example, environmental effects.

We can visualize the GEEM factors, therefore, as a series of hurdles over which the marketing manager will mentally have to jump (see Figure 7.3).

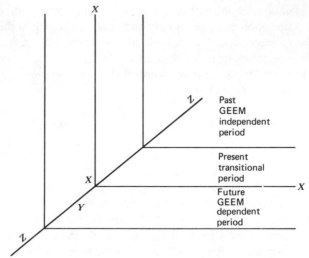

Figure 7.2   Z, GEEM factor: dependent, transition, and independent phases.

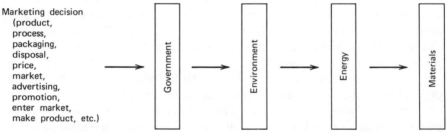

Figure 7.3   GEEM hurdles in marketing decision-making. Theoretical = all have to be considered as of equal concern. Practical = all have to be considered. However, some may be more important than others at any given time, but may shift in importance as a function of time and both intrinsic and extrinsic factors.

Unfortunately, this visualization is somewhat limited in that it indicates the hurdles as if all were equal, which is not the case since at any given point in time the relative importance of any one of the four factors may differ. Part of the decision-making process incumbent upon the marketing manager will be a determination not only of the specifics involved in terms of considering any of the four factors, but of the relative importance of the four factors (see Figure 7.4).

As if this problem itself were not enough, we have an additional complication: The relative significance of the factors is a time-dependent variable. That is, we are dealing with a dynamic situation. Although government may be the predo-

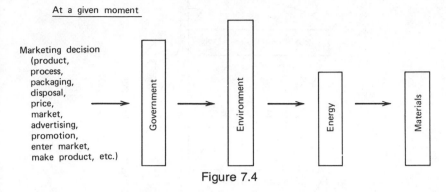

Figure 7.4

minant factor for a particular product or market at a particular time, environment may be the more important factor for that same product or market at some future time. Similarly, the relative importance of any of the four factors is a market-product-dependent variable. At any given time the relative importance of any of the four factors will vary with respect to variation in the market-product, which means that we must constantly bear in mind this additional dimenson of the problem.

Graphically, we can represent the time-dependent variation of the GEEM effects as illustrated in Figure 7.5.

The point regarding the relative difference in importance as a function of a market or product-by-product analysis should be sufficiently clear to all. It is an additional multivariable in that it is a product/market-dependent function but at the same time it is a time-dependent function—that is, a specific product or market will have various thresholds in regard to the four factors which will vary for that product or market as a function of time.

All of the foregoing may seem overly complicated, but unfortunately, it does represent a series of multiple variables which do reflect a rather complex extrinsic as well as intrinsic set of operating parameters. The essential point is that the future clearly implies the need to include the GEEM factors in the marketing decision-making analysis and evaluation process, but one must remember that they are variable in terms of their application at a given point in time or as they apply to any specific market or product; and that they are time-dependent variables in that their relative merits will change as circumstances and time change.

Contemporary and future marketing management must be extremely sensitive to the influences of the Z and GEEM factors and learn to deal with the rather complicated series of additional analyses that will have to be made. In terms of both internal and external constraints, they may well be the major ones against which all marketing decisions will have to be made. They will also be the primary determinants in the success or failure of new products or existing products in terms of their viability in the marketplace.

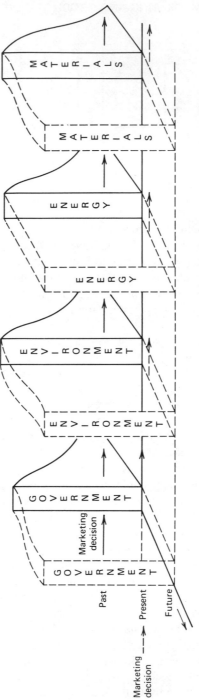

Figure 7.5   Practical utilization of GEEM factors on a two-factor (time-dependent variable basis).

190

Later we discuss in more detail the actual practical utilization of these factors in terms of developing marketing techniques and strategies that are related to identification and translation of these factors as the active dimension of the external efforts of the marketing activity. That is, how the marketing manager can utilize his new knowledge and insights of the Z and GEEM factors in active marketing programs such as sales, advertising, promotion, distribution, consumer appeal, establishment of perceptual value. Obviously, these must be done. Merely acknowledging the existence of these factors and their effect in terms of the internal activities (i.e., product identification, process identification, etc.) is not sufficient.

In reviewing this use of the GEEM factors no mention has been made of economics. Clearly influences such as capital availability, investment, and all of the other internal economic factors that affect and influence the company, as well as all of the external economic factors that affect and influence the customer have to be considered. However, as mentioned, the GEEM factors are described as the new dimensions of concern. They are added to the already traditional concerns of marketing such as economics. Since economic factors are so important, and since economic conditions are changing rapidly and radically there is no doubt that this area will take on ever increasing importance to the marketing manager.

Economics also deserve comment in another context, and that is that many of the GEEM factors are intimately related to economics on both a cause and effect basis. Inherent then in this broader involvement of marketing to including GEEM factors will be a broader examination and consideration of economic factors, both independent of, and related to the GEEM factors.

Vested Interest Theory: Competitive Analysis

The analysis of competitive actions and the ability to anticipate competitive action and reaction is extremely important. Historically, marketing has been concerned with its ability to analyze competitive action/reaction and of the constraints or opportunities created by the activities of the competitor in any given market. The problem with traditional competitive analysis is that, to a large degree, it has been too superficial. We have tended to concentrate on either a product-by-product comparison—that is my product versus his product—or on a market-by-market basis—my product in a particular market or a product need in a particular market versus his product or his ability to identify a product need in a particular market. We have tended to think on this one-to-one basis, and we have failed to perceive the realities of the effect of the perceptual value cluster as an ultimate determination mechanism.

The customer doesn't really care which product he buys as long as he achieves his desired function or effect. He doesn't really care who he buys from, provided he has a certain confidence level in the supplier, which is one of the psychological factors that is an element of the perceptual value judgment. When we look at marketing from this viewpoint, we get new insights into the realities of competitive action and the competitive marketplace. Such insights merely revalidate that rarely, if ever does a truly totally noncompetitive market exist for any particular product.

In the future we must understand the relationship of the perceptual value concept, Z factor and GEEM factors marketing theory, and the customer's attitude in relationship to identifying market needs and wants. This has to be done from the perspective of market research, new product development, innovation, and commercial development. At the same time we must recognize the action of any particular competitor in any marketplace as an after-the-fact situation with regard to his ability to identify similar market opportunities and what he may do. In terms of analysis of actions in a given marketplace, whether on a one-to-one direct competitive product basis or an effect analysis basis, we need to examine some of the older concepts—for example, nearest equivalent product (NEP) and nearest equivalent market (NEM)—to visualize better the realities of what our competition is or may be. We must also look to much deeper analysis in an area we term *the vested interest*. A vested interest theory will go a long way toward explaining actions of specific competitors in specific markets—both their identification of new market opportunities and their marketing efforts with existing products vis-à-vis our own new products in those markets. We can visualize our competitors in terms of their reaction to actions we might take in the marketplace with existing products. What this really says is that in addition to the conventional evaluation on a product-by-product or market-by-market basis and examination of nearest equivalent product or nearest service, we want to take an extensive look at the manufacturer or supplier of that particular product in that particular market, from the viewpoint of the basic position and interest of the particular supplier of the particular product or service.

If a particular supplier is only a jobber of a product, his degree of interest in the market will be extremely low; and the effort and expenditure he is willing to undertake in protecting the product or market will be correspondingly low. His interest in a market for a new product introduction and the effort and expenditure he is willing make is correspondingly low. Thus, the theory is comparable whether we are talking about identification of opportunity and introduction of new products into markets or protection of existing products in markets against either new products from another supplier or existing products.

If the jobber is also the distributor, his degree of interest is correspondingly higher, and the efforts he will expend in regard to that market are of a higher order. We can follow this chain through the logical sequence of jobber, distributor, formulator, manufacturer, basic producer, and raw material supplier. At this point we come to the most fundamental and most basic vested position—that of the producer who is also the supplier of the original basic raw material from which the product is either constructed or manufactured. Obviously, if we are dealing with back integration to the degree of raw materials supply, we are dealing with the most elemental set of circumstances. The amount of capital and fixed assets employed, for example, in terms of the basic raw material supplier will be far more consequential than those of even a basic manufacturer of a particular product. Therefore, the degree of vested interest is significantly higher, and the basic activities of the manufacturer/seller in the market will be of a correspondingly higher order.

This is shown graphically in Figure 7.6.

This concept is extremely important because it can be a predictive tool in terms of projection of the action or reaction of a company in any market as it relates to either its new product identification and potential entrance into a market or its actions with regard to protecting products and markets. A similar concept also applies in the service sector, although determinants would be the degree of investment and the share of market rather than the degree of back integration. Obviously, there is little if any opportunity for back integration in the same sense in which we can apply this in terms of manufactured products. The general concept, however, is equally valid if we relate it to market share, degree of investment, capital and fixed assets deployed in terms of a particular service. Moreover, there are examples of integration of service in terms of whether the service is a total service—for example, providing all repair and maintenance in all types of products—or whether it is a highly specialized service—for example, providing repair and maintenance only for durable goods such as household major appliances. Such an evaluation is necessary; it will provide this predictive ability.

Of course, we can apply a similar analysis in relationship to our own decision-making. When we make a determination regarding interest in a poten-

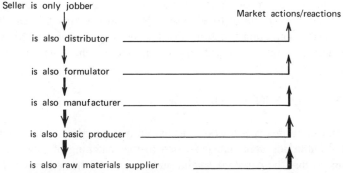

Figure 7.6   Vested interest parallels degree of basic back integration and investment which in turn relates to marketing decisions.

tial new product, new market, or new service or when we make a decision with regard to protecting our interest in a particular market or for a particular product or service, we will obviously need to analyze our own vested interest position. This should be quite fundamental in terms of making marketing decisions. The criticality of such analyses will take on increasing significance as we move into the GEEM dependent period. Marketing will naturally be far more concerned with the return on investment of fixed assets and the preservation of markets where vested interest activities are prevalent because these may be the more important concerns for longevity—to the optimum interest of the corporation.

Alternative Use of the Fixed Asset

Clearly, there are opportunities for alternative utilization of equipment or materials. Marketing management has always been faced with the challenge of making choices—for example, either product introduction or market introduction or the utilization of financial resources in advertising and promotion activities to expand. The classic trade-off situation in terms of optimization of the marketing effort is not alien to the marketing manager. What we are addressing here, however, is slightly different in that utilizing equipment or fixed assets for some other purpose must be possible. To accomplish this the marketing manager must be better informed. This will require much closer coordination in the future between marketing management and production and engineering or manufacturing services.

In Chapter 10 we discuss the need for the development of a new marketing team that will include in its structure and composition a vital new dimension——manufacturing and engineering. This is an inherent consideration in the evolution of the new approach to marketing in which the vested interest theory is recognized as well as the need to optimize in areas that are the foundation of the corporate interest—return on investment and fixed assets and assurance of continued high utilization rate of fixed assets. We will see how this can be better integrated in the marketing function. For the moment, know that this will be a key ingredient in terms of identifying and protecting the long-term corporate interest.

PUTTING THEORY INTO PRACTICE

To have merit any theory must be translatable into practical application.

The new marketing approach is related to the matching of buyer and seller perceptions so that the perceptual value judgements of the seller and the buyer will be as closely attuned as they can be. If this occurs, both in market research, product development, product innovation, commercial development and sales, advertising, promotion, distribution, marketing will be in a far better position to insure success in the future in spite of and in fact, in response to GEEM constraints.

A rather simplistic approach can be established in an idealized formula for marketing success. As with most simple things, there are many complex quantitative and qualitative determinants that will go into the actual construction of such a formula. However, we must move into this new dimension that is predicted on the establishment of the function/effect perceived value as the basis for full marketing activities within the operating parameters of all elements.

To look at this in even more finite terms, we can list the following traditional marketing activities in the context of some decision elements relative to GEEM and perceptual value as they relate to function and effect. Table 7.4 is not meant to be inclusive but only illustrative of some finite considerations in these areas. It should serve as a guide to the application of the theory in regard to specific marketing decision-making, planning, and activities that include both the positive assertive action mode as well as the responsive or passive mode.

Multiple Analysis Requirements

We have been describing an increasingly complex series of events that reflect the increasing complexity of the real-world marketing situation. None of us can expect that the demands will diminish or that any significant simplification will occur. The marketing manager is going to be asked to do even more.

Recognizing that this is the case, we present another analytical and evaluative consideration—the necessity for multiple analysis as it relates to any of these specific factors within the new marketing theory.

The multiple analysis requirements are summarized in Figure 7.7 It involves a matrix to allow for the analysis of product, market, and customer—both ours and the competition—as well as the consideration of nearest product, service, or market, in three temporal parameters: past, present, and future. Adding the analysis of the past to an already extensive analysis is necessary if we accept the Z and GEEM factors. Past practices as determined by retrospective analysis are important because they can point to present and future events and alterations as they relate both to ourselves and to our competition. In addition to the identification of the areas of analysis, the major factors to be analyzed as they relate to the matrix are listed in Figure 7.7

This analysis is a difficult and complicated task. It is revolutionary in terms of traditional concepts relative to visualization of marketing responsibility and activity and, if adopted, unquestionably poses some significant challenges to marketing management. One cannot dismiss lightly the implications of the additional burdens that will be assumed by marketing to accomplish these analyses. Nor can one take lightly the imagination and initiative that will be required to meet these

TABLE 7.4 IDENTIFICATION OF GEEM AND PERCEPTUAL VALUE FACTORS IN KEY MARKETING ACTIVITIES

Key Marketing Activity	Exemplary Relevant GEEM Factor(s)	Exemplary Relevant Perceptual Value Factor(s)
Market research	All GEEM factors prioritized relative to product/service need identification before marketing or acceptance, improvement, modification, appeal after marketing; all related buyer/market data from GEEM and Z factor marketing theory	All perceptual value factors, oriented towards (a) identification of specifics, (b) priority of factor(s), (c) criticality of factor(s), (d) appeal of factors, (e) sensitivity of factors, (f) ultimate buying decision effects
Research and development	G Legislation, rule, regulation E Environmental effects including health and safety on humans and ecology M Availability, cost, potential allocation, substitution	Efforts targeted to satisfying prioritized elements and objectives deriving from market research (above) or new product/service criteria internally established, recognizing the importance of perceptual value (PV)
Product design/specifications	G Legislation, rule, regulation M Availability, cost, potential allocation, substitution, alternatives	Primarily quantitative factors in industrial and government markets; primarily qualitative factors in consumer markets
Performance	G Legislation, rule, regulation (warranties, guarantees, proof of efficacy) M Durability, alternatives	Primarily qualitative factors
Packaging	E Environmental effects, disposal, recycling, recovery M Availability, cost, alternatives	Primarily qualitative factors
Manufacturing/production	E Health, safety and environmental effects E Energy, cost and availability M Availability, cost, alternatives	Negligible from buyers immediate perspective, but could be of great importance from the "aura" effect viewpoint if any of these elements are seized upon as public interest issues as they often are with subsequent adverse media coverage

Category	Code	Description	
Price	G	Antitrust, restraint of trade, truth in lending, and various other specific statutes or limitations and controls	Function/effect achievement as perceived on a cost/effectiveness basis
	E	Energy conditions, policies	
Sales	G	Antitrust, restraint of trade, fiscal policy, related regulations from ICC, FTC	Quantitative and qualitative, but with focus on factors that are paramount in particular buying decisions; should be closely coordinated with post-marketing market research
	E	Energy conditions, policies	
Advertising and promotion	G	Several statutes and regulations including significant court decisions and important consent judgments	Qualitative factors, especially to determine appeal and reaction
	E	Energy as a subject and object	
	E	Environment as a subject and object	
Service	G	Guarantees, warranties, labeling	Qualitative reactions
	M	Durability, replacement	
Competition	GEEM	Analysis of all factors from viewpoint of effect on existing or potential competitor's policies, actions, and reactions	All qualitative and quantitative factors to determine buyer perceptual value of competitor and competitor's product
Planning	GEEM	Should be formally integrated into planning process on both absolute and contingency basis	All qualitative and quantitative factors should be integrated into relevant planning areas (e.g, marketing, product, R&D)

Areas to analyze

		Past	Present	Future
Product				
	Ours	x	x	x
	Competition	x	x	x
	NEP/S	x	x	x
Market				
	Ours	x	x	x
	Competition	x	x	x
	NEM			
Customer				
	Ours	x	x	x
	Competitors	x	x	x

Factors to analyze in the context of Z and GEEM factors

Cost/price/value effects
Sensitivity/vulnerability
Comparative need/desire/value effects
Alternatives
Options
Alternations
Substitutions
Perceived value effects

FIGURE 7.7   Multianalysis requirements in marketing decisions.

challenges. However, marketing has always had the strength of flexibility, resiliency, and responsiveness. One of the basic validations of traditional marketing theory has, in fact, been the vitality that marketing has introduced into the corporation. Even recognizing the enormity of these recommendations, we are convinced that marketing can and will respond positively, affirmatively, and aggressively to these new challenges.

SUMMARY

In the preceding sections of this chapter we have identified a new marketing theory with many specific elements. To put them into better perspective and to serve as a brief recapitulation: we summarize these in a rather elemental fashion.

1. As we traditionally conceive of them, products are, incidental to the actual marketing transaction.

2. Ultimately, we are neither selling, nor is the customer buying a product, but rather a function or an effect.

3. Price is not necessarily the primary determinant in the buying/selling decision-making process; perceived value is the basic determinant.

4. Perceived value is based on both quantifiable and unquantifiable criteria.

5. Marketing success is dependent upon the identification of the function or effect to be accomplished and the basis of the perceived value judgement. Inherent in this idea is the utilization of determinations; such as criteria for identifying new products, or services, and markets and for designing and affecting marketing activities relative to the introduction of new products or to sustained efforts for continuation of successful activity with products (e.g., advertising, promotion, sales).

6. Superimposed over these considerations are those of government, energy, environment, and materials—GEEM factors.

7. Superimposed over the GEEM factors is the Z factor—that is, the continuum of past, present, and future events that must be visualised.

8. Analysis of marketing decisions and activities must proceed on the basis of the recognition of the preceding elements and also encompass multiple analysis which allows for the identification and assessment of specific factors as they relate to our product and those of our competition and the market and our actions therein.

9. Competition must be examined, not only from product-by-product or market-by-market evaluation, but in terms of vested interest determinants.

10. A new marketing team must be established for optimization of the accomplishment of corporate objectives, with particular emphasis on utilization of the vested interest concept.

NATIONAL, INTERNATIONAL, AND MULTINATIONAL COMPANIES

As markets have been characterized as consumer, industrial, and government, companies have of late been placed into three generic categories—national, international and multinational—depending on where and how they operate.
These terms have definite and specific meanings to owners and operators and to lawyers, although they have come to have some different meanings to the public. Some of the inferences in the public and even government minds are not too favorable, particularly in regard to the so-called multinationals.

Although we cannot fully examine this vast and complicated subject here, we should understand this categorization and the business realities that result from

public and government opinions related to it. Many additional laws and regulations apply to both the importer and the exporter. They represent additional
elements to be considered in marketing activities. Since we are primarily concerned here with domestic events, we can only mention these with the recommendation that they not be overlooked or ignored. In addition to specific legislation that deals with international trade (quotas, tarriffs, trade restrictions, etc.),
new legislation is binding on imports and exports. New laws, such as the Toxic
Substances Control Act, are dealing with imports just as if they were domesti-
cally produced materials. This provides a whole new set of considerations for
both the importer and the exporter. Such matters have to be addressed in practical
terms, and new relationships between importers and exporters have to be devised
to comply with such legal requirements.

As with legislation in other areas we can expect more attention to be focused
on this subject, especially as it concerns multinationals. What new marketing
problems and opportunities this will give rise to cannot be examined here, other
than to say that they do have to be considered by those to whom they will apply.

CONSUMER AND PUBLIC REACTIONS

While not so prominent as it was once, the consumerism era is far from over.
Having achieved certain goals, the strategy by which to achieve others has
changed. We now see some encouraging signs of recognition that all arguments
are not one-sided and that business, government, and the public interest can best
serve society's interest and the ultimate public good by mutual problem
identification, prioritization, and objective solution.

However, there is still a long list of consumer advocate demands with which
business may not completely agree, and solutions are not going to be easy.
Narrowing our focus to those that are of most immediate concern to the marketing manager, we can clearly identify a few. They must be considered as we look
to short-term marketing activities.

Basic challenges to marketing activities and products have taken the form of
three basic tenets that have been postulated by Ralph Nader:
1. All products should be thoroughly and completely tested before marketing.
   No responsible manufacturer would disagree with this approach, but problems
   and questions certainly do arise in attempting to translate this into practice.
   Clearly who determines what is reasonable and necessary by way of testing
   (and what testing is therefore undertaken) is going to be controversial. A
   thorough examination of the possibility of safer substitutes for existing or
   proposed new products and safer uses or proposed new uses for existing
   products should be conducted. This seems sound and reasonable until one

starts to examine certain questions: What is safe? How is this determined? Safe to whom and under what conditions? And, most importantly, who ultimately makes this decision and how is it enforced?

2. Reorganization of business is necessary. Suggestions have been made ranging anywhere from sweeping reform of antitrust statutes to federal chartering and verticle divestiture. Such basic alterations go beyond the scope of this book because they involve some fundamental societal and legal issues. However, we must recognize them and their implications in terms of consumer attitude and responsiveness to specific marketing activities, particularly in industries that have been identified as targets for such actions.

3. There is a need for additional consumer legislation up to and including the proposed but defeated bill that would have created the Consumer Protection Agency. We discuss this bill in some detail in Chapter 11 in examining the future since it will probably come up in the next Congress. For now let it suffice to say that it must be considered in any serious attempt at constructing a model of long term markets.

Legislation and altered consumer attitudes will pose many problems and disadvantages for marketing, but there are some advantages, which the creative marketing manager must identify and utilize. Many will be company-, product-, and market-specific. We cannot provide solutions to specific problems, but we hope the following list will stimulate some constructive thinking. In the context of Z and GEEM factors future marketing must:

1. Focus on specific areas rather than nebulous generalizations.

2. Develop ability to judge consumer attitudes.

3. Identify product opportunities.

4. Develop product rationalization elements.

5. Develop market rationalization elements.

6. Develop specific advertising and promotion campaigns.

7. Recognize specific market research targets.

8. Identify areas for consumer education.

9. Identify specific elements in long-term business decision-making.

10. Integrate legislative and regulatory considerations in all business activities and decisions.

EIGHT

Marketing:
STRATEGIES
FOR SURVIVAL

In Chapter 6 we saw how legislation and regulation affect each area of the marketing function and how they affect the total company and market. In Chapter 7 we explored a new approach to marketing based on inclusion of government and public action and external events, such as energy and materials, which to a significant degree are outside the direct control of government and the public but which also have profound effects. Recognizing that these effects are here to stay and that we must learn to deal with them realistically and effectively, we considered the Z factor in the new theory of marketing and the GEEM factors. All of this combines to give us a new outlook and a new perspective by which to manage and operate the marketing function and the company.

These alone, however, are not enough, for they tend to deal with theory rather than practice, and we are still confronted with translating these conceptual approaches into concrete everyday practical business policies, practices, and actions. In this chapter then we accept the theory as given and explore tools and techniques that can be employed to accomplish the new marketing and management objectives that these theories impose upon us. Many of the newer and well publicized management practices, such as management-by-objective and zero-based budgeting, are as appropriate to the new requirements of government effect integration as they are to conventional management, even though they must be employed in a different way. They must be used in a way that captures the elements of the regulatory and the public dimension. These newer management techniques, which evolved as a function of general business and economic conditions, not as a direct consequence of the regulatory or public interest activity, are familiar. Thus, we concentrate on (1) tools and techniques whose primary intentions and derivations are specifically the result of regulation and government action, (2) the need to find effective mechanisms by which to integrate them into the company, particularly marketing, and (3) the need for the company to reach out to the market, as it has traditionally done, to better understand its needs, behavior, and response. However, even this latter must take into account these new aspects of public involvement, public reaction, and the changing social climate.

There is a simultaneous need to interact with the government. Integration of government actions does not stop with the unilateral effect of these actions and activities on the company and marketing. Also required is recognition of the effects of business on the public, the market, and the government and the need, if not obligation, of business to make its voice heard in the entirety of the legislative and regulatory process. This is a topic that we address in this chapter and in later portions of the book.

For the moment, however, our primary objective is to see how we can practically and effectively combine all of these new concerns, perspectives, and activities with those of marketing. This is far from an easy assignment and will impose extreme demands and pressures in addition to seemingly innumerable existing ones. The following strategies for survival are advocated with the full knowledge and recognition of these new burdens. Later we consider organization, staffing, and budgeting. We cannot and will not ignore the three Ms: money, manpower, and materials. Before doing this, however, examination of specifics will assist marketing personnel in more precisely determining what these needs are and convincing management of the commitments required for their accomplishment.

WHAT WILL BE NEEDED?

Looking at the business in a new way is not enough. We must also approach it in a new way and run it in a new way. To do this requires not only a new outlook but several operational prerequisites:

Identification of sensitivity and vulnerability factors
Information
Documentation
Compliance programs
Specialized training and education
Market research
New functions or relationships
Planning
Overall short- and long-term strategies

This list is in no particular order; all the elements are important, and therefore, we examine each in some detail. However, we do not try to review existing or more recent management practices even though they may be applicable in certain cases. We also realize that in some instances you may already be doing many of these things, or have in place the same or similar functions or operations. With the expectation that even those who have some of these elements or operations functioning may not have all or may gain some new insights we ask forebearance in reviewing what could be somewhat elementary information. To the majority of readers, however, this will probably not be the case.

IDENTIFICATION OF SENSITIVITY AND VULNERABILITY FACTORS

Every company, no matter how large and no matter what its capabilities, is finite. Its resources are not limitless and it is ultimately dependent upon the success or failure of its marketing operation for continued growth and prosperity or, conversely, for decline and failure. It is both sensitive and vulnerable to certain effects or events. The larger company may be better insulated, and such events may not so quicly take their toll, or because of diversity a large number of events might have to occur before their full effects are felt. This in no way negates the basic premise; it merely attenuates the consequence.

The problem that confronts us is to determine the factors to which the company—or more specifically, the marketing function—is both sensitive and vulnerable. Such determination will be important and useful in a number of ways including general business conduct, determination of actions and reactions, but probably most importantly in the planning process. In studying sensitivity and vulnerability factors we might start by examining some of our objectives and then proceed to more detailed consideration of definitions, examples, and application.

OBJECTIVES

Although the following list is not inclusive, it certainly reflects the primary objectives that should be inherent in the determination of sensitivity and vulnerability factors:

1. To plan the more important business activities, somewhat analogous to 80/20 determinations of what are in fact the most important.
2. To plan on a contingency basis for actual and anticipated events affecting these major activities.

3. To prevent being "caught short" by external (or internal) events insofar as possible (e.g., cyclamates and food color bans, PCB bans, raw material shortages, oil price increases).

4. To provide for immediate response to such events thereby preventing loss of marketing position, competitive advantage, loss of revenue.

Before we can utilize these objectives in constructing the most reasonable and practical approach, we must define what we mean by sensitivity and vulnerability factors.

Sensitivity factors are elements or events that seriously affect a business (dominant influences on the business). Examples include capital formation, materials, energy, disposable income, regulation (actual/pending), and legislation (actual/pending).

Vulnerability factors are elements or events on which a business is dependent (continuation or discontinuation effects). Examples include key product, key account, key market, key R&D effort, regulation (actual/pending), and legislation (actual/pending).

Perhaps we can make the distinction between sensitivity and vulnerability factors more meaningful with actual examples. An example of a sensitivity factor would be the events of the Arab oil embargo and resultant oil price increases of a few years ago and reoccurring now. Clearly companies that were dependent upon oil as a source of energy or as a raw material encountered a direct and immediate effect. They were obviously sensitive to the events of Arab actions. As this book is being written, consideration is once more being given by OPEC to additional price increases. Obviously, those that are sensitive as a primary influence, that is oil producers, refiners, petrochemical users, will once more have to wrestle with the numerous questions that occur as a consequence of this kind of action. Obviously, the Arab oil embargo and price increases can be looked upon in an even broader context—that is, as they affect all of the complex of manufacturing and material availabilities as well as the direct out-of-pocket expenditures for gasoline, home heating, and similar uses. We cannot here examine the direct consumer effect other than for goods that go into the consumer market (e.g., gasoline, home oil). From the viewpoint of sensitivity determination, we can see that those who have immediate dependencies have immediate sensitivity.

An example of a vulnerability factor is the recent proposal for limiting the use of chlorofluorocarbons in aerosol propellant formulations, particularly the advocacy for banning all aerosols containing chlorofluorocarbon propellents other than those for essential uses (e.g., pharmaceutical formulations). Here is a potential limitation through a ban or at the very least a significant consumer influence as a consequence of the government's recommendations. Either leads to revenue loss; hence, the business is vulnerable to such action.

Next we should consider the characteristics of these factors so that one can proceed to identify them within the specific company.

Characteristics

1. Sensitivity and vulnerability factors represent key business success or failure elements or events.
2. As shifts from controllable to uncontrollable events occur, business control obviously decreases.
3. All of these factors represent fundamental consideration in all business decisions—both long- and short-term determinations.
4. The actual factors differ from company to company.
5. The factors are time-dependent, varying both in terms of the exact factors involved as well as their magnitude of influence.
6. The factors in reality consist of a mixture of both internal (essentially controllable) and external (essentially uncontrollable) elements.

Determination

To utilize this approach one has to have a basis to determine the specific vulnerability and sensitivity factors that are applicable to a particular company. Basically the process by which these can be determined lies in their definitions, characteristics, and objectives. If the rationale for the approach is clearly understood, based on these considerations, it should be fairly easy to determine and use them on a company-to-company functional basis—that is, separate factors for each function. Some of the criteria one should employ in making such specific determinations, as you review each function such as R&D, M&E, product management, sales, and so on are:

1. Vested interest
2. Capital versus labor intensification
3. Market share
4. Profitability
5. Proportioning of costs—materials, labor, marketing, R&D
6. Cash flow
7. Long- versus short-term intentions
8. New products/innovation importance
9. Interrelationship of identified sensitivity and vulnerability factors (how far risk is spread over a number of functions or over a range of products)

These criteria measured against the definitions, characteristics, and objectives presented should enable the establishment of specific sensitivity and vulnerability factors in various functions such as we have already exemplified and as they also apply to elements such as price, availability, advertising and promotion, liability, insurance, cost, and competitive viability.

Uses/Actions

Obviously, for all of this to be meaningful, the establishment of sensitivity and vulnerability factors must be useful and should be translatable into specific actions.

In exemplifying objectives we have already seen one of the most important of these—the ability to prevent being ''caught short in the marketplace.'' The following simplified flow chart (Table 8.1) illustrates how these determinations can be useful in constructing a series of activities leading to eventual direct market effects in the area of product, production, marketing, and environment.

The second chart (Table 8.2) is even more detailed. Each of the primary responsibilities within the marketing function are examined, and some specific examples of sensitivity and vulnerability factors are cited, with exemplary potential marketing/business actions.

The usefulness of this approach lies not only in being able to determine what affects the business (both internal and external elements) today but more importantly tomorrow and in the future. By identifying these central elements, we can devote the time, attention, and management direction that is most appropriate to the basic business interests. This will marshall resources (money, manpower, or materials) and assure that they are applied to aspects that truly warrant such allocation. *One of the surest means to survive in the regulated environment is the ability to separate management trivia from management essentials.* There is too much going on, too many frontiers. We cannot devote the time and attention we would like to all, and so we had better know which are critical and which are incidental. Identifying sensitivity and vulnerability factors is a good beginning to providing this kind of essential management guidance.

INFORMATIONAL REQUIREMENTS

Information is needed for marketing in a regulated environment the same as for conventional marketing, but it is significantly altered and expanded. The marketing manager needs first and foremost to establish an effective informational network (although those less sanguine about marketing have been known to call this a web rather than a network). Traditional needs are well known, so we do not review them here. We devote our attention to the new information requirement in four categories of concern:

TABLE 8.1 USING SENSITIVITY AND VULNERABILITY FACTORS IN MARKETING ACTIVITIES

Sensitivity or Vulnerability Is in		Anticipated or Actual Event		Planned Action		Action Step		Result
Product	→	Banning or restriction	→	Modification or substitution	→	Marketing plan for modified or substitute product	→	Release to market
or								
Production	→	Ingredient banning or restriction	→	Modification or substitution	→	Marketing plan for modified or substitute process derived product	→	Release to market
Marketing	→	Increased cost	→	Cost reduction program	→	Price retention	→	Undistrubed market
or								
Market	→	Adverse public image	→	Revised A&P	→	Implement specific new A&P program	→	Retain market

TABLE 8.2 OPERATIONAL ANALYSIS OF SENSITIVITY AND VULNERABILITY FACTORS, USES AND ACTIONS DIRECTLY AFFECTING OR INVOLVING MARKETING

Research and development	Sensitivity factor	NIOSH identifies a substance as a suspect carcinogen.
	Vulnerability factor	OSHA declares substance a carcinogen and regulates its use.
	Uses/actions	Consider not using this substance in R&D efforts. This, therefore, alters the R&D program (selection) but conversely could identify an area of replacement opportunity which could even be of competitive advantage (product opportunity).
Process development	Sensitivity factor	In-process quality control standards imposed by EPA/TSCA.
	Vulnerability factor	In-process substance banned by EPA/TSCA.
	Uses/actions	Undertake process development to comply with standards.
		Undertake process development to identify substitute.
Manufacturing and engineering	Sensitivity factor	OSHA proposes noise standard.
	Vulnerability factor	OSHA establishes noise standard.
	Uses/actions	Analysis and implementation of administrative and engineering controls.
Product	Sensitivity factor	Aerosol container employing chlorofluorocarbon to require labeling.
	Vulnerability factor	Chlorofluorocarbon propellents are banned.
	Uses/actions	If using chlorofluorocarbons, initiate product replacement or shift to alternate forms (roll-ons, etc.)
		If not using chlorofluorocarbons, consider marketing efforts in promoting alternatives offered.

TABLE 8.2 OPERATIONAL ANALYSIS OF SENSITIVITY AND VULNERABILITY FACTORS USES AND ACTIONS DIRECTLY AFFECTING OR INVOLVING MARKETING (*continued*)

Advertising and promotion	Sensitivity factor	FCC announces review of all advertising oriented to children.
	Vulnerability factor	Specific bans ensue (e.g., Spiderman vitamins).
	Uses/actions	Review all child-oriented programs to anticipated requirements. Utilize FCC approach in positive terms as part of broader A&P to parents.
Sales	Sensitivity factor	Proposed Consumer Protection Act.
	Vulnerability factor	Passage of Consumer Protection Act.
	Uses/actions	Preparation now of industry and company position vis-a-vis act and subsequent rule and regulation. Critical impact analysis and initiation of voluntary programs to be "ahead of the curve."
Market research	Sensitivity factor	Trends and directions of public and government.
	Vulnerability factor	Unpredicted, undiscerned significant behavior in environment (market).
	Uses/actions	Revise market research techniques and focus to gain new insights; redefine market research objectives and priorities.
Management	Sensitivity factor	Personal civil and criminal liability in some statutes.
	Vulnerability factor	Actual prosecution under prevailing statutes.
	Uses/actions	Informed decision-making, compliance programs.
	Sensitivity factor	Existing product liability, legislation, and public attitude toward product liability.

Risk	Vulnerability factor	Major product liability suit.
	Uses/actions	Clear understanding of law, informed decision-making, product design, adequate warning and instructions, clear statements of guarantees and warantees.
Distribution	Sensitivity factor	Legislation on spills and leaks, transportation of hazardous materials.
Physical	Vulnerability factor	Limiting rules and regulations, fines, penalties, freight rate increases, refusal to carry, refusal to insure.
	Uses/actions	Examine limitations, minimize risk through modified packaging, reduce unit size to lower risk, develop clean-up and emergency procedures.
	Sensitivity factor	Proposed divestiture and possible federal business chartering.
Methods	Vulnerability factor	Active divestiture and federal chartering.
	Uses/actions	Development of industry position (of those not already directly involved) and legislative action, public and government education.
Profit	Sensitivity factor	Cost increases created through legislative and regulatory action.
	Vulnerability factor	Raw material, energy allocation.
	Uses/actions	Projective cost accounting, price planning, stock piling.

Nature of information required
Sources
Uses
Communication

When examining them we have five objectives underlying each:

1. Effect on organization activities and operation
2. Effect on competitor's organization, activities, and operation
3. Effect on the market and the buyer
4. Development of marketing strategies based on this information
5. Development of specific actions based on this information

NATURE OF INFORMATION REQUIRED

The new informational needs are many. This applies not only to the number of new elements and areas that must be considered but also to the depth and detail of data required. Once more we present a tabulation summarizing essential new information requirements (Table 8.3). Individual company needs may not necessitate information in all areas or may dictate a greater or lesser degree of detailed knowledge in each or any. The number of variables is extensive; however, by becoming familiar with these you should be in a far better position to make effective selection.

SOURCES OF INFORMATION

Today there are almost as many sources as there are generators of information. Considering that there is so much to know and so many ways in which information can be presented or analyzed, this is perhaps not all bad. Choices are many, and selection should be made only after careful review of all available sources in a particular subject area, not only from the viewpoint of cost but also to determine which best meets your needs. Consider frequency, level of detail, availability of complete texts or abstracts, interpretation, analysis, anciliary service, and so on. Because many of the sources are commercial operations, you will have the opportunity in several instances for "trials." The following is an abbreviated tabulation of some of the major ones which are of government, public interest, private, or commercial origin. No particular advocacy is intended or implied and no infernces or conclusions should be derived from the absence of any particular "report," "service," document, or source. Such exclusions are based merely on

TABLE 8.3 INFORMATION REQUIRED

Type	Example	Data required	Source
Legislation	Existing	Nature, intent, scope, authority, agency, department or commission, responsibilities created, penalties, applicability, effect on company and marketing.	Senators/members of Congress, Congressional library, law library, corporate counsel, various commercial services
	Pending	Same as above except information is prospective. Additionally, want to know probability of enactment and and have ability to monitor progress in Congress.	Congressional Record, media, appropriate Congressional committee or sub-committee, trade associations, various commercial services.
Rules and regulations	Existing	Basically same as on legislation plus office/officer within agency, department, or commission to contact; effective dates; compliance requirements; reports; forms; records; etc. mandated or logical on voluntary basis.	Responsible department, agency, or Commission; Code of Federal Regulations; trade and professional associations.
	Pending	Same as above but especially interested in development of regulation to have input at various stages—preliminary development, hearings, posthearing comments, agency contacts. Also need to monitor progress in administrative proceedings toward final promulgation.	Federal Register; responsible agency, department, or commission; trade and professional associations.

213

TABLE 8.3 INFORMATION REQUIRED (*continued*)

Type	Example	Data required	Source
Litigation	Suits filed, decisions appealed	Identification of litigants and issues.	Corporate counsel should be advised of your areas of interest and establish a procedure by which to inform you of legal activities accordingly.
Court decisions	NRDC/EPA, FWPCA settlement	This settlement was the outcome of a suit filed against EPA by NRDC (and others) that resulted in several new actions and activities by EPA that will affect industry directly relative to the FWPCA. All relevant data required.	Same procedure as with litigation.
Executive orders	Inflationary Impact Statements	While most often these orders do not affect the company directly, they do indirectly. The requirement to conduct Inflationary Impact Statements (which applies to Executive Branch) is a case in point.	Office of the White House, Congressional Record, Appropriate commercial services, trade and professional associations.
Agency, department commission actions and intentions	FDA laboratory inspection program	Many overall actions or intentions are not the result of or part of the formal regulatory process. Agency policy statement also fall into this category. Because they affect the company, data is essential.	Agency, department, or commission communications (most have mailing lists you can get on), appropriate commercial services, trade or professional associations.

Public interest group activities	Advocacy for federal business chartering	Nature and purpose of position, likelihood of government or public effects, likelihood of resulting legislation or regulation, market effects, and ability to monitor progress.	Public interest groups (mailing lists, publications, etc.), media, presentations at hearings, congressional committee or sub-committee meetings.
Public opinion	The public believes business profits are too high	Effect of opinion on all of the above and even more specifically on individual product performance and all marketing activities. Also useful in the determination of educational activities to correct erroneous impressions.	Media; polls and surveys; public interest groups; comments at proceedings, hearings, and committee and sub-committees.
Legislative opinion	Some form of guaranteed employment should exist.	Nature and direction of executive and Congressional thinking in order to anticipate events.	Media, Congressional debates, legislation or regulation proposed, voting record.

space limitations or other factors not related to any judgments or personal recommendations.

Short-Term Outlook	Long-Term Outlook
Federal Register	All of those included in Short-term
Federal Briefing	outlook, plus
Congressional Record	Federal policy statements
Trade associations	Agency or commission policy state-
Professional associations	ments
Public media	Media
Consultants	Congressional offices
Contracted studies and surveys	Congressional committees
U.S. Government Publications	
(list available form GPO)	
Agency, commission, department	
mailing lists	
Specialized "services" in specific	
areas (e.g., BNA Reporter)	

Information in the legislative area is desirable, but it represents a category that
may be less familiar to marketing people. Hence, the following more expansive
summary of commercial and government legislative full text and summary reporting services is provided (with the same limitations mentioned before) (Table
8.4).

When considering any informational requirements do not forget your internal
resources—departments such as legal, public relations, government relations and
the marketing classic personal contact and personal interview. Personal contact
works well in garnering marketing intelligence; it will work equally well with
legislative and regulatory intelligence.

In terms of most frequently used references, the following should be available
to you:

Federal Register. Daily government publication of department, commission,
agency actions, regulations, proposed regulations, hearings, meetings, notices
and so on.
Congressional Record. Daily government publication reporting on activities
in both houses, including full text of all legislation discussed or voted upon as
well as other actions of the Congress.
United States Government Manual (issued annually). Detailed information on
agencies and departments, including responsibility and authority; also includes

TABLE 8.4 SUMMARY OF EXISTING MAJOR FEDERAL LEGISLATIVE AND REPORTING SERVICES

Service	Frequency	Cost*	Comments
Congressional Quarterly Congressional Quarterly, Inc. Washington, D.C.	Weekly	$ 532	Covers all major activities by Congress and the White House with running status for about 15 major bills. Does not deal with regulatory affairs in general.
National Journal Government Research Corp. Washington, D.C.	Weekly	$ 300	Specializes in half a dozen lengthy interpretive articles each issue on major legislative and regulatory issues, discussing the background and position being taken by all sides.
BNA Environment Reporter Bureau of National Affairs Washington, D.C.	Weekly	$ 450	An 11-volume set of loose-leaf binders covering legislations and regulations involving environmental issues. Includes full texts as well as weekly bulletins on current developments.
BNA Report for Executives Bureau of National Affairs Washington, C.D.	Daily	$2400	Covers key developments in Congress and White House; includes summaries and reports of selected documents.
Federal Briefing McGraw-Hill, Inc. New York, N.Y.	Weekly	$ 227	A newsletter summarizing legislative and regulatory developments directly affecting chemical manufacturers.
Toxic Materials Reference Service New Business Publishers, Inc. Silver Spring, Md.			Typical of a variety of newsletters such as *Solid Waste Report, Air/Water Pollution Report, Energy Resources Report*.

*Approximate at time of preperation (1976).

217

nonfederal Washington offices and activities in related areas of topical concerns (e.g., employment and labor, economic and business).
Specialized commercial "service" in your area of particular concern. There are many services ranging from dailies to monthlies. Coverage extends from very specialized fields such as toxicology (e.g., TOXLINE®) to coverage of agencies or commissions (e.g., BNA, OSHA Reporter). A little exploration will uncover the service or services for the topic and area you want.

USES

For information to be of value it must be used. We have already considered this in general terms when establishing the five objectives mentioned before. Later in this chapter we examine several other techniques and managerial approaches that can be effective only if they are constantly fed information. Therefore, the uses to which this information will and should be put go far beyond the specific responsibilities of marketing. Uses within marketing, however, will become more apparent based on the remainder of this chapter and the next.

COMMUNICATION

Most discussions of needs within the organization begin with communication. There is no doubt whatsoever that this is critical. It has been left to last here so that it is the last thing reviewed and therefore ideally the first in mind when thinking through your own informational needs and systems, which we trust you will do. Although it is clear that all of the information received must be analyzed, interpreted, judged, and then acted upon, how this will happen may not be so clear. In a large corporation, for instance, where there are multiple needs and vast resources, this may occur through a centrally located function with responsibility for obtaining this information and its selective distribution throughout the company. This is an ideal that is seldom achieved, even in the most sophisticated concern. Unfortunately we cannot address the redress of this distressing situation. So for the moment, at the risk of being selfish, we can only advocate that marketing look to its own interests by selecting informational sources that are most pertinent and then establishing responsiblity for obtaining and distributing this data within the marketing operation. In our discussion of other approaches to the overall problems of incorporating consideration of government in the total business (Chapter 9), we will see how marketing can play a central role in the management of such operational practices and in expanding its information-gathering and distributing activities. For now, suffice it to say that any information obtained must be distributed, analyzed, and acted upon. Otherwise we are only draining the corporate coffers to no avail.

DOCUMENTATION

Once more we are dealing with a concern that has existed within most companies, but the requirements of old must now be modified to satisfy and encompass the new. Documentation is an area that may be somewhat ignored or taken for granted by the marketing executive, who may feel that it falls within the domain of the legal department. When visualized from the standpoint of past objectives, this might well have been the case. Today, however, we have added reasons for being concerned with documentation, and many of these fall squarely within the responsibility of marketing.

All of this leads to examining once more the traditional versus the new needs. These can be exemplified as:

TRADITIONAL	NEW
Reference	All above plus
Record	Legal requirements
Verification	1. As mandated in specific statutes or by rule and regulation
Accuracy	
Insurance	2. As desirable for
	(a) Use in proceedings
	(b) Use in litigation
	(c) Defense in litigation
	(d) Demonstration of action and good faith
	Judgmental requirements
	1. In anticipation of legislation or regulatory requirement
	2. Voluntary programs
	3. Specific use in internal or external programs or activities

These categories lead to a further distinction, again one that we have elaborated upon before—that is, elements that are mandatory and those that are voluntary. Examples of each are:

MANDATORY	VOLUNTARY
EEOC affirmative action plans	Customer complaints (all types)
	Adverse reactions (some are already mandatory)
FWPC reports and records of effluent discharges .	Customer service
	Cost analysis
	Energy consumption (and reduction) programs
	Materials consumption (and reduction) programs
	Labeling activities (other than required)
	Actions regarding guarantees and warranties

All of these actions, whether mandated or voluntary, require the establishment of new records, reports, and data systems. To attempt to describe in detail how these can or should be developed is beyond our scope. What the marketing manager must be concerned with is that they be accomplished. The following are some steps in developing a documentation program that could be helpful:

1. Review all existing documentation, records, and related programs to be sure of complete knowledge and familiarity with what your company is already doing. This will avoid duplication and perhaps allow building upon existing systems and capabilities.
2. Review statutes, rules, and regulations that pertain to your business and be sure that you understand and are complying with existing legal requirements.
3. Review present business activities, both internal and external, from the documentation viewpoint and determine if you wish to install any new procedures or practices on the voluntary basis discussed.
4. Monitor carefully for any new mandated or desirable voluntary requirements.
5. Obtain legal advice on both existing and proposed systems.

COMPLIANCE PROGRAMS

As with documentation, there are mandatory and voluntary (or anticipatory) aspects of compliance programs. Since most of the compliance programs involve either socially oriented legislation and regulation that apply to other functions (e.g., personnel, accounting, finance), our purpose here is to mention them in passing so that the marketing manager knows of their existence; is better informed so as to be openly and willingly cooperative in all that is required; and becomes an active participant in programs that usually originate elsewhere in the company.

There is yet another series of compliance programs that, although also based on socially oriented legislation, have as their objective protection of health, safety, or the environment. Although requirements for clearly delineated compliance programs do not parallel exactly those in other areas, they are no less necessary. Specific action programs—for example, to assure meeting water or air pollution control requirements or to bring an OSHA violation into compliance—may have to be developed. New legislation brings new demands—for instance, the effects of the fairly young CSPC have yet to be felt completely in terms of compliance programs. This is probably even more the case with the October 12, 1976 Toxic Substances Control Act.

Although some of these programs may not fall directly within the purview of marketing, they will affect the marketing operation in various subtle (and often not so subtle) ways. Effects can and will range all the way from the availability of product to cost of goods; other effects are evident in the marketplace (e.g., reactions to labels that may be required or to consumer "scares" like the cranberry incident of a few years ago).

The effects may not be immediate; they may occur both as a function of rules and regulations under a particular statute and as a function of increased cost or decreased availability as the company comes into compliance. Marketing personnel must therefore but only be closely attuned to any rules and regulations that affect these areas and also to compliance programs so that they can include provision for the effects in marketing plans. Knowledge of compliance programs and scheduling will allow for better integration of these effects—phasing—into marketing planning. Clearly, the opposite is also true. Compliance, particularly in terms of reviewing options and establishing schedules, especially where voluntary programs are concerned, could benefit enormously from close integration with the marketing operation. In this way the ultimate objective will be obtained with minimal business and marketing disruption. This certainly is an additional argument in favor of long-term assessment and effort toward anticipating government action so as to be prepared. We examine this latter aspect in more detail when discussing anticipation of government legislation and regulation and planning.

SPECIALIZED TRAINING AND EDUCATION

Finding the right people, we often hear, is a problem. If this is already a problem, when there are many experienced people available and comprehensive educational and training programs exist to provide experts in virtually every field, then what must this problem be when we start to look for educated, trained or experienced people in the more esoteric field of government and regulatory effects. Few schools teach these subjects, and the practical specialists are rare or already well situated. This is to be expected because, despite what has been said of government incursion, many of the most pervasive activities are of only comparatively recent origin. The response by the educational community has yet to take full effect. The job market has yet to respond fully. Both will come. But what can we do in the interim?

There are several options open, as there usually are. (1) One can hire away from industries that have been regulated for some time (e.g., pesticides, pharmaceuticals) or from the government (not too uncommon a practice in the past); or (2) undertake recruitment from the few select schools that have programs that even closely parallel the needs (however, for the moment graduates tend to be too academic and educationally and experientially lack the necessary business background; or (3) as is most often the case, one can resort to in-house development of existing staff.

Development of existing staff is in many respects by far the most common and for several reasons the most advantageous solution, at least for the present and under prevailing economic and business conditions. We are not necessarily discussing the development of a corporate government relations expert or a lobbyist, although this may well be the progression. Rather, we are attempting to locate and develop an individual within the marketing operation who can be responsible for determining the myriad effects of government action on the business and market and perform the integrative functions that we have been describing. The person chosen should have the following characteristics:

Knowledge of the business
Knowledge of marketing
Knowledge of company policy and programs
Knowledge of the company's products and services
Practical business experience
General education in business or one of the specialties
Compatible personality
Ability to think and articulate clearly and under pressure
Ability to learn
Ability to adapt
Ability to communicate

Admittedly, this is quite a long list. However, we want this contemporary Leonardo da Vinci to perform a number of vital but diverse functions, which will require most, if not all, of these aptitudes. The person will have to use them both within the organization and outside as he or she represents the company in areas such as government departments, agencies, or commissions; legislators; public interest groups; and appropriate trade or professional associations. A multitalented person is required for the job to be done effectively. Naturally, locating people with all of these skills is practically impossible, so one does what one must always do and compromises to obtain the optimum mix of talents that correspond to the particular objectives, techniques, and plans of the company.

Once selection is made, education and training is possible through many courses, programs, and seminars that now are held with seemingly endless regularity. More to the point will be immediate practical exposure through trade and professional associations, which can be most helpful in "learning the ropes" from peers.

As needs develop, in-house training programs can be contemplated that draw upon the many consultants available for such specialized services. Top management support combined with an unusual degree of patience is necessary, for the results of this effort are often slow to be realized and difficult to quantify precisely.

MARKET RESEARCH

For all intents and purposes, market research has missed the target with regard to government and its effects on business and the market. Missing, or perhaps even more appropriately ignoring, the effects on the business can be rationalized, if not justified, in that this is not their responsibility. Missing or ignoring the effects on the market (here *market* means not only the amorphous "they" but the individual "him" and "her") is more crucial. This criticism of marketing research should be taken in the spirit of objectivity, for it is more a criticism of management than of market research itself.

Lest one think this criticism too radical, in the light of some efforts made by excellent market research institutions such as the Chemical Marketing Research Association (CMRA), we must understand that the efforts are minor, compared to their efforts in other areas of more conventional concern.

However, market research is beginning to recognize the importance of this area and is making an effort to apply its expertise and experiences. In addition, realization that government can seriously effect so many markets and buyers has only recently come about, and therefore market researchers are also in a learning mode. Because of their responsibilities related to anticipation, perception, and prediction, perhaps more has been expected of them than of the more internalized functions whose operations deal more with the day-to-day needs of running a business than assessments of the general social and cultural climate and similar factors.

Allowing that with some modifications these assertions are correct, what then has been the problem and how can it be rectified? Do we still need market research, and if so, what should it be doing?

The problem is that existing market research:

Essentially misses the effect of government on business and markets
Essentially misses the effect on the individual
Focuses on "markets," not individuals in too many instances
Is oriented toward traditional market information needs
 Market size
 Market duration
 Market share
 Competition
 Consumer product response
 New market opportunity
 New product opportunity
 Consumer attitudes (to company, product, competitors)
 Advertising and promotion campaigns (creating and measuring response)
Does not examine or assess effect of public interest groups
Is oriented toward conventional planning requirements

This tabulation should not be misconstrued. It is not meant to imply that market research does not make valued and valuable contributions to the marketing effort. The contributions have been important and are still needed to a major extent. However, because the focus has been misdirected—that is, in terms of contemporary needs—market research has failed to provide the guidance and leadership that we in marketing need in view of our new requirements relative to government and its effects.

Do We Still Need Market Research?

We do need market research to perform its normal duties; however, we also have to consider what new duties should be added and how the balance can be struck between old and new. That this is worth doing is based on the firm conviction that there is need for the talents and knowledge of the professional market researcher, provided that the orientation is altered.

Alteration of the market research focus can be accomplished by considering some of the new aspects that ought to be addressed:

How does government legislation affect the business?
How does government legislation and regulation affect the buyer (disposable income, attitudes, confidence, product selection, service package, expectation, response to advertising and promotion, etc.)?
How can determinations of effect on "buyer" be translated into more effective marketing efforts?
How does "he" or "she" feel about the company in light of government and public interest activists' allegations?
Is there an "aura" effect created by banning or "blacklisting" a particular product?
How do all of these factors affect the competition and the market?
What new market or product opportunities are created by virtue of legislation and regulation?

All of these and many more specific questions must be considered and included within the scope of market research concerns. All clearly reflect a redirection, one that includes effect of government and the public in all aspects of activities and places a high priority on making such determinations. These should encompass not only macroeffect (on the company and the market), but very particularly microeffect (on the individual).

The subject of microeffect leads us to several basic questions. They must be answered if we are to know anything about our products and our business.

1. Who buys my product? That is, who makes the actual purchasing decision

whether in a corporation, the government, or the family versus who influences the buying decision? Only by knowing this can we truly focus the marketing effort and make determinations of effects on the buyer by business, government, and the public interest groups.

2. Why does "he", or "she" buy my product? What are the elements that go into the individual purchasing decision?

3. Why does "he" or "she" buy my product and not that of my competitor? This is a most difficult and seldom considered question when contemplated on a one-to-one, person-to-product level.

4. Why doesn't "he" or "she" buy my product?

Where from Here?

With some redirection and reorientation market research can perform a valuable function. The opportunity exists to provide a creative and needed service within the company, a service that is not now being performed. There is also need, however, for marketing management to come to grips with what it expects and wants from market research. These suggestions may help to put this into perspective and with a realignment of objective and outlook combined with the establishment of new priorities within market research, we will be able effectively to combine the old with the new.

New Functions and Relationships

Not necessarily directly within the marketing function but closely allied in the sense of needs is consideration of government and public relations functions. Many of the concerns we have expressed do involve elements that cross the boundaries of marketing. Later we examine how this crossover can be attended while preventing duplication and potential misdirection of emphasis or confusion over responsibilities or priorities. At this time we wish to merely call attention to the two separate but related functions that more and more companies are adding to their organizations—government relations and public relations. Although many responsibilities are not within the marketing function, the marketing manager should know that more companies are beginning to employ the talents of specialists in these fields. When and where they are being added, marketing should have a say in the determination of their efforts, objectives, and priorities.

To avoid duplication or misdirection, close contact and ongoing relationships have to be established. These will ensure that a commonality of objective is reached and that the important services these new staff functions can perform include the specific interests of marketing. The objective is clearly to establish a good relationship between marketing and government relations and public relations personnel.

In the event that addition of such staff cannot be supported, thought must be given to how to accomplish these functions within the role of market research or through the creation of a new management marketing response team, which we will examine in Chapter 10.

ANTICIPATING GOVERNMENT LEGISLATION, REGULATION AND PLANNING*

Our focus now is on trying to determine what legislation and regulation will come next so that it can be incorporated into the planning process. Of course other objectives can be realized by predetermining what may take place in government, and other changes in the planning process may be desirable.

The other uses to which such "anticipations" can be put include such formal or informal activities as:

Identification of product or market opportunities/problems
Determining actions
Determining reactions
Immediate, short- and long-term decision-making
Assessments of involvement in the legislative or regulatory activity

The list could easily be expanded; however, the implication is clear: These are all essentially reactive, not creative, uses. When we look to prediction of government activities, particularly as they relate to the planning process, our emphasis will be on this last aspect—the creative and active mode.

Other planning changes could include:

Reduction in planning complexity
Alteration in planning schedules
Flexibility in planning
Change in perspective (What is a short- or long-term plan? How far into the future should we plan?)

Again the list could readily be lengthened. Since we cannot address all of these, we limit our attention to two dimensions that are more in concert with our

---

*The material that follows (pages 226–244) is based on a lecture delivered by the author at the Chemical Marketing Research Association Meeting held on September 19–21, 1976, in Virginia Beach, Va. Material in the speech is copyrighted by the Chemical Marketing Research Association and is used here by permission.

objectives: (1) inclusion of government legislation and regulation in the planning process (both existing and anticipated), and (2) contingency planning as a survival technique.

Anticipating Government Legislation and Regulation

Predicting government action is an uncertain and imprecise task. However, the attempt must be made to anticipate and deal with government activity as part of the business and planning process.

No one needs to be convinced of the need for, or the desirability of, anticipating government legislation and regulation. Our problem is how to accomplish this highly desirable objective. In an effort to systematize ''anticipating'' we should answer the following questions:

What is our timing?
What do we want to know?
What sources of information are available?
What mechanisms are available for accurate and reliable anticipation of government legislation and regulation?

Before examining these questions we need to establish our temporal references as they relate to legislative and regulatory concerns.

What is our timing? As usual, we have both long and short-term considerations, and they differ in the context of government actions as they do when considering normal business planning elements. When considering these effects we can make the following distinction:

Short term: Basically oriented toward anticipating rules and regulations.
Long term: Basically oriented toward

1. Major federal policies or shifts in policy; interpretations by agencies, reinterpretations by agencies
2. Pending legislation (e.g., Clean Air Act Amendments)
3. Creation of new agencies
4. Political and social changes that could affect or result in any of the foregoing.

In all cases we have some fundamental needs. Table 8.5 might help in giving some additional perspective and focus to these needs.

What do we want to know? This is another of those deceptively simple obvious questions. However, when we examine some of the operational options that

TABLE 8.5 INFORMATIONAL NEEDS IN ANTICIPATING GOVERNMENT LEGISLATION OR REGULATION

Nature of proposed action (as specific as possible)	Identification of agency and its specific office and responsible personnel (through all stages at all levels of activity)	Date of proposed action (as specific as possible)	Date of proposed implementation (as specific as possible)	Possible effects on industry (technical, compliance, economic) during development prior to finalization	Effect on industry after finalization (problems and opportunities in compliance, technology, science, marketing, finance, legal, manufacturing, distribution, personnel, management, liability)	Alternatives and options to government and industry

derive from the information gained in the previous analysis, there are new perspectives here as well. The basic reason we want to know is, of course, directed ultimately toward decision-making. Leading to such decisions, however, is the need for complete understanding of actions proposed and their consequences. Consequences are closely related to examination of all options and alternatives. In evaluating any decision logic related to position (before actual legislation, rule or regulation—longer-term activity) or compliance (after legislation, rule or regulation—shorter-term), we should formalize approaches to option analysis.

Table 8.6 identifies some of the primary options that are available both before and after legislation, rule or regulation. The list is not inclusive, but it is illustrative of the analysis and considerations that are essential. This entire exercise has value for determination of what course of action should or should not be undertaken and provides an excellent foundation for feedback into mechanisms for predicting legislative or regulatory action. The entire sequence of questions and answers developed through the analysis suggested here is designed to be interrelated. Each may be considered separately and has value as such, but should also be visualized as a total system.

What sources of information are available? A few sources mentioned earlier in this chapter are repeated here for convenience.

Short-Term Outlook	Long-Term Outlook
Federal Register	All of the preceding, plus
Federal Briefing	Agency policy statements
Congressional Record	Federal policy statements
Trade associations	Political and social developments
Professional associations	Major national and international
Public media	events
Personal contacts	Direction of academia
Consultants	Public interest group activity
Contracted studies and surveys	Adverse environmental health reports
Data determinations for previous	Commercial services
analytical steps mentioned	

What Mechanisms are available for accurate and reliable anticipation of government legislation or regulation? Since we must still translate the results of the preceding analysis into some form by which we can arrive at specific "anticipations," the question now is what, if any, mechanism exists for such determination. In this instance we can borrow from existing marketing research techniques and employ them as a basis to construct or test our own decision logic. Admittedly, it will be relatively crude and unsophisticated; however, it can be the basis for determinations, recognizing that as knowledge and experience in this area develop, it will be refined.

TABLE 8.6 OPTION ANALYSIS

Do nothing (identify all consequences—legal, ethical, social, image, etc.)	Include provisions of proposed or actual rule or regulation in planning	Participate in legislative and regulatory process; enactment of laws, promulgation of regulations. This involves	Actions after enactment or promulgation. These involve	Compliance options. This involves complete evaluation of all alternatives that could be employed for compliance.
		(a) Hearings (b) Action through trade or professional associations (c) Lobbying (d) Public relations (e) Legislative or agency contacts (f) Industrial studies or surveys	(a) Hearings (b) Review of proceedings (c) Submission of post-hearing comments (d) Agency contacts (e) Legislative contacts (f) Amendment efforts	

From marketing research we can borrow three basic techniques:

1. Delphi determinations
2. Models
3. Surveys

To these we add the common-sense approach of analogizing to past experiences—in this case, legislative agency and regulatory. Combining these should enable us to approach a structure by which to make reasonably projections.

We must admit that market research approaches probably will not be employed in most companies. They are quite time-consuming and expensive and, therefore, beyond the reach of many small and medium-sized concerns, in addition, they seem to be more applicable to the longer-term determination than to the short-term.

Let us therefore concentrate on the simpler, even if admittedly more subjective approach—the one that relies more on analogy and "common sense" than on statistical methodology. We can represent this decision logic and its elements diagrammatically.

INDICATORS		TESTS			ANTICIPATION
Data ⟶ From information sources including personal judgment rumors experience	Pertinency	Reliability	Accuracy	Completeness ⟶	Short term Rules Regulations Long term Agency action New laws Federal policy

Using this subjective model involves making an initial determination from the indicators, then testing it against the criteria shown. Thus, a scale can be developed (again, for the time being, a subjective one) of 1 to 10. (1 is lowest in terms of accuracy, reliability, etc.; and 10 is highest). This will enable comparative assessments from indicators and judgments as a function of time/experience with the decision logic itself. By inputting the indicators and measuring against the tests, anticipated legislative and regulatory actions can be determined (the degree of accuracy, while highly speculative, is a subject again of time/experience refinement). Where one can afford the more expensive market research techniques, they can be used to make the determination in the "test" areas.

The resultant anticipations are then used in the planning process itself in any one of several alternative methods.

What of potential practical value do these analyses demonstrate? Interesting as the exercises may be, we must ask of what practical value they could be. Can they be employed as the basis for actual prognostication of government legislative or regulatory action? The answer is yes for using them in accordance with the following additional suggestions they can form the basis of such predictions.

1. We need to separate our long- and short-term information and analytical requirements as well as the concurrent business objectives.
2. Varying informational sources would be employed, and emphasis would vary depending on what we seek to ascertain.
3. Analytical tools exist for making "anticipations." They can be further refined through employment of some standard market research techniques for validation, such as Delphi.
4. New analytical tools and techniques must be developed to refine "anticipations" in this highly specialized area (e.g., regulatory decision logic development).

INTEGRATING GOVERNMENT REGULATIONS IN BUSINESS PLANNING

While not exactly true, let us start with the premise that there is little or no formal consideration of regulatory effects in contemporary business planning. What little provision we see is ad hoc, rather than based on any sound, systematic, programmed, and carefully analyzed and reasoned assessments. It is usually more reactionary than anticipatory. It is, in other words, essentially unstructured and certainly, where present even in this rudimentary form, unsatisfactory. A regulatory effect in terms of Federal Water Pollution Control Act compliance is, for example, not integrated into the planning complex from the standpoint of its short- and long-term effects on cost of goods, volume of production, availability of product, product rationalization, effects on total plant overhead, cost allocations—the list could go on and on and on.

Given that government regulation has been affecting us for sometime (e.g., Federal Water Pollution Control Act, Occupational Safety and Health Act, Consumer Product Safety Act), that new regulations are issued continuously, and that new legislation with even greater impact exists (e.g., Toxic Substances Control Act, Energy Conservative and Recovery Act, Clean Air Act Amendments), why should this planning void exist?

There are several reasons. No single one is probably the basis. The following list (Table 8.7), however, may serve to identify some of the factors, We already know that their effect is no formal plan integration.

TABLE 8.7   INTEGRATING REGULATORY REQUIREMENTS IN PLANNING

Arguments against	Arguments for
Uncertainty	Policy formulation
Unfamiliarity	Program identification
Complexity	Positive compliance scheduling
Personnel limitations	Cost Analysis/documentation
Lack of experience	Problem/opportunity analysis
Cost	Coordination of compliance effort
Magnitude of task	Integration of concerns
Questionable relevance	Assurance of proper/full consideration
Frequency of rule/regulation change	Assignment of responsibility
Documentation of problems	Focus on regulatory requirements
Confidentiality vs. disclosure	Determination of sensitivities and vulner-
In-house security	abilities
	Statutory civil and criminal penalties
	Liability identification and analysis
	Risk/benefit analysis
	Compulsory aspects mandate some
	planning/documentation
	Optimum efficiency

FORMALIZING PLANNING

Now let us assume that regulatory planning needs outweigh regulatory planning risks. The pros have won. We will undertake formalized regulatory planning.

Logic now leads to determination of

What our options are
What elements should be considered
How this construct can be made to function

Planning Options

Although integrating, which has the clear connotation of fitting into an existing planning framework, might be preferable, it is often not the case. In fact, it represents only one of several options:

1. The creation of a totally new planning base predicated on complete planning reassessment in recognition of the fundamentality of regulatory requirements—a totally new way of looking at planning.
2. Introduction (integration) into existing planning structures
   (a) Total business plan (integrated management plans)
   (b) Functional plans—marketing, manufacturing, and so on.
   (c) Operational—product, sales, and so on.

3. Contingency planning
4. Separate regulatory plans
    (a) Overall on existing business plans
    (b) Fully operative but separate
5. Ad hoc (to the purist clearly not planning but reactionary to the given situation)—limited and restricted to reacting to specific situations when and as they occur. Planning as the need arises.

When we explore each of the options, keep the following underlying assumptions and distinctions clearly in focus.

Although we address the subject from the viewpoint of "options," this means here only options from the perspective of approaches (mechanics) and formality (management posture), not in the context of voluntary versus involuntary or mandated actions. There are clearly several existing regulatory requirements that mandate some planning actions (e.g., EEOC, EPA Water Permits, ERISA, etc.), they are certainly not optional. However, there is yet another sense in which we can discuss options, for even in the mandatory areas there are compliance options and alternatives. It is even more correct to speak of options in terms of actions and programs when we examine the second set of conditions—voluntary actions. These are short- or long-term self-imposed requirements that are not statutorily mandated. They derive either from legislative/legal prognostication or as aspects of the corporate ethic.

Option, then, has at least three separate and precise meanings:

1. Mechanics—planning inclusion/exclusion, techniques, and so on
2. Alternative mandated compliance approaches
3. Self-imposed limits, standards, performance, and so on

Examining the Planning Options

The best way to examine the five planning options (mechanisms, techniques) is, perhaps, to summarize them, which we have done in Table 8.8.

What elements should be considered? Although there is some disagreement regarding the precise elements that should be considered even in conventional business planning, we should include the basics that are generally agreed to:

Objectives and goals
Strategies
Review and analysis
Problems and opportunities
Budgets
Action programs
Assumptions

They are obviously approached from the regulatory viewpoint.

In addition, if there are functions such as government relations or regulatory affairs within the company, these should be addressed in the plan. Alternatively, where such functions do not already exist, the planning process might well include consideration of their need within that company.

The similarities and dissimilarities in the elements and their focus are highlighted in Table 8.9.

How can this be made to function? We now come to a basic and practical consideration—that is, putting the plan into action. This problem is certainly not unique to the regulatory planning or integration process. It is common to conventional planning, and in the main, the resolution here is the same as it is for the normal business plan implementation.
We must have all of the following:

1. Corporate awareness
2. Corporate recognition
3. Corporate commitment
4. Organization for compliance
5. Budgets for compliance
6. Formal planning
7. Review and evaluation

All of these ideals, however, will only function properly within any company or system if there are dedicated personnel. Therefore, one of the essential ingredients here is personnel that are qualified, trained, and experienced in the area of government regulations, the legislative process, and where necessary, in the disciplines that will be affected by such regulation—whether they be scientific, marketing, administration, or finance. More is said on these topics in Chapter 10 where we examine in depth an approach toward putting this all together in the company.

Contingency Planning

Whether we attempt contingency planning in total or selectively is a choice that must be made by each company. To do this, however, one should be sure to understand what contingency planning is and how it can be approached.

Most simply stated, contingency is "what if" planning. It proceeds on the basis of identifying probable events and those effects and actions that would or should be consequent to the event. Obviously, it could be applied to the entire company—that is, to all departments, functions, and operations—or on a limited basis. Equally obvious is the fact that the number of contingencies that could be planned for in any given function is virtually limitless. Both of these mean that

TABLE 8.8   REGULATORY PLANNING OPTIONS

Planning Option	Summary of approach	Advantages	Disadvantages	Application
1. Totally new planning base	This would involve a basic restructuring of the planning operation. It would start from the premise that existing laws, rules, and regulations, plus those pending, form the framework in which business can or will be conducted and, proceeding on this basis, would analyze the corporate activity and options.	Would allow for extremely thorough evaluation and business restructuring where needed; would provide a totally new way of visualizing the business.	Radical, expensive, not needed in many instances.	Limited at this time to a relatively few highly regulated industries but may well be the future mode.
2. Integration into existing plans	Basically involves considering the legislative, regulatory perspective in the existing planning framework.	Aside from the difficulties mentioned regarding data gathering, uncertainty, etc., this approach is relatively simple and builds upon an existing foundation.	Not as thorough or basic as Option 1; some factors may be missed.	Short term, this option would appear to be the best intermediate between Options 3, 4, and 5, which are clearly inferior, and Option 1, which may not be appropriate for many at this time.

3. Contingency	As the name implies, this is "what if" planning; the "ifs" in this instance would be legislative and regulatory factors; actually this approach can be subdivided onto contingency plans for exploring various options from the viewpoint of various alternative legislative or regulatory possibilities.	This is a limited approach but would be somewhat simpler and less costly; for some companies, not so highly regulated, it may, in fact, be the more logical choice.	Quite limited; much could be missed.	While of limited value to the larger company as its basic approach, it would be useful to the smaller; the second aspect of planning alternative courses based on alternative legislative or regulatory possibilities could be a useful adjunct to fully integrated planning of the larger company.
4. Separate regulatory plans	This would involve developing separate (essentially functional) plans built around specific existing or projected regulation (e.g., personnel, packaging, manufacturing, pollution control); this is, in fact, just what many companies are doing.	This is a simple and comparatively inexpensive (administratively speaking) approach; however, it is limited and fails to achieve the integration needed.	Fails to integrate either the business around the requirements or the regulatory requirement around the business.	Would be suitable only for limited application by smaller companies on the short term.
5. Ad hoc	Reacting to specific situations.	Least expensive (administratively); however, least effective	Fails to integrate; only reactive and not anticipatory; To many it would not be considered true planning at all.	Extremely limited application.

237

TABLE 8.9 COMPARISON OF LEGISLATIVE AND REGULATORY PLAN ELEMENTS AND FOCUS VERSUS CONVENTIONAL PLAN ELEMENTS AND FOCUS

Conventional plan elements	Similarities	Dissimilarities	Legislative and Regulatory Plan Elements
Analysis	Plan has to be logically and systematically approached.	When analyzing from the regulatory viewpoint there are several major considerations that differ from conventional planning; these must be assessed with proper value judgements applied: (1) Voluntary vs. (2) Involuntary (compulsory) aspects (3) Regulation interpretation (4) Enforcement aspects (5) Inclusion/exclusion of pending or Projected laws, rules, regulations (in long-range planning they obviously should be included).	Analysis
Opportunities and problems	Assessment requires identification and prioritization. Also, all opportunities should be examined to see if they present any problems, and conversely, all problems to see if they provide any opportunities.	A more complex analysis is required; issues dealt with involve liability, possible criminal sanctions and are potentially highly controversial and sensitive; the public relations and emotional aspects are relatively new factors; categorization, to provide focus, should identify individual problems and opportunities as short- versus long-term and as internal versus external; establishing a grid is helpful.	Opportunities and problems

238

| | Short term | | Long term | |
	Vol	Comp	Vol	Comp
Problem Int				
Ext				
Opportunity Int				
Ext				

Assumptions

Assumptions

The basis for decisions should be clearly stated; assumptions are both fed into and derived from the analytical phase.

In short-term planning there is ironically less uncertainty in terms of compliance because basically it addresses existing rules and regulations. The basic questions requiring judgement are:

(1) Do they apply to me and my product/market?
(2) How are they to be interpreted?
(3) How are they to be implemented/enforced?

When dealing with long-range planning requiring prognostication of:

(1) Statutory modification
(2) Amendments
(3) Agency interpretation (new or modified)
(4) Agency policy assessment
(5) Changes in enforcement (either in direction or effect)
(6) Influence of extrinsic factors, public interest, group activities, litigation, court decisions

239

TABLE 8.9 COMPARISON OF LEGISLATIVE AND REGULATORY PLAN ELEMENTS AND FOCUS VERSUS CONVENTIONAL PLAN ELEMENTS AND FOCUS (*continued*)

	(7) Penalty changes (8) Shifting political and social attitudes (9) Legislation and Regulation which in turn affect the regulatory process, assumptions become simultaneously more meaningful and necessary, but more complex. Since in the long term these are the events that will, to a major degree, shape, control; and determine the structure and conduct of the business overall and of R&D, manufacturing and marketing, in specific assumptions will have to be made.	Objectives and goals
Objectives and goals	Have to be established essentially as in conventional planning. Based on the distinction between voluntary and compulsory aspects some objectives and goals are imposed while others will be self-determined. As a practical matter this can be an important distinction when (1) Establishing priorities (2) Committing resources (especially where limited) Since essentially all objectives and goals here are not profit or sales oriented, consideration of profit/sales must be effected indirectly (e.g., effect on cost, market, competition, etc.).	

Strategies	Have to be established essentially as in conventional planning.	As with objectives and goals, some strategies will be externally imposed (e.g. compliance programs under FWPCA or EEO), while others are company developed; in these latter (and in some instances even in the former) marketing considerations can and should be introduced; aspects such as possible inclusion in advertising and promotion plans, public relations, utilization of government certification or endorsement, and direct government contract bidding represent some of the aspects warranting inclusion	Strategies
Action programs	Derived in same manner.	To a large extent action programs follow the logic of those derived from or specifically mandated by the involuntary elements imposed by regulation; additionally, there may be others that result from court decisions or litigation that are compulsory. Where voluntary programs are initiated from objectives, goals, and strategies, they would follow the normal course in plan development. However, from the viewpoint of (1) Documentation of corporate activity (2) Assigning responsibility (3) Building a record for compliance review, adjudication, or for evidence in any proceedings, they are of tremendous significance and value, especially if feedback reports are developed and maintain demonstrating activities undertaken to fulfill the actions planned.	Action programs

TABLE 8.9 COMPARISON OF LEGISLATIVE AND REGULATORY PLAN ELEMENTS AND FOCUS VERSUS CONVENTIONAL PLAN ELEMENTS AND FOCUS (*continued*)

Budgets		Budgets
Similar from the mechanical viewpoint since specific regulatory compliance budgets are necessary.	When examining budgets and budgeting in the regulatory area, the following factors represent some psychological and procedural differences from normal planning:	

(1) Not profit oriented

(2) There are a large number of uncertainties; hence, more inaccuracies (plus and minus) have to be expected.

(3) Specific budgets for compliance have been a relatively neglected area; there is little in the literature from which to draw.

(4) Inherent in budget establishment is cost analysis and identification; few, if any, accounting procedures within the company provide for this; therefore, they must be created. They will also be useful and necessary

    (a) To determine cost of compliance

    (b) To determine allocations

    (c) As a determinant in pricing decisions

    (d) As a basis for argument in the legislative/regulatory process pending, existing, up for revision or amendment.

    (e) As a possible element in public relations

    (f) As an element in sales/price discussions and justification to government internally and to the customer

    (g) Evidence in formal legal proceedings

Control and review procedures	Again, similar, from the mechanical viewpoint.	Once more, distinction can be made on the basis of those that are essentially voluntary as opposed to those mandated. Therefore, these procedures are (1) More essential and formal because of OSHA, FWPCA, ERISA, etc. (2) Even where pursuant to voluntary objectives/ actions, they provide advantages similar to those indicated above for budgeting.	Control and review procedures
	Not normally explicitly planned.	Because these are areas of (1) High concern (2) Substantial regulation existing and pending (3) Great sensitivity, formal planning provision should be made.	Health and environmental concerns
	Not normally explicitly planned.	Obviously, legislation and regulations emanate from the government — whether federal, state, or local; formal government contacts can and should be established; where such a function is included in the company, either by direct representation or through a consultant or lobbyist, formalization in planning is desirable, even if only to the extent of monitoring and reporting on existing and pending legislation and regulation.	Government relations
	Not normally explicitly included.	As business vulnerability and sensitivity to legislative and regulatory action increases contingency (or what if) plans become of increasing necessity; formalized analysis and planning provision will be required.	Contingency planning

243

careful thought has to be given to implementation of contingency planning or we could generate more wasted paper than we often accuse the government of doing.

The first consideration is the objective of the planning operation—which in this case is basically not to be caught short in important areas—and then using this criterion to examine each of the departments' functions and operations from the viewpoint of the sensitivity and vulnerability factors as they apply. Thus, we will be able to limit potential contingency plans to meet the objective of anticipating and planning for major events in critical areas that relate to the basic sensitivities and vulnerabilities of the company. Then we can establish a list of areas for which contingency plans should be developed (e.g., R&D, M&E, sales, product management, packaging) and then a set of specific assumptions regarding these areas that would represent probable future events and conditions. Here again a selective process is involved, one that identifies those that have the highest degree of possible reality, and it is for these that specific contingency plans are drafted.

By doing this we cannot prevent events or provide for all uncertainties, but we should be able to minimize "surprises" and their negative effects on the marketing operation. We need think back to only one example, that of the dietetic beverage industry that was caught by the cyclamate ban a few years ago. The result was months of revenue loss because of the lack of suitable replacements or substitute products of commercial acceptability. Certainly the ban could not have been prevented, nor would one want to if the conclusion regarding risk were valid (and this remains a highly controversial issue today). Nevertheless, contingency planning would have placed the companies in a more advantageous position in terms of substitutes. Such planning need not have been limited to noncaloric or low caloric sweeteners alone but also include, for example, advertising. This kind of planning would have a program ready to put in place to facilitate product conversion such as we are now seeing with deodorant "roll-ons" versus "sprays" manufactured and offered by the same company.

Overall Short- and Long-term Strategies

To survive in a highly competitive marketplace requires implementation of carefully predetermined strategies. To survive in a highly regulated market also requires implementing carefully predetermined strategies. In this chapter we have tried to provide some indication of the shift in orientation and perspective that will be needed to formulate these strategies. More to the point, we have identified many operational alterations that will be necessary and elaborated on several tools and techniques that are immediately available to all marketing executives. The message is not to wait but to initiate policies and programs now even acknowledging that they may not be total, inclusive, or in any sense final. Obviously here, as in other managment areas, there will be evolution, an expansion of knowledge, and sophistication in approach. This, however, only comes with time, experience, and the benefit of refining existing programs.

While these broader provisions must be made eventually—and needless to say, the sooner the better—there are several strategies described in Table 8.1 that can be employed within marketing that require a minimum investment and can be accomplished in most instances with existing personnel. While definitive, each of these specific strategies is still broad enough in concept to be applicable to most companies in the majority of situations. One vital last thought before you examine this tabulation: *Disabuse yourself of the "this is none of my business" attitude when it comes to government and its effects. The "my job is marketing, or sales, or R & D, or whatever," attitude is a sure road to business disaster. It will not work any longer—and if too many people stick to it, they may not either.*

TABLE 8.10 STRATEGIES FOR SURVIVAL AND GROWTH

Marketing Area	Strategy Synopsis	Illustrative Elements/Actions
Management	Establish organization and set responsibility for integrating legislative and regulatory effects.	(1) Identify and review pertinent legislation and regulation. (2) Establish assigned responsibility for compliance. (3) Establish assigned responsibility for information gathering.
	Create correct employee attitude regarding effects of legislation and regulation.	(1) Provide for internal education in this area. (2) Assure recognition of importance of this area on a general level to ensure consideration in decision-making.
	Provide for customer education.	Plan for inclusion of appropriate customer education either formal (through booklets, A&P, etc.) or informal (through salesmen). Let the customer know what you are doing both responsively and voluntarily in those areas of his interest including environment, safety, product, quality, energy, etc. Turn your actions into positive marketing-related activities that also raise the level of awareness regarding factors such as added cost, reduction of innovation, etc.
	Increase internal productivity.	(1) In part this can be a result of the other strategies provided. (To some degree as the level of awareness of the problems increases, responsible voluntary productivity should increase on the part of employees.) (2) Make affirmative efforts for improved job and performance revisions and reviews; open dialogue on production expectations. (3) Reduce all paperwork to absolute minimum.

246

Establish an interdisciplinary approach to problem identification and solution.

(1) Review primary areas of concern including consideration of Z factor theory and GEEM elements.

(2) Provide for formal planning integration of legislative and regulatory effects.

(3) Create a new marketing team with direct representation of other functions (R&D, M&E, legal, etc.).

(4) Secure top management involvement and support.

Create an atmosphere of adaptability.

(1) Recognize that rapid change will be necessary.

(2) Avoid rigidity of approach and response.

(3) Establish a flexible response mechanism that is also rapid.

(4) Delegate what authority is needed to make this truly an operative approach. See Chapter 10.

(5) Utilize contingency planning to assist, but do not allow even this type of planning to forestall nonplanned actions where they are obviously needed.

Adopt Z factor.

The elements of the theory that are applicable to the particular business should be adopted.

Adopt GEEM factors.

The individual company must examine its position in relationship to these factors and employed them in both its decision-making and planning operations.

Sensitivity and vulnerability factors should be identified.

Both factors should be carefully analyzed; result will be a clear understanding of the company's sensitivity and vulnerability factors; appropriate inclusion should be made in both decisions and planning.

TABLE 8.10 STRATEGIES FOR SURVIVAL AND GROWTH (*continued*)

Marketing Area	Strategy Synopsis	Illustrative Elements/Actions
	Establish investment controls and criteria.	(1) Reexamine investment plans in the light of all of the considerations mentioned. (2) Revise investments where seemingly desirable. (3) Although many aspects of uncertainty remain total investment withdrawal is not only illogical but undesirable.
	Provide for profitability examination and revision.	(1) Within the limitations of profitability control and accountability, review profit objectives; in a highly regulated market these can be different from those in a nonregulated market; as the transition is made in some business from essentially nonregulated to regulated profit objectives may have to be shifted. (2) Examine other mechanisms for profit improvement or perhaps even settle for stabilization. (3) Maintenance of existing profit margins in an inflationary and highly regulated period does represent growth; some of our basic precepts here have to be reconsidered on this more realistic basis. (4) Traditional as it is reexamine short- versus long-term profit objectives, this time taking into account the legislative and regulatory effects combined with the GEEM factors; distinction based on market and competition can lead to short-term profit losses or stabilization with expectations of gains in the long run thru thru market alteration or decline in competition. Companies with a greater vested interest or capital investment position may be in a

far better position "to weather the storm", and emerge with an improved consolidated position.

Inventory control measures should be reexamined.

Examine inventory control from the normal considerations of economics, replacement value, etc. and as government legislation of regulation might affect you. Some factors to provide for are:

(1) Possible recalls and replacement provisions in some legislation (e.g., FDA, EPA–pesticides, toxic substances).
(2) Banning or restricting provisions (e.g., CSPA, EPA).
(3) Rule changes that affect packaging or transportation (e.g., DOT, DOC, EPA).
(4) Safety considerations such as explosiveness; flammability; toxicity; and the risk of accident, leak discharge, etc.
(5) Liability in the event of accident or discharge (e.g., EPA).
(6) Control of package size to minimize risk (liability, insurance).

Provide for complete consideration of product liability in marketing decision making from R&D to post-marketing service.

(1) Product liability is fast becoming a major concern, and it should be factored into all decision-making.
(2) All aspects should be considered:
  (a) Extent of liability
  (b) Insurance
  (c) Minimization
  (d) Risk/benefit to the corporation when adding a product or program that incurs liability
  (e) Potential for limitation to control liability such as labeling, product use information, packaging, size and quantity, shipping, distribution channels, etc.

TABLE 8.10   STRATEGIES FOR SURVIVAL AND GROWTH (*continued*)

Marketing Area	Strategy Synopsis	Illustrative Elements/Actions
	Procedures to minimize risk.	(1) Three types of risk have previously been identified: economic, technical, and psychological; each has the dimension of the conventional or present-day effect and the new or projected effect; each has to be carefully evaluated and fully recognized in planning and decision-making.
		(2) All programs and activities should include provision for full evaluation of all of these risks and various methods for their reduction such as:
		(a) Interdisciplinary approach that assures input from all areas so that no important aspects are missed.
		(b) Carefully studied, developed, and implemented compliance programs (remember here that in some statutes executives are clearly held liable based on their assigned responsibilities in their respective areas).
		(c) Legal department or external counsel review.
		(d) Periodic reassessment to incorporate changes in rules and regulations based on agency, department, commission, or court decisions.
	Establishment of new informational networks.	(1) Informational requirements to capture legislative and regulatory effects differ from those that are traditionally considered in marketing; therefore, they must be provided for.
		(2) Information obtained must be communicated after interpretation—upward, downward, and laterally.

(3) Be certain to include legal judgements on information obtained and distributed.

(4) Provide for the inclusion of such information in planning and decision-making.

Development of accounting systems based on new needs.

(1) Review existing accounting procedures and practices to determine if they are adequate for contemporary needs.

(2) Develop new systems to capture compliance and related costs to:

(a) Pass through those that are appropriate.

(b) Determine quantatively the company investment and cost of compliance.

(c) To use as a basis for presentation in hearings, litigation, proceedings, either individually or as part of a trade or professional association activity.

(d) As an element in cost/benefit and cost/effectiveness determinations.

(e) As a basis for predictive cost calculations for purposes indicated above and for internal planning.

Establishment of cost control measures.

(1) As with consideration of profits, to maintain costs can be a significant and positive accomplishment in view of legislative and regulatory and general external events that result in so many increases.

(2) Specific systems for review and cost analysis should be developed and employed.

TABLE 8.10   STRATEGIES FOR SURVIVAL AND GROWTH (*continued*)

Marketing Area	Strategy Synopsis	Illustrative Elements/Actions
	Establishment of profitability objectives.	(1) The establishment of profitability objectives is not new for marketing management; what is needed now is not only another analysis of what profit performance should be but the creation of profit objectives by: (a) Product. (b) Market. (c) Market sector. (d) Account. 2. Account-by-account profitability is admittedly the most difficult but can be most helpful in controlling marketing costs. 3. Keeping costs constant.
	Integrate other nonmarketing areas in marketing decision-making.	Legislative and regulatory effects, limitations, problems, and in some cases opportunities are felt throughout business and do not respect normal business function boundaries. Some functions may not exist in the company, such as government relations or public relations, and it is necessary therefore to consider first the need for them and the role of marketing in identifying and supporting such need and, if needed, their integration into the marketing effort. In addition, areas such as R&D and M&E, which have had a traditionally close relationship to marketing, will have to grow even closer in the future. Relating market research, for example, with R&D from the Z, GEEM, and PV viewpoints can be of enormous value to the viability and vitality of the organization.

Determination of positions to take in pending legislation, rule or regulation.

Depending upon the organization, this responsibility may not fall directly within the marketing function. However, there can be a direct effect on marketing from such decisions, and those responsible should be consulted when considering any position to be taken by the corporation. In this instance the lead may well be taken by, for example, legal or government relations, but the need for close working relations with marketing is not minimized.

Identification of sensitivity and vulnerability factors.

(1) All companies are both sensitive and vulnerable to a number of external factors and events. The number of factors and the degree of sensitivity and vulnerability differs.

(2) Such factors should be clearly identified and considered seriously in planning and decision-making.

(3) Reexamination is necessary because this is not only a time-, but product-, and market-dependent phenomenon.

Look both ways at legislative and regulatory effects.

(1) Examine the effects on your supplier—that is, look back.

(2) Look forward to what the effects will be on your customer—as your supplier is affected so are you.

Think in terms of the totality of effect.

A regulation involving production affects product availability, and a restriction on a customer's use affects sales; learn to detect and determine what these are.

Use consultants.

This is a new and complex arena of operation, and professional assistance can be beneficial and in the long run economical.

Participate in legislative and regulatory affairs.

Only by being directly involved will you really know what is going on and be in a position to influence events.

TABLE 8.10 STRATEGIES FOR SURVIVAL AND GROWTH (*continued*)

Marketing Area	Strategy Synopsis	Illustrative Elements/Actions
Sales	Price planning.	(1) Product pricing has always been considered critical; perceptual value factors may be more important in the overall, but price is still a vital element.
		(2) Variability in extrinsic events may cause increased pricing uncertainty but must be considered.
		(3) Cost pass through based on legislative and regulatory compliance, plus energy and material considerations should be provided for via planning and accounting mechanisms.
		(4) Preplanned pricing is of increasing importance.
	Buyer identification requirements.	(1) To identify the actual buyer or at least those responsible for the buying decision is even more important now and for the future in order to make A&P and overall marketing efforts better.
		(2) Pose the rather simplistic but important questions: Who buys my product? Why do they buy my product? Why do they buy my product instead of some other product sold by my competitor? Why don't they buy my product?
		(3) Develop answers to these questions which should then be translated into positive marketing campaigns which should include product development, A&P, sales, etc.

Increased return of sales call investment.

(1) Sales calls cost money. Sales-support efforts (letters, brochures, etc.) cost money. These costs are increasing and thought must be given to controlling these costs and improving the return on this investment.

(2) Cost controls are relatively clear and have been rather extensively treated in the literature. The other aspect, improving return on sales calls has not. Therefore,

(3) Look to the salesmen to:
   (a) Provide education to the customer.
   (b) Conduct limited market research based on clear instructions from marketing management.
   (c) Conduct sales research.

Justify account retention.

(1) Develop an account rationalization program.
(2) Be as ruthless in examining the justification for accounts as you are with products.

Review all contracts and contract policy.

(1) Curtail long-term agreements or contracts.
(2) Look carefully at any "evergreen" contracts—existing or potential.
(3) Incorporate provision for price or supply adjustments in any long-term agreements or contracts.
(4) As with the recommendation of considering effects on suppliers and customers, here too you had best look both ways.

Utilize legislation and regulation as well as extrinsic events as a basis for advertising and promotion campaigns.

(1) Many of the company efforts relating to legislation or regulation can be employed in advertising and promotion. Several examples exist today from hot dog ads to those for oil and gasoline.

TABLE 8.10 STRATEGIES FOR SURVIVAL AND GROWTH (*continued*)

Marketing Area	Strategy Synopsis	Illustrative Elemenents/Actions
		(2) Voluntary measures that go beyond those mandated can also be used, particularly if the comparison of what is being done to what is required can be effectively communicated.
		(3) External events that do not fall within legislative or regulatory affairs can also be used as positive A&P (e.g., oil crisis, energy crisis, recession).
		(4) Close review and examination of A&P budgets should also be established with full justification for any A&P investment.
	Revise advertising and promotion to reflect changes in consumer attitudes.	Consumers are distrustful of business; they are better informed now than they were in the past; they are confused by too many claims and counterclaims; they are smarter than they are often given credit for being—all of these and other realities are good cause for revisions of all A&P approaches.
Distribution	Reexamine all aspects of distribution—both channels of and physical—from the viewpoints of compliance with the law and to minimize risk and to identify business opportunities.	(1) Establish a team to review all aspects of distribution (physical and methods of)
		(2) Be creative in identifying new methods in both areas to
		(a) Reduce costs.
		(b) Comply with laws and regulations.
		(c) Anticipate new laws and regulations.
		(d) Prolong product or market life.
		(e) Anticipate events that might require alterations.

(3) Do not prejudge any approaches even if they are at first seemingly inappropriate as radically different from present practices. Carefully review and analyze them before making any final determination.

Product management

Establish product control procedures.

(1) Determine optimum product line size and initiate efforts to obtain and maintain it.
(2) Examine carefully all effects on new and existing products.
(3) Examine carefully all effects on all R&D products at whatever stage they may be.
(4) Establish procedures for product audits.
(5) Establish product-by-product profit objectives.
(6) Review and justify the continuation of each product in the line.
(7) Examine all products from Z and GEEM factor viewpoints.
(8) Introduce product planning (if none exists) or modify planning process to include Z and GEEM factors in future product planning.
(9) Explore all perceptual value factors for inclusion in product decisions.

Product life cycles should be examined and plans modified where necessary.

(1) Life cycle analysis should now take into consideration Z and GEEM. Don't forget PV factors.
(2) Use life-cycle principles to extend product longevity.

TABLE 8.10 STRATEGIES FOR SURVIVAL AND GROWTH (*continued*)

Marketing Area	Strategy Synopsis	Illustrative Elements/Actions
	Establish packaging policy.	(1) Examine all legal and regulatory aspects of packaging; many of these have changed or are in a state of flux.
		(2) Examine not only the requirements but costs of packaging and ecological effects, which will be the subject of increased future concern and attention.
		(3) Start in the development of appropriate alternative packaging approaches now wherever it can be projected that legal or GEEM factors will come into consideration in packaging.
	Establish quality control review procedures.	(1) Examine all legal and regulatory aspects of quality control.
		(2) Many of these have changed and are being reviewed with potential new regulatory requirements (e.g., Toxic Substances Control Act, Resource Conservation and Recovery Act of 1976).
		(3) Explore the possibilities of quality control modifications to control costs.
		(4) Examine the relationship of quality control to product performance and liability in addition to costs under guarantee and warranty.
	Product policy.	Try to extend the life of all products rather than introduce new ones; this is especially necessary for "me too" products.

Examine labeling requirements and attempt to use them for marketing purposes in addition to straight-forward compliance requirements.

(1) One of the most pervasive aspects of legislative and regulatory requirements is labeling covering requirements from safety data to mandated nutritional information, from disposal information to the Universal Price Code.

(2) Establish a labeling committee to be sure that you can do the following:

   (a) Comply with the myriad labeling requirements of the law.

   (b) Prepare for future labeling requirements (e.g., Toxic Substance Control Act).

   (c) Use labeling as an illustration of your voluntary actions in instances where you are ahead of the legislated requirements.

   (d) Employ your labeling in positive A&P campaigns so that while you are either complying or anticipating you can also use to some marketing advantage.

Planning

Provide for the inclusion of legislation and regulation as well as Z and GEEM factors in all phases of planning.

(1) All of the recommendations provided previously should be included in:

   (a) Price planning.

   (b) Cost planning.

   (c) Marketing planning.

   (d) Contingency planning.

(2) Examine the planning options reviewed and include the most appropriate one in your basic planning operations.

TABLE 8.10 STRATEGIES FOR SURVIVAL AND GROWTH (*continued*)

Marketing Area	Strategy Synopsis	Illustrative Elements/Actions
Market research	Examine present market research activities objectively and modify them in the light of legislative and regulatory effects; also focus on Z, GEEM, and PV factors.	In the broadest possible sense all that has been written here regarding legislative and regulatory effects and all of the other intrinsic and extrinsic effects both expressly and implicitly involved in Z, GEEM, and PV factors consideration should be used as the basis for reexamining market research practices and modifying them accordingly. They create many problems, but they also create opportunities both for existing products and for new ones and existing and potential markets. The object is to recognize this potential for new marketing efforts based on such redirection. Those who learn to do this early and efficiently can obtain substantial marketing advantage.
Competitive analysis	Prepare for a new way of examining, analyzing, and appraising yourself and the competition.	(1) All that has been discussed also applies to the competition. (2) Analyze the competition from this viewpoint to determine actions, predict reactions, and assess strategy and tactics. Combining this with some overall management assessments, which include consideration of the vested interest theory and present financial state appreciation, can provide many strategic and tactical insights for your company. (3) Such determinations should be included in market research objectives and then included in day-to-day operational decisions and all planning activities.

NINE

THE NEW
Legal Framework

There is an adage about one man's poison. If it applies anywhere in the business world, it certainly must be in the area of the effects of legislation. If nothing else, our legal brothers in the firm, the private world of legal practice, or the government, are secure. In addition to the specifics of new legislation and regulation, several important developments in the overall category of business and the law warrant further examination. Gone are the days of the slow and seemingly ponderous actions of the legislators in terms of enacting new statutes, and gone too are some of the delays in the judicial processes. Moreover, we have seen the growth of the fourth branch of government—the regulatory branch—whose action in terms of issuing rules and regulations impose more numerous and specific business requirements than the statutes from which they are derived.

Recent years have seen literally thousands of bills introduced in each Congress, hundreds of which are subsequently enacted into law. As an example, there were over 24,000 bills introduced into the 94th Congress (17,015 in the first session, and 7,268 in the second). Of these 588 public bills and 141 private bills were enacted into law (total for both sessions). True, not all of these are major legislative events, but each one adds some pieces to the overall puzzle and imposes some effect on someone somewhere. Many do not have such indirect effects. Remember when thinking about this number it represents only two year's activities—imagine what that means over the course of several years.

In the area of regulatory actions recent issues of the *Federal Register* have reported approximately 25,000 new regulations per year. Again, not all affect business directly, but many do—more fences in the maze. Some of the immediate problems for marketing management are related to the basic volume of legislation and regulation and the problems posed in keeping informed, reviewing, digesting, interpreting, and acting upon those that require action. In an earlier chapter we discussed the informational needs of marketing and the establishment of new intelligence networks to produce data about statutes before enactment or the proposed rule or regulation before promulgation. Such systems must provide for the legal aspects as well as the other more normally sought market-oriented or economic information.

The second major change has been in the nature and thrust of legislation and regulation. That is, the redirection from economic to socially oriented perspectives and resultant restrictions and sanctions. Although we have mentioned this before, it bears brief repetition here because it has a relationship not only to the question of numbers, but to the thrust and direction of future legislation and regulation, both in degree and kind. There are any number of examples that could be given, ranging from concerns with occupational safety and health, which resulted in OSHA, to social benefits and equality considerations, as reflected in EEOC. These trends are the direction of the future.

The courts themselves have shifted toward upholding the actions of agencies, departments, and commissions as well as awarding substantial amounts in private litigation. When considering the results of litigation, this trend should be uppermost in mind. This is not a direct or implied accusation of any bias or favoritism; it is merely an observation of the contemporary climate. It perhaps reflects some of the essential cultural and value alterations that were the subjects of earlier expostulation.

These changes have also resulted in a shift from classical concerns of economic controls to those that regulate the internal activities of the company and affect the basic product and process from R&D through marketing and even into the home in the sense of warranties and guarantiees. What this means to the marketing manager is that he must go beyond the Robinson-Patman or Sherman Antitrust legislation in terms of his knowledge of the law that affects marketing and controls or directs his marketing efforts.

As if these alterations were not sufficient, there have been others; but perhaps the most important from the corporate and personal viewpoints is ths trend toward establishing personal, civil, and criminal liability, which is attached not to the inanimate corporation but to the very animate individual. Historically, the corporation was held responsible and its actions were the subject of restriction and the object of sanctions or penalties if there were legally upheld violations. When the company examined a statute and looked to related violations and prohibitions, it clearly assessed the liability on the basis of the penalties imposed. There were, no doubt, instances in which because the corporation, not the person, was liable and the cost of penalties may have been far less than the cost of compliance, some companies elected to pay (if caught). One cannot condone this, nor is there any attempt here to do so. We can only trust that this was the exception rather than the rule. But exception or not, business and industry cannot contend that it did not occur.

When it comes to questions of the environment, safety, health, equal rights, job and income or retirement security, some fundamental issues arise—issues that no responsible person wants to push aside. This had led to many contentions on both sides, but the prevailing attitude of the Congress regarding these issues is that they are obligations of the corporation. Our environment must be protected, and the use of natural resources and the preservation of environmental quality is not only the right but the duty of the state. Private enterprise does not have the right to utilize or pollute the resources that are rightfully those of the public at large, thereby in effect converting them to their own use and profit. Similarly, arguments are directed toward protection of the individual—whether from unknown or undisclosed hazards or from economic, sexual, racial, religious, or social inequities or injustices.

So much for political and social philosophy. The result is that Congress and the public found a way to enter the essentially anonymous corporation or company and reach the real and identifiable responsible executive who resides therein. The motivation here is not difficult to see. If one can reach the individual and apply penalties against which the company cannot idemnify, there should be a different and far more response reaction to compliance. When these penalties are made criminal (in some statutes) as well as civil, which means not money out of the pocket—painful as this may be—but years out of lives, the motivation is even stronger. The result is the inclusion of personal, civil, and criminal penalties in several of the newer statutes. (Incidentally—and it is not so incidental —corporate liability still obtains.) To see how this is expressed and what the typical penalties are the following is extracted from the October 12, 1976, Toxic Substance Control Act (TSCA).

TABLE 9.1   PUBLIC LAW 94-469

SEC. 16. PENALTIES.

(a) CIVIL. (1) Any person who violates a provision of section 15 shall be liable to the United States for a civil penalty in an amount not to exceed $25,000 for each such violation. Each day such a violation continues shall, for purposes of this subsection, constitute a separate violation of section 15. — 15 USC 2616.

(2) (A) A civil penalty for a violation of section 15 shall be assessed by the Administrator by an order made on the record after opportunity (provided in accordance with this subparagraph) for a hearing in accordance with section 554 of title 5, United States Code. Before issuing such an order, the Administrator shall give written notice to the — Hearing.

TABLE 9.1 *(continued)*

person to be assessed a civil penalty under such order of the Administrator's proposal to issue such order and provide such person an opportunity to request, within 15 days of the date the notice is received by such person, such a hearing on the order.

(B) In determining the amount of a civil penalty, the Administrator shall take into account the nature, circumstances, extent, and gravity of the violation or violations and, with respect to the violator, ability to pay, effect on ability to continue to do business, any history of prior such violations, the degree of culpability, and such other matters as justice may require.

(C) The Administrator may compromise, modify, or remit, with or without conditions, any civil penalty which may be imposed under this subsection. The amount of such penalty, when finally determined, or the amount agreed upon in compromise, may be deducted from any sums owing by the United States to the person charged.

(3) Any person who requested in accordance with paragraph (2) (A) a hearing respecting the assessment of a civil penalty and who is aggrieved by an order assessing a civil penalty may file a petition for judicial review of such order with the United States Court of Appeals for the District of Columbia Circuit or for any other circuit in which such person resides or transacts business. Such a petition may only be filed within the 30-day period beginning on the date the order making such assessment was issued.

Petition for judicial review.

(4) If any person fails to pay an assessment of a civil penalty —

(A) After the order making the assessment has become a final order and if such person does not file a petition for judicial review of the order in accordance with paragraph (3), or

(B) after a court in an action brought under paragraph (3) has entered a final judgment in favor of the Administrator—the Attorney General shall recover the amount assessed (plus interest at currently prevailing rates from the date of the expiration of the 30-day period referred to in paragraph

TABLE 9.1 *(continued)*

(3) or the date of such final judgment, as the case may be) in an action brought in any appropriate district court of the United States. In such an action, the validity, amount, and appropriateness of such penalty shall not be subject to review.

(b) Criminal. Any person who knowingly or willfully violates any provision of section 15 shall, in addition to or in lieu of any civil penalty which may be imposed under subsection (a) of this section for such violation, be subject, upon conviction, to a fine of not more than $25,000 for each day of violation, or to imprisonment for not more than one year, or both.

There are similar provisions in the Federal Water Pollution Control Act (FWPCA).

TABLE 9.2 PUBLIC LAW 92-500

"(e) (1) Any person who willfully or negligently violates section 301, 302, 306, 307, or 308 of this Act, or any permit condition or limitation implementing any of such sections in a permit issued under section 402 of this Act by the Administrator or by a State, shall be punished by a fine of not less than $2,500 nor more than $25,000 per day of violation, or by imprisonment for not more than one year, or by both. If the conviction is for a violation committed after a first conviction of such person under this paragraph, punishment shall be by a fine of not more than $50,000 per day of violation, or by imprisonment for not more than two years, or by both.

Penalties.

"(2) Any person who knowingly makes any false statement, representation, or certification in any application, record, report, plan, or other document filed or required to be maintained under this Act or who falsifies, tampers with, or knowingly renders inaccurate any monitoring device or method required to be maintained under this Act, shall upon conviction, be punished by a fine

TABLE 9.2   *(continued)*

of not more than $10,000, or by imprisonment
for not more than six months, or by both.

"(3) For the purposes of this subsection, the   "Person."
term 'person' shall mean, in addition to the definition contained in section 502(5) of this Act, any
responsible corporate officer.

"(d) Any person who violates section 301,
302, 306, 307, or 308 of this Act, or any permit
condition or limitation implementing any of
such sections in a permit issued under section 402
of this Act by the Administrator, or by a State,
and any person who violates any order issued
by the Administrator under subsection (a) of this
section, shall be subject to a civil penalty not to
exceed $10,000 per day of such violation.

"(e) Whenever a municipality is a party to a
civil action brought by the United States under
this section, the State in which such minucipality
is located shall be joined as a party. Such State
shall be liable for payment of any judgment, or
any expenses incurred as a result of complying
with any judgment, entered against the municipality in such action to the extent that the laws
of that State prevent the municipality from raising
revenues needed to comply with such judgment.

In the event that one might think this is academic, the first case that is clearly in
this area, the so-called Park Case, proves that it is not. There are some differences in terms of legal technicalities but not in principle.

Liability of Corporate Officers: The Park Case

Illustrative of the liability of corporate officers in areas other than antitrust or
restraint of trade, is the case that involved alleged violation of the Food, Drug,
and Cosmetic Act. The issue in the Park case was whether Park, President of
Acme Markets, was guilty within the law of violating the Act. Violations that
had occured, although within the areas of his jurisdiction, did not involve him
personally but were attributable to employees within the organization.

The lower court decision was that he was guilty and that the traditional awareness of violation or intent need not be used for a conviction under the Food,

Drug, and Cosmetic Act. The court also said that a corporate officer was liabile if he has a "responsible share in the furtherance of the transaction which the statue outlaws." Thus, the issue was what constitutes a "responsible share." In this instance when the case went to the Supreme Court they decided by a six to three decision on June 9, 1975, that Park was guilty and confirmed a lower court decision. In making their decision the justices did not say that guilt can be determined solely on the basis of an officer's position, but that there must be some measure of "blameworthiness." However, this can be demonstrated by the fact that the officer had the responsibility and authority to prevent or correct a violation and failed to do so. The judgement of the Court was that this was in fact the case with Park. Although he had testified that he had delegated responsibility to subordinates, the Court said that Park had notice that his delegation system was not working. FDA had notified Park of earlier violations in a warehouse and thus his testimony was rebutted.

This decision is important not only because it opens the way for holding corporate officers responsible for violations under the Food, Drug, and Cosmetic Act, but because others under similar statutes can be held liable where courts have or will apply "strict liability."

What this tells us is that any corporate officer who has both the responsibility and the authority in any given area, when delegating specific authority must not only make the assignment but also introduce a system of checks on the use of that delegated authority. There must be a system of reporting, investigation, and positive action.

Will there be more Mr. Parks? Only time will tell. The actual prosecution under these statutory provisions is a relatively new area of law and therefore one that remains to be clarified in terms both of utilization and conviction. What does not need any clarification is that the laws are, as they say, on the books and that these penalties can be invoked. Whatever one has to say about the need or lack of need for them is not the point. They are the here and now of the law. Moreover, they are the direction of penalty provisions of the future, and when taken with the events of recent years in terms of judicial actions, to "knowingly or willfully violate" is less than a calculated risk. This means that life, liberty, and the pursuit, as most of us know it, is on the line when it comes to understanding and complying with these laws. What follows is that clear unequivocal policies and programs are required by management. Despite the limited use of this authority to date, there is little doubt that it will be increasingly invoked. Even if it were not, it could be, and therein lies another motivation in itself.

All of these developments are not so negative as they first appear, but they do impose new ways of looking at and doing things. They do affect the basic nature and conduct of the company. One has to recognize that the complexities of these laws, regulations, and the entire legal process is such that one conclusion is inescapable: We need legal help.

LABELING

There is a new and growing concern over labeling. Many of us are familiar with product labels that contain information such as the name and use of the product; others are familiar with mandates such as weight, composition, contents, nutritional value, and the Universal Pricing Code. There are still others. For instance, there are a whole series of DOT labels that are necessary as shown in Figures 9.1 and 9.2.

Although these labels may be directed more toward physical and safety or health hazards, the direct marketing constituencies are important. In some cases they are clearly required by law, and in some instances they are being applied voluntarily. Where the law requires them—assuming that everyone is in compliance—all are equal. However, where they are being used voluntarily, many questions of commercial significance arise. For example, if a company elects to apply some form of warning label and others do not for similar or comparable materials, will the first seller be at an advantage or a disadvantage? Some buyers will prefer to know what potential hazards might be represented by the product and react favorably; others who will feel that this information merely presents new problems and will react negatively. Questions of voluntary labeling and notification represent matters of judgment. Therefore the company and the lawyers must take into consideration aspects suct as risk and mitigation of liability when labeling. This must include labeling that goes beyond the strict legal requirements, and consideration must be given to the commercial risks involved. To this must be added some of the other considerations such as government reaction and credibility to the public that we have examined before. A complex decision, one more that lends weight to our "team" suggestion, (see Chapter 10) is involved.

Legally, labeling and its requirements are not limited to a sticker placed on a drum or a label on a package; it includes all representations and descriptions of the material so that what is said on the label may well also have to appear in product literature, bulletins, catalogues, and so on. Once a determination on labeling policy is made, where, when, and how such "labeling" should be undertaken to provide the most adequate protection means that close coordination with the company's legal counsel is necessary. Clearly, previous decisions related to labeling policy, which essentially relate to policies that reflect only the strictest mandatory requirements as opposed to broad and comprehensive labeling on a voluntary basis, also requires the close coordination of the "team."

NEED FOR COUNSEL

From what little has been said here, supplemented by the many and varied references that have been made throughout this book, we can see that the benefit of legal advice is essential. There are several ways in which this can be obtained:

Figure 9.1   Illustrations of DOT labeling requirements. *Source: Federal Register,*
Vol. 41, No. 188, Government Printing Office, Washington, D.C., September 27,
1976.

Figure 9.2   Illustrations of DOT placarding requirements. *Source: Federal Register*, Vol. 41, No. 188, Government Printing Office, Washington, D.C., September 27, 1976.

EXPLOSIVE C

NON-FLAMMABLE GAS

FLAMMABLE GAS

POISON

OXIDIZER

IRRITANT

EMPTY

271

Permanent in-house counsel or staff
Outside counsel on retainer
Outside counsel on an issue-by-issue basis
A combination depending on the circumstance and the need

Even large companies use the last approach because the complexities of the law are such that various specialists are required from time to time to supplement the basic in-house expertise. Smaller companies, however, may well have to rely on the advice and assistance of a single individual. This should in no way be construed as to impune such individuals or their contributions, it is merely meant to indicate a range of possibilities. Whichever the approach, legal support is required not only in interpreting legislation and regulation, but in determining if specific actions are or are not in compliance or at least constitute a best good-faith effort. Needless to say, counsel is also required to initiate or defend in litigation or to assist in a number of other vital activities. With the complexity of the regulated environment, using the talents of lawyers is not a luxury, not only a necessity, but an imperative.

WHAT THE LAWYERS CAN AND CANNOT DO FOR YOU

Recognizing that we need legal assistance, however, is not the same as expecting that it is or can be a panacea. While there are many things lawyers can do for us in marketing and general management, there are also many things that they cannot. For marketing executives, and senior managers to utilize the vital contributions of counsel, we should all clearly recognize both the potential ''can and cannots.'' Many of the most important of these are summarized in Table 9.3.

TABLE 9.3   WHAT LAWYERS CAN AND CANNOT DO

Can Do	Cannot Do
Counsel	Establish marketing policy
Monitor statutes	Make marketing decisions
Monitor regulations	Represent marketing activities
Advise on compliance programs	Replace marketing judgement
Consult on compliance programs	Assume responsibility for business
Review marketing activities	decisions based on legal advice
Initiate or defend in litigation	Replace marketing management
Monitor case law	
Participate in information system	
Participate in decision-making	
Advise on labelling	

LITIGATION AS A NECESSITY

One of the many changes we have noted is that there seems to be little reluctance on the part of the public interest activists to resort to the courts to attain their objectives. They willingly and frequently take industry or individuals as well as the government to court to advance their positions. This has resulted in a new era of litigation. We have alluded to the fact that this has in some instances gone so far as to create special problems in terms of the courts dealing with scientific and technical issues, resulting in court decisions that are tantamount to the establishment of national priorities and policies. These important concerns are somewhat beyond us for the moment. What we must be concerned with is our ability to respond to these suits when brought against us or when initiated against the government over issues we should support because they represent positions that are in accordance with business interests. Here again lawyers, and in many cases trade associations, can be most helpful.

Since the trend toward litigation is evident, and since the decisions, once rendered, as well as out-of-court settlements are so important, industry too must consider initiating such litigation. While no responsible person would advocate or encourage litigation for its own sake or because it seems to be the contemporary "in" thing, there is ample justification for filing suit or joining litigation in areas of substantial business concern. If equity is what is sought, clearly there should be equality for business just as there is for the government and the public. The timely and appropriate use of litigation, therefore, must be considered by the corporation. This is an area in which counsel is most definitely needed and represents one of the many reasons why in constructing the new marketing team inclusion of the legal perspective is vital.

TEN

Putting It
All Together
WITHIN THE COMPANY

In Chapter 6 we examined the historical role of marketing and traced its evolution from relative obscurity to its present central position in the corporation. This development was the consequence of changes both within and without the company. The company had traditionally manufactured what it deemed to be most appropriate and necessary and continued to make essentially what it could sell regardless of changes in consumer attitudes, market response, or other external events. Only as the company began to perceive that externalization was necessary did marketing come into full being. At this point, recognizing the need to understand and relate to actions based on reactions to the market, the company altered its basic premise and began to make what it could sell. This seemed like a radical approach and for the time it probably was.

Later came other ideas, which in many respects were nothing much more than refinements of this basic new perception, although no less important. The public—the market—was ultimately in control, for only through satisfaction of the market comes success in the market. As things progressed, however, application of these refinements became more important, as did marketing itself; we saw not only the added sharpening of the new perspective of the market but areas such as market research, which enabled us to more effectively understand, define, appeal to, satisfy, and predict markets. New product research and development derived benefit from these techniques, as they did from increased sophistication in advertising and promotion, which in many respects both added to and learned from the marketing research activities. New theories came into being such as product management, which actually started, not with products per se, but rather with brands; thus, the industrial producers refined what they called product management while the consumer goods producers refined their brand management. In many ways the objectives, tools, and techniques were the same. Both were predicated upon the fact that while organizations provided for direct control over conventional functions, they made no such provision for the product. And, ultimately the product provided the corporate revenue, and the product determined the company's success or failure. Product management, which was designed to fill this gap to provide the needed specialized management focus on the product, also provided for the integration and coordination of internal functions such as optimization of operations, cost and profit planning. All of this must be accomplished while assessing the external marketplace to determine new product opportunities and optimal marketing techniques for both old and new products.

These ideas are reflected in the following illustrations of an organization without product management (Figure 10.1) and one with product management (Figure 10.2).

The idea of the product providing the basic revenue and profit and therefore being central to the corporation is aptly described as the concept of product centrality and is one of the major contributions of product management theory to contemporary business operations. The person responsible for all of this, the rproduct manager, remains unique in the field of management, for he is assigned numerous responsibilities both in his direct operations within the marketing function and in his sphere of influence outside the marketing function. For example, in his role as coordinator and optimisor of internal functions, his ultimate focus is on the product as it wends its way through the various corporate functions illustrated in Figure 10.2. The objective clearly is to reduce time, optimize performance, prevent slow-ups, minimize difficulties, and obtain maximum profits. At the same time he balances the external interests in the marketplace with the product and activities such as sales, advertising and promotion, and distribution. To accomplish these objectives he must relate to and participate in activities in many other disciplines such as R&D, M&E, market research, legal, sales, and advertising and promotion. He therefore plays a central role in the forefront of a business backdrop which relies heavily on marketing not only to

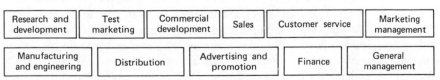

Figure 10.1   Organization without product management.

Figure 10.2   Organization with product management. Integrating and coordinating between functions are achieved through product management.

identify and successfully market new products or expand sales and markets for existing products, but which also looks to marketing for profit optimization and business leadership. All of this is important and all involves a number of complex skills, close cooperation, and teamwork.

A later and important development has been the expansion of the marketing horizon through the thinking of outstanding marketing theoreticians such as T. Levitt and economists like J. Galbraith. Both, and of course many others, have directly and indirectly contributed greatly to marketing's understanding of itself—for example, defining and understanding the business in or desired to be in, and marketing/economic dynamics.

This thumbnail sketch of marketing theory and practice, including the distinctive role of the product manager, may seem to be somewhat anomalous in a book about legislation and regulation written for practicing marketing managers who probably know all of this already. However, this was done very deliberately for two reasons. First, it demonstrates the inherent strength of marketing, which originated in change, responded to and flourished in change, and continues to be self-critical and to change. This demonstrates an attitudinal posture necessary for, and conducive to, understanding what is now needed and to provide it. It also reflects another of the great strengths of the marketing concept and marketing management—flexibility. The second, but equally important, reason is that the function of marketing overall, and that of product management in particular, can be employed to advantage to analyze what is needed to respond effectively to demands of the government, the public, and legislation and regulation.

The idea of change is inherent in the situation that breeds product management and today's needs. The concept of recognition, integration, and coordination of both internal and external events to optimize performance, response, product, and profit is clearly parallel. All of this leads to the conclusion that although integration of these legislative and regulatory controls may not be best conducted totally in the marketing discipline, it may be far from the worst choice. Even if this is not the case, there is reason to consider seriously the experience and talent of the marketing function when considering effects and how to approach translating them into effective organizational response. The direct experience of the marketing expert and the product manager can be most instructive and helpful even if the specific responsibility is not within marketing. The relationship between people, function, operations, and the internal and external needs and demands of the market are clearly similar to such demands as they relate to integration and optimization of performance when considering marketing in a regulated environment. The ideal may well be placement of at least a major emphasis, if not all responsibility, within the marketing operation

Before we come to any conclusions with regard to organizational structure and the assignment of responsibility, we should examine some of the needs regardless of locus. These should include:

Relationships with other functional and operational areas
Relationships with the external environment—agencies/departments/trade and professional associations/public interest groups/media
Coordination of internal efforts
Legal considerations
Functional factors
Determination of business objectives
General Management Considerations

Underlying these overall considerations are the specific tools, techniques, and concerns that we have been discussing in the preceding chapters. By now they have provided sufficient background to clarify the "how" of our effort. Therefore, as we examine each of these elements we do not refer any further to specific approaches such as planning and budgeting. What we want to concentrate on now is what is needed within the new organization, the one that is designed to function optimally in a regulated environment and how and where we can put all of this together within the company.

RELATIONSHIPS WITH OTHER FUNCTIONAL AND OPERATIONAL AREAS

We have seen that there is a need for close coordination between the efforts of the various functional and operational units. Legislation and regulation present a new area of need in terms of interfunctional effects and in mechanical considerations such as information flow and response. A few examples should make this amply clear.

Let us take the actions of EPA as a case in point. When EPA implements a section of the Federal Water Pollution Control Act and makes it mandatory for each relevant plant to have an effluent discharge permit, it establishes effluent limitations for that plant. These limits represent the maximum quantities of specific pollutants that the plant can legally discharge during a given period of time. Although we could consider any number of ramifications of effect consequent to this action—from treatment investment to operating expenses—for our purposes we need only investigate some that affect marketing. Again we could choose from a number of possible alternative effects but a few should suffice for our purposes:

1. To reduce effluent to permissible levels may require the discontinuation of some products.
2. It might require an alteration in the product mix.
3. It might require production rescheduling thereby affecting inventory policy or availability of goods.
4. It adds cost that will have to be absorbed in one way or another—either through overall allocation or via ascription to a particular product.
5. If unequally applied, it could pose competitive advantage or disadvantage.

These are only five alternatives. To extend them would not take much imagination or experience. For instance, we can immediately extend them dramatically by pointing out that in any given instances all five or any combination of them could occur simultaneously if the production facility were large enough and producing a variety of products.

Another of the newer socially oriented laws provides a good example. This time let us look at OSHA. The effects of OSHA are again both direct and indirect and, depending on the plant and its operations, could involve the following:

1. Production rescheduling
2. New requirements for employee training and education
3. Installation of new safeguards
4. Product discontinuation

5. Effect on downstream users (compliance problems)
6. Additional testing and informational demands
7. Maintenance of OSHA records and reports
8. Imposition of additional allocated or direct product costs

Once more we are looking at only a few effects; to these we could readily add the inclusion of OSHA considerations in R&D objectives and the application of all or any of the above simultaneously. Moreover, there are very serious questions of liability and risk.

In another vein, but again using the more socially oriented statutes as an example, we could cite the effect of EEOA on operations. These include the need for new hiring policies and practices, new employee education, potential reduction in productivity, and potential retroactive penalties. Each or all of these can and will have effects on efficiency, productivity, and cost.

Again, an example of a recent law provides an illustration, this time a newer act—the Employee Retirement and Income Security Act (ERISA). Although its intention is admirable, not only are there questions of ultimate benefit, which we will leave aside completely, but effects on investment, corporate resources, and cash flow. All of these have, albeit indirect, consequences on the marketing function.

Our last example, the effects on marketing of the Securities and Exchange Commission (SEC), is perhaps the most insidious. It affects the corporation, and ultimately marketing, but there are more direct effects. We have only to look at the existing and proposed disclosure requirements to see this. Environmental, safety, and health violation disclosure is being proposed, much of which is specifically product oriented. We can see how this will influence the shareholder, actual or potential, as well as the consumer with regard to particular companies and their products.

The effects or influences are myriad. Not only do the regulations and the legislation cross all organizational boundaries, but so do their effects. We can place them into two categories: the effects on the organization by legislation and regulation and the effects of actions within one segment of the organization on another vis-á-vis such legislation and regulation.

Examples could help put this aspect into perspective: A new product is being considered. However, based on limited animal studies, one of the ingredients is listed as being a suspected animal carcinogen. R&D must be advised of this finding—an informational problem. Toxicological advice must be sought—a scientific problem. Risk must be assessed—a combined toxicological, medical, and legal problem. Coordination and integration are needed.

Under new legislation, the Toxic Substance Control Act (TSCA), new testing requirements and the identification of suspect substances of high priority for testing a so-called "priority list" are authorized. An existing product is on this list and requires extensive testing. Although the testing may be justified, serious questions of marketing interest, testing costs and their justification, time for testing, competitive displacement, and "black listing" effects all have to be considered. Decisions requiring input from a number of functional areas will be necessary.

Marketing is employing an advertising campaign addressing the juvenile market. An FTC ruling revises what is or is not permissible for children's advertising programming. Revisions, both time consuming and costly, are called for.

A substance is banned, presumably for just and good cause. The questions include those of recall and existing stock. Certain industries are no strangers to the practical and integrative problems associated with these, but others who will be subject to such provisions in the future (e.g., TSCA provisions), are not. And so provisions for records, distribution, batch or production lot numbers, and so on will have to be developed, retained, and resorted to. Out-of-pocket costs and market disruption are other factors.

None of the foregoing examples are improbable; in fact, with the exception of the projections based on recently enacted legislation, all have already occurred. These examples are not proposed as criticisms or condemnations of responsible actions by government. Where such actions are warranted, responsible members of business or society do not object. But even where they are justified, they are expensive and so have to be considered when we are reviewing effects on organization, integration, information, and coordination. When they are not warranted, which may be the opinion of industry and independent experts in some cases at least, the situation is worse: Not only are the costs incurred, but the public is not served.

What have these examples shown us? They prove the need for integration of effect, consideration of interrelationships, informational exchange, coordination and inclusion of government actions, as well as public demands within the totality of the corporate activity. Moreover, they demonstrate that many of these effects eventually come to be felt in the marketing discipline and parallel quite closely some of the relationships that have been traditionally assigned to marketing.

They do not prove that only marketing can cope with them. This may well be far from the case. However, they do support the contention that at least we should benefit from the knowledge and experience of the marketing organization both conceptually and pragmatically in approaching consideration of effects that so closely resemble the requirements that have long been familiar to marketing. By long experience marketing has learned to handle and respond to them effectively.

RELATIONSHIPS WITH THE EXTERNAL ENVIRONMENT

There are least six discrete areas of contact:

Legislators (and their staffs)
Federal agencies
Federal departments
Trade and professional associations
Public interest groups
The media

Each of these contacts possess different requirements and the establishment of different approaches with various objectives. Because we have considered the legal aspects of external operations, including the Lobbying Act, we forego any further discussion of legal limitations and lobbying and presume that action will proceed within the confines of the law up to and including lobbying or the hiring of a lobbyist. Although our discussion does not include any further reference to legal limitations or requirements, we do remind you that they exist and that if you have any doubts in a particular situation you should consult with counsel before acting.

No specifics can be suggested regarding any of these contacts because they vary with different companies and situations. The following are overall recommendations, aspects that should be carefully preconsidered before making contacts.

Objectives

What are your objectives in making any contact? Obviously these differ from contact to contact, in different situations, or even when contacting the same agency or department. They also differ if the meeting or presentation was initiated by you, by the agency or department, or by some external association or group of which you are only a member. Whatever the case, you should review your objectives for the meeting or discussion beforehand and plan and prepare accordingly. Try to foresee the objectives of the people you are contacting. This can be helpful not only in determining your own but in planning your specific actions and reactions during the meeting.

Planning

Preplan your meeting. Thorough preparation is extremely helpful. Besure you know the facts or that you can obtain them readily in time for any discussion. In many cases a written statement is beneficial. This helps the people you are dealing with, assures clarity, assists in quotations, assures accuracy, and provides a written record.

Public Disclosure

Remember that meetings with federal agencies and departments and records of them are a matter of public record. What transpires is open to public review.

Minutes

Prepare your own minutes of your meetings. These can be useful not only in the conventional sense of minutes but also as a written record that may at some time be beneficial to you in later proceedings.

Information Flow

Feedback mechanisms should be established. As we have considered informational needs, you should consider who needs to be informed of the results of your meetings and be certain to establish mechanisms by which this can be accomplished.

Debriefing

Where meetings occur with several business participants, even if they are from the same company, arrange for a debriefing session as soon after your meeting as possible. It is often surprising what comes of this. Not only is the collective memory often better, but interpretations and the significance placed on different statements, inferences, and conclusions drawn differ.

Documentation

Consider writing a "memo to the file" if some particularly important conclusion was reached that you think ought to be documented.

Counsel

Carefully consider the desirability or undesirability of having a lawyer present. Obviously, there are some instances in which this will be essential. We are not considering such situations but rather those in which it could or could not be appropriate. Consider the circumstances, the people you are meeting with, the atmosphere to be created, the objectives, and most important, if a lawyer for the other side will be present. There can be no absolutes here, but logic, experience, and common sense will go a long way in guiding you correctly.

Leader

Give a lot of thought to who will lead the meeting for you. Your governmental relations person (assuming you have one), or the marketing vice president, or even the company president may be the person, depending on circumstances. There are the usual pros and cons associated with all of this. Once more consider who you are meeting with, what you intend to achieve, and the importance of the situation to you and your company. Logic, experience, and common sense will aid you in the right decision.

Forum

Consider the forum, the circumstances, and location of the meeting. Is it a public hearing, a formal procedure, a position to be written for the record, a possible statement for future use in formal proceedings including litigation, or a response to a specific request? These and other possibilities occur. They require careful thought not only of what is to be said but how it should be said, documented, and presented—orally, in writing, or combinations.

Information-Data

Try to obtain a precise indication of what either you or they want to know or communicate. This will aid greatly in your overall planning and preparation.

Recommendations/Alternatives

Have positive suggestions, alternatives, and particularly recommendations. The basic posture of "we are against" without the corresponding "we are for' only gets everybody nowhere, dispels confidence, destroys credibility, and lacks any semblance of recognizing reality. This is not to say that you must or should compromise your principles, sacrifice your rights, or put yourself in an untenable position. However, even where you are against a specific piece of legislation or regulation, the terms in which this is couched are important. Even a negative "we are against" can be translated into the "we are for" aspects by pointing out, in positive terms, why you are against, what is wrong with the proposal, and what the negative effects would or could be, while also demonstrating the improbability of the intended beneficial results. This is not always an easy task, but one that will go far in attaining your objectives.

Media

The media imposes additional advantageous and problematical dimensions to the "contact" question. A book that is longer than this one could well be devoted to the subject of business/media contacts and relationships. Obviously, we cannot even begin to cover this topic, but we can spotlight a few thoughts.

1. Speak or write out. Be heard.
2. Make all oral or written statements understandable to the public.
3. Consult with the public relations department whenever possible.
4. Consult with the legal department whenever possible.
5. Prepare written statements or summaries whenever possible.
6. Train key executive in public speaking and appearances.

These recommendations are remarkably close to the planning and review that you would give to almost any sales call or business contact. Sometimes they may require a greater degree of diplomacy and because you are operating in the public arena, require more care and preparation. Nevertheless, they should not pose any insurmountable difficulties. Following these simple "rules" should aid greatly in successful and productive interrelationships. And you are looking to building relationships. Just as in sales, it is often impossible to tell immediately whether you have attained your objectives or not. Moreover, one cannot always quantify the results, nor may they be apparent for some time. Neither factor should be allowed negate the significance of these contacts or be allowed to forestall their development.

COORDINATION OF INTERNAL EFFORTS

Since we have already seen that the actions of external agencies can effect a number of internal operations, the need for coordination internally is obvious. Not so obvious, however, may be some of the effects, and how in the present organization this integration does take place. If this latter is the first question to arise, it completely validates the basic premise from which we start—that is, that most companies do not know how to integrate these considerations into the business operationally.

Let us take a case and follow it through at least its primary effects. NIOSH (essentially the research arm of OSHA) recommends that use of a series of chemicals be regulated. OSHA heeds the NIOSH recommendation and appoints an adivsory board to review the recommendation and in turn make its recommendation to OSHA/DOL. This takes place and DOL promulgates a work-place standard for those substances and products containing certain quantities of those substances. From the moment of the announcement of the NIOSH recommendation to the completion of the standards rule-making procedure, a series of internal company activities should be set in motion:

The substances and proposal should be brought to the attention of

Management
Marketing
Manufacturing
Engineering
Research and development
Legal
Safety and health

so that they are aware that:

Potential action is being considered.
Research can consider the advisability of using or dropping any such material
from any existing or contemplated projects.
Review of usage can be undertaken.
Review of processing (if using) can be undertaken.
Sensitivity/vulnerability can be determined.
Preliminary legal and other assessments can be made.

Deliberations of the proposal should be monitored and decisions, even if only
provisional, along with company interpretation should again be brought to the
attention of the above areas within the company to continue efforts in relevant
decision making. As the situation progresses toward firmer positions, further
refinements in the company assessment and decision-making process should
occur.

When the recommendation is adopted by the agency, formal procedures, such
as hearings, are set in motion. This is the time to take the information developed
in the previous steps and utilize it as the basis for deciding how to proceed (e.g.,
statement, oral presentation, participation in trade association activities, etc.)
and in making more finite internal determinations (e.g., effect on sales, profit,
product, marketing, production based on assumption to continue/discontinue,
compliance options and costs). Some of these may still be preliminary in that the
final position of the agency and standard to be developed (if any) is not known;
however, the preparation is more than worth the effort.

When the proposed standards are issued, there are again a series of procedural
possibilities (e.g. written statements, appearances at hearings, and post-hearing
comments). There are also possibilities of litigation and questions over interpretation, inspection, compliance, and so on. All of these involve a number of
internal functions. Marketing will have to determine, for example, the value of
the product in terms of the compliance cost. This entails knowledge of:

The existing market

The market potential

Sales volume now and future

Profit now and after compliance costs are added

Compliance costs under various options

Marketing risk (Will the customer continue to buy or are there psychological or other reasons why, even if you continued to produce, he would not continue to buy.)

The effect on the customer in terms of any compliance problems that he might encounter.

Determination of liability.

This should suffice to show the nature of the information required, the functions that will be involved in obtaining the information, and the decision-making required. From the nonmarketing viewpoint there are, of course, others, such as investment, overall financial effects, capital problems, cashflow, shareholders' reactions, and personal liability.

The example we have used is not an overly complicated one, nor is it atypical of the many concerns evolving from economic or social legislation or regulation. Employing virtually any statute, regulation, or agency, we could draw similar and often far more detailed and complex scenarios of internal communications, coordination, information, and decision-making requirements.

LEGAL CONSIDERATIONS

Although we are not dealing with legal considerations here, we must mention that one of the most important of all factors is the legal aspects of any particular situation. In this overall review of the major requirements for effective internal integration, we must reiterate the need for inclusion of the legal function. If internal counsel is not available, external aid should be given even if it is only on an issue-by-issue basis.

FUNCTIONAL FACTORS

Every company function is or can be involved. We have drawn organization and management comparisons to product and marketing responsibilities. One of those is to provide for the integration and optimization of internal functions as they affect the product. This responsibility was the consequence of a need, which was based on the recognition that each function had its own perspectives, its own problems, its own viewpoints, its own vested interest, and its own assigned responsibilities. Its particular success or failure was based essentially on its performance within these somewhat narrower constraints and perspectives. The plant manager is judged on meeting production schedules and cost control and not on his ability to interpret regulations. Similarly, the salesman is measured on sales and profit performance and not on his ability to predict legislation. And so it goes. To this must be added the usual psychological factors of functional concern over interference, lack of expertise from the "outsiders," and all of the usual suspicions and reluctancies that occur when those from without the function or operation want to involve themselves in it. This was true when product management and marketing evolved, and to a significant degree it is still true even though this was one of the first clear rationales for both.

Here, we once more see parallels between what we would like to accomplish in terms of integrating legislation and regulation into the total company activity and concern and what we want to accomplish in marketing and product management. The same barriers exist and will be an influence and concern when trying to create a position or function that will undertake the determinative and coordinative role in accomplishing or catalyzing the legislative and regulatory integrative objective. Experience has taught us that the barriers can be overcome. However, we must recognize that they exist as they did in the past, and some of the techniques that we employed successfully in implementing product management can be of assistance here.

DETERMINATION OF BUSINESS OBJECTIVES

In Chapter 8 we discussed the need for a new type of planning, with special emphasis on contingency planning and the need to establish objectives. The objectives considered there were specific to the issues confronting marketing. Thought also must be given to the more generalized objectives and intentions of the total corporation.

In the final analysis marketing is only one of several affected areas. The entire corporation is involved. If marketing is to do its job, we must give credence to these more pervasive organizational needs. Therefore, the corporation must establish its overall objectives when contemplating integration of legislation and regulation into the corporate structure and operation and in terms of its outreach to both government and the public. Such objectives must be harmonious with the more specific objectives of the various functions and must be communicated to them. However, often either such objectives are not established by the corporation overall, or if they are, they are not communicated to marketing. Although in some instances this is deliberate—the corporation perhaps taking the "signal" from marketing—in others it is not. It is an accident of circumstances or the outright failure of the corporation to set its own overall objectives. Whatever the

cause the immediate concern is that they be established. If marketing must take
the lead, fine; if the corporation takes it, as it should, and passes the objectives on
to the functions, better yet. Some suggestions for possible corporate objectives
can be helpful. Very briefly stated, and without any attempt at justification or
elaboration, they might include:

To participate actively in legislative affairs
To participate actively in the legislative process
To participate actively in regulatory affairs
To participate actively in the regulatory process
To integrate federal legislative and regulatory effects and requirements into the
organization
To establish an organization that is responsive to social needs
To establish operations and functions within the organization with specific
responsibility in this area
To provide for ongoing liaison with government legislators and regulators
To provide for ongoing liaison with public interest groups
To Establish Practices And Procedures that will provide for such liaison, in-
tegration, and interrelationships
To establish ongoing compliance programs
To participate in voluntary standards programs
To establish voluntary industry or company codes of conduct

The list could be lengthened extensively, but these examples should more than
suffice as a conceptual foundation of the nature, scope, or thrust of corporate
objectives in this area. These should, of course, be supplemented by more
specific departmental or functional objectives, including strategies, action plans,
and review procedures to assure their accomplishment.

GENERAL MANAGEMENT CONSIDERATIONS

Certain areas are the responsibility of general management. At least two immediately come to mind: (1) overall responsibility for the conduct of the corporation, which includes any societal aspects and those attending the success of the
total enterprise, the discharge of obligations to shareholders, and those that
pertain to the employees; (2) the legal aspects of these responsibilities and the
additional legal responsibilities, obligations, and liability that are present in the
more recent statutes. The possibility for personal liability should assure management interests, and it demands management involvement and attention.
    General management, whose perogatives involve the basic nature of the cor-

porate direction and who have the opportunity and the authority to implement changes, should initiate them in the interests of good business. Most managers already realize this. The ones who are able to perceive what is desirable and necessary are not only those outside of the corporation. Moreover, that the initiative has been taken within the corporate confines can be demonstrated. Good common business sense leads one inexorably in the direction of responsible management with all that this implies in the running of a contemporary business in the light of both present private and public demands.

Assuming that we will have this most important of ingredients—top management support—the remainder of the challenge is definitely eased. First we need the explicit interest, involvement, endorsement, and commitment of management; then the organization for implementation of integration and coordination, inclusion and outreach; and last, the staffing and budgeting required. These complete the basic requirements. Things are never really simple, and certainly we recognize that this skeleton needs flesh, blood, and brain, that is, the outline must be filled out. Now we can do this by pursuing in some detail at least one approach to such internal organizational provisions.

NEED FOR ORGANIZATION RECONSIDERATION AND RESTRUCTURING

Business must objectively analyze the present corporate purpose, organization, and structure. One decision involves the company's redefining its relationship to the government and to the public. A reconsideration of the role of the corporation and the corporate conscience and consciousness is required. Thought must be given to organization, staffing, budgeting, and redefinition of purpose and the establishment of new objectives.

There are many options and alternatives to reconsideration and reorganization, as there almost always are in decision-making. To the adage "death and taxes are inevitable" we can now add legislation, regulation, and the need to fulfill and satisfy the public demand. We cannot examine all the options in great detail; to a certain degree this would be presumptuous in a book primarily directed to the concept of marketing in a regulated environment. We can mention some possibilities for inclusion of government effects—to organize around a corporate staff position, or an entirely new function, or via some assignment to an existing committee (e.g., the management committee), or even through some function outside of marketing (e.g., legal). But explorations are better left to future consideration when dealing with the broader topic of the total effects of government and society on the whole of the corporation. Here we confine our recommendations to effects that directly involve marketing. With this limitation in mind we can still propose several alternatives:

Assign all responsibility to marketing Á la product management.

Make marketing a central participant but have ultimate responsibility and authority as a corporate activity.

Assign partial responsibility within marketing (activities that are clearly mainly within marketing, with other functions assigned similar responsibility for their areas).

Assign basic responsibility to another function (e.g., legal).

Create a new management team that would allow implementation of effort on a flexible, or even provisional basis, which could then lead to modification later.

Each of these suggestions has a number of advantages and disadvantages. Since they are self-evident, rather than elaborate on them, Table 10.1 summarizes many of the most obvious ones and provides some recommendations for where implementation of each might be most appropriate.

The most logical and appropriate approach seems to be the last option indicated—creation of a new management team with responsibilities in this area. At first this may seem somewhat contradictory to the earlier bias to marketing, but careful reflection and study will reveal that this is not so. It would not place all of the authority and responsibility within the marketing function, but it still allows for a prominent marketing involvement and application of the techniques and experiences of marketing and product management which can be extremely useful.

THE NEW MANAGEMENT MARKETING TEAM

Rationale of the New Management/Marketing Team

In creating this new management-marketing team we are simultaneously accomplishing two objectives: (1) providing an organization for integration of governmental concerns; (2)providing for the new marketing approaches we have discussed (implementation of new marketing theory and GEEM factors). If we approach the subject with these in mind, the logic of the situation can be visualized as the new management/marketing team acting as a fulcrum for balancing the needs of the business with those of the market. Understanding, of course, that both terms are being employed in the fullest sense and the needs of business include survival, and those of the market include the public interest; both in turn are involved with government. This is diagrammatically represented in Figure 10.3.

TABLE 10.1 ALTERNATIVE ORGANIZATIONAL APPROACHES

Alternative	Advantages	Disadvantages
Assign all responsibility to marketing.	Simple. Fits into most existing structures. Economical. Benefits from marketing experiences.	Limited perspective. Limits marketing options. Poses difficulties in coordination. Poses possible conflicts of interest. Only really suitable for the small firm.
Make marketing a central participant with ultimate authority in the corporation.	Simple. Fits into existing organization frameworks. Economical. Facilitates coordination.	Perspectives may still be limited. Can cause confusions and jurisdictional overlap. Suitable essentially only for small to medium companies.
Assign partial responsibility within marketing with other functions having similar limited responsibilities.	Broadens the base. Allows for direct involvement of other functions. Fits into existing organizational frameworks.	Can be confusing. Can cause redundancies. Can lead to conflicting decisions; still relies heavily on upper management for ultimate coordination. Essentially suitable on only a very selective basis.
Create a new management team that encompasses the various functions.	Allows broad direct involvement. Fosters coordination. Fosters integration of approach. Facilitates planning. Establishes common objectives. Broad application in any size company.	May create some internal problems in differentiating its responsibilities from those of general management. Requires careful delineation of authority. Diffuses authority and decision-making (the committee problem).

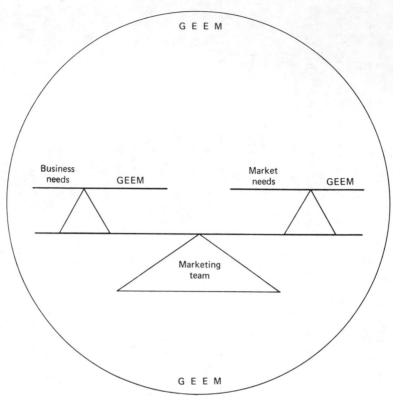

Figure 10.3   Interrelationship of GEEM and business and market needs.

Benefits of the New Team

This approach, even if provisional, has several benefits.

1. It can be implemented immediately and with little preparation.
2. Existing personnel can be used—assuming that they must have time available and are provided the proper education and support.
3. All will benefit from the learning and practical experiences involved and will make for stronger more versatile managers.
4. The approach is flexible and allows for change within itself.
5. As organizational requirements demand change, this approach allows for such change up to and including centralization of operations within the corporation, but with the continued use of this team as a technique for continued corporate effectiveness.

6. Expenditures can be kept to a minimum; obviates the need for too much in the way of new, expense, and extensive preparation, personnel, and support; we must always be cognizant of Dr. Parkinson and his immutable laws.

7. It imposes some new insights on the marketing function itself by virtue of new relationships and new perspectives. This broadening of the marketing horizon must be ultimately beneficial to the discipline. It will compel marketing to break its own stereotype.

There are of course disadvantages.

1. It may not be inclusive and therefore may fail to represent fully some important general management concerns(e.g., finance).

2. It may not be permanent and thereby lack inherent stability and continuity.

3. It may not be suitable to all organizations, especially those that are already weak in the marketing area.

4. It still relies heavily on top management involvement for integration of other management factors.

5. As with most committee approaches, there are problems with committees (authority, delegation, avoidance of decisions, delay, etc.).

None of these seem insurmountable or of sufficient importance to outweigh the advantages. For the small to medium-sized company, which has yet to learn much or to afford more it seems very appropriate indeed. It may well also be the most desirable first step for many of the larger concerns.

Composition, Organization, Requirements, Objectives, and Functions Responsibilities

What would be the composition of such a team? How would it be organized? What would be the requirements? What are its particular objectives? How would it function and what would be the responsibilities.

In Table 10.2 these questions are answered in detail. Although the recommendations provided cannot be inclusive or representative of the ultimate, they are a good working beginning—a beginning that can be refined and adapted to the particular needs of the individual company now and later.

WHAT COMES NEXT?

The option we have elected here is related to interim consideration. Of necessity, there may be alterations later. These should be based on factors such as size of

TABLE 10.2 MANAGEMENT/MARKETING RESPONSE TEAM

Composition	Organization	Requirements	Objective	Functions/Responsibilities
V.P., Director, Manager* of Marketing R&D Legal Production/manufacturing Public relations Government relations Safety, health, ecology	1. Reports directly to board or executive management committee. 2. Chaired by marketing representative. 3. Meets on a regular monthly basis with reports from each area on key developments, progress reports, etc. 4. Ad hoc meetings as required. 5. Subteams created and activated as required for major specific events (e.g., ERISA, EEOA, TSCA).	1. Top management commitment. 2. Delegation of specific authority required to accomplish objective. 3. Budget (a separate budget is advocated so cost can be identified, quantified, and allocated).	To integrate and coordinate corporate resources based on new recognition of and sensitivity to internal and external demands made on the corporation, or opportunities for business as reflected in Z, GEEM, and PV factor considerations to assure their inclusion in the establishment and attainment of corporate objectives.	1. Analyze effects of events, legislation, etc. 2. Develop and examine options and alternative reactions, responses, actions. 3. Recommend specific reactions, response, actions to management. 4. Implement[†] approved programs, policies, actions. 5. Advise management on policy and, where appropriate, make policy recommendations. 6. Develop marketing strategies and tactics. 7. Implement marketing strategies and tactics. 8. Provide marketing and business planning input. 9. Implement approved marketing and business plans. 10. Provide standing, experienced forum for response to immediate situations.

11. Develop compliance programs and schedules.

12. Implement approved compliance programs and schedules.

13. Develop and implement mechanisms for cost analysis.

14. Act as source of experts for the company in litigation, testimony, trade associations, professional associations, etc.

15. Act as focal point for responding to inquiries, surveys, report preparation, whether self-generated or externally requested or required.

16. Provide interpreted communication to management and subordinate in relevant GEEM areas.

17. Provide flexible and quick response when and where required.

---

*Where separate individuals are not responsible for these functions membership will be numerically smaller, but these areas should be represented.

†Implementation here is not to be effected through the team, but through assignment to the appropriate function(s). However, the team can be helpful in reviewing progress, advertising, etc. Policy would be established by the team, but responsibility for implementation would be individual/functional.

company, number and diversity of products, organizational structure, physical locations. Examination of these will lead to decisions regarding continuation of the new management/marketing team or the evolution of some more sophisticated approach. In all probability the small to medium-sized company, operating more in the mode of the general manager approach, could well retain the team, with the chairman being the general manager. The larger or more diversified company will probably extend to some form of central or corporate control through the establishment of a corporate function with overall responsibility and authority operating through vehicles such as a management/marketing team in each division or in specific geographic locations, depending on the nature of the business and other organizational factors.

WHERE ARE WE?

We are now left with a basic understanding of what happened, where we are, and how we got there. More to the immediate point, we have examined some of the things that we might do and some of those that we ought to do. Two things yet remain: implementation, which is up to the corporation, and a consideration of what the future holds in store, which is discussed in the last chapter.

ELEVEN
What of the Future?

No attempt at comprehensive and critical assessment of the many fundamental issues we have dealt with would be complete without some consideration of the future. Obviously, the future concerns us all. Regardless of our perspective—that of consumer, businessperson, or government official—we are all equally curious about and affected by the future. What it portends and what its ultimate effects are on us, as individuals and within the context of our various societal roles, is a fascinating topic. We are also curious and concerned about the future of our society and society in general.

We have visualized the progression that has resulted in our contemporary situation as the result of an evolutionary process. Darwin's theories as they applied to the evolution of species seem to have application in the broader sense of societal evolution and, logically, of business evolution. What this means, therefore, is that we must look forward to a continuation of the evolutionary trend. From the marketing perspective, what we can expect is more consumer activism, more antibusiness attitudinal shifts, more legislation, and more regulation, and more problems for the marketing manager.

Having made these generalizations, our efforts toward predicting the future must attempt a greater degree of specificity despite the risks that we all know attend any effort to divine expectations in precise terms. The caveat about the future is that the only thing we can say with absolute certainty is that we can't say anything with absolute certainty. Nevertheless, some attempts must be made. This ''glimpse'' of what may come is important, even if it proves to be substantially inaccurate. We are not attempting postulation of specifics; we are trying to look to broad dimensions of the future market environment.

As we do this we must ask some primary questions: Why are we even attempting such prognostication? For what purpose? To what avail? Intellectual curiosity and personal concerns over the effects on and the conduct of our lives are two reasons for our attempt. However, for marketing managers, pragmaticism demands that our objective should be the translation of projections into more concrete application in the marketing process.

The answer is in developing, retiming, and applying survival strategies or in creating new and more appropriate ones as our awareness and knowledge expands. The term *survival* should not be taken too literally. Although the next few years may be ones that can be more accurately characterized as those of survival, in the long run growth may well return. Therefore, an added dimension of future concern is the ability to determine when this transition will occur and to be prepared to shift from survival to growth.

If we keep these objectives firmly in mind, to a very significant degree, the exactitude of projections is not the primary factor. What we should be looking for are the indicators of the trend of evolution and what it will dictate logically in terms of external events, such as legislation, regulation, buyer attitudes, and responses; as well as internal events and their effects.

Although our primary purpose is not to deal with the broad and complicated subject of corporate conduct, the evolution of the concept and conduct of the corporation itself, and the influences this brings to bear on the marketing discipline, this is a legitimate and realistic consideration. As there is market and government evolution, there will continue to be a business evolution. Part of this evolution will be responsive—behind the curve as it were. However, there will also be a business evolution which is ahead of the curve—that is, one that anticipates and provides in advance a corporate structure, philosophy and milieu that is, in its own way, as "business progressive" as the "socially progressive" elements of our society and our government have been. We cannot explore these aspects in depth here, but we do have to recognize that these dual influences—the external combined with the internal—are going to have their effect on the marketing discipline, the marketing manager, and marketing practices.

With all of this in mind, we explore major future directions in a few key areas. Their influences on the marketing activity should be extremely clear and, therefore, no attempt is made at any exhaustive analysis of their business effects.

MAJOR GOVERNMENT ACTIVITIES

The trend toward more rather than less government will continue. Despite the cry of regulatory reform and despite the inclusion of sincere commitments on the part of legislators toward critical review and examination of the regulatory process, we will probably not see any significant alteration in the regulatory activity over the next few years.

This rather pessimistic viewpoint is not because of any lack of belief in the genuine concern of the administration and of the Congress and in many of the regulatory agencies themselves, but rather because of the reality of the existing statutory obligations and of the existing vested interests within the regulatory establishment that will perpetuate overall regulatory activity. To apply the same yardstick of vested interest measurement and vested interest entrenchment to the bureaucrat as to the businessman is not cynical; it is realistic. To recognize the enormous difficulties in any attempt to dismantle the already existing regulatory, agency, statutory, and judicial framework is equally realistic.

Many people in government have already said that business has been quick to seize on the rubric of ''regulatory reform'' without recognizing the government perception of what this really means. The business community, they say, believes that this is a commitment to less legislation and regulation, whereas in fact many of the proponents of regulatory reform, by their own admission, do not mean this at all. Their commitment is to more, but different, legislation and regulation. The difference, with which we can agree in principle, is that legislation and regulation should be more specific and more realistic. That is, it should be enacted or promulgated in areas of clear need and address issues of consequence, dispensing with trivia or excessive regulations that have unfortunately characterized, to the eventual dismay and disappointment of many of the legislators themselves, activity within OSHA, EPA, CPSC, FTC, and others. Although we can agree in principle with this laudatory objective of regulatory reform, we must still be vitally concerned with the two assurances this does not provide:

1. Elimination or alleviation of existing regulation
2. The possibility that new legislation and regulation, even on this basis, will not create additional marketing burdens that may not be necessary or justified.

This should not be construed, however, as meaning there is no potential for at least some relief. The fact that regulatory reform is a prominent concern has a dampening effect on agency actions; this cannot help but be beneficial. Second, it will influence the intention of legislation and regulation to reflect more clearly the reality of need that is based on some rule of reason.

A few other major events or trends in government that are important to use within this context.

Sunset Legislation

Bills have been proposed that provide for the review and rejustification of certain agencies on a periodic basis. This is to ensure that agencies that are created to fulfill certain specific perceived needs do not continue long after the needs have been satisfied. The general intent and concept of Sunset Legislation is an encouraging sign. But we cannot rely too heavily on this approach for several reasons:

1. The high degree of probability is that most agencies will, in effect, be extended, although perhaps modified, rather than discontinued at the point of their "sunset."
2. The legislation that has been adopted does not apply universally, and therefore, there are agencies that are not included.
3. There is a certain logic in arguments made over the difficulties of continuity that obviously occur when dealing with an agency whose existence is in question.
4. Despite the possibility of the termination of any particular agency, there still may be the problem of existing rules and regulations that it has initiated all of which would apparently not terminate; some would continue although the agency itself might not. This line of reasoning brings us back to point 1—(the high degree of probability of continuation of the agency—or the equally logical conclusion that although the agency might be eliminated, its responsibilities will merely be reassigned for implementation under some other agency.

So, although we talk of sunset, the probability is that most of us will merely get sunburned!

Executive Department Review Program

Most of you have probably read that high on the agenda of President Ford's administrative concerns was the issue of regulatory reform. Prior to the expiration of his term in office he did propose a program requiring administration agencies and departments to complete reassessments of their aims, objectives, and programs and to submit to the Executive Department a detailed agenda for necessary revisions. Combined with this was the clear commitment that, over a four year period the appropriate congressional committee would have before it either its own agenda or an agenda created by the Executive Branch.

This, obviously, is another approach that has some potential for regulatory relief, but it is also problematical from several viewpoints:

1. By the nature of the administration's program, it could take years before we would see even the initiations of revision of any particular agency or department.
2. The reforms that might be proposed could be those suggested by the responsi-

ble agency itself. This may be analogized to the chickens cheering for Colonel Saunders.

3. There is the real problem that because this was an executive proposal one cannot say with any degree of certainty as to whether President Carter will reactivate it or consider it as important. However, we might also take some encouragement from this fact because it is equally possible that Mr. Carter will not only continue such a program but initiate an even more comprehensive and potentially more meaningful one—a program that might specifically require external agency examination and reform recommendation.

Zero-Based Budgeting

We have read a great deal about the introduction of zero-based budgeting in government operations. In this case we already know that Mr. Carter is committed to the zero-based budgeting concept, and the Congress has already moved in this direction. The relative advantages and disadvantages of zero-based budgeting are familiar to us in marketing because this technique has been employed in the business world for several years. Its application in government represents, however, a different set of circumstances, and it is easy to foresee limitations in its application even if introduced with the best of intention. Because, on a federal level, we have yet to see actual implementation, it would be both unfair and unjust to precondemn. However, to point out that from the viewpoint of the marketing manager we cannot look to zero-based budgeting as a panacea is neither unfair nor unjust. There are several reasons:

1. As with the sunset legislation, zero-based budgeting as a technique was not designed around application in situations where there are strong political and social forces involved that must take into account a substantial number of external uncontrollable requirements.

2. It does not consider the serious dimension of expensive activities that result from court decisions. The effect of the courts on the interpretation and implementation of legislation, rules, and regulations has been discussed in this book from the viewpoint of the extension of the court's authority into decision-making areas that are questionable and are questioned by many within the judicial system itself. Some of these decisions do result in additional agency action, which is, of course, costly both to the agency and ultimately to business and the consumer.

Congressional Budgets

For many years one of the great shortcomings of the Congress was the rather startling fact that nobody really kept count; no one really knew what federal spending was by virtue of Congressional action until after the fact, despite the existence of annual budget reports and notwithstanding the efforts on the parts of individual members of the legislative branch and the executive branch. This year marked the introduction of congressional budget committees that "watchdog" this expenditure before and during rather than after the fact. While clearly the original intent was not to provide regulatory reform or relief but rather to respond to substantial and valid public criticism of Congressional financial inexactitudes and to the need to balance the budget one cannot deny that it can have beneficial effects in the areas that concern us. Clearly, this review process can lead to limitations that could result in a greater degree of selectivity in legislation that is passed as well as in agency and department actions.

SPECIFIC LEGISLATION ON THE HORIZON

Thinking about the future requires that due consideration be given to legislation that has not been passed in the last Congress or stands a high possibility of passage in the next. The reasons are many, but the most important is that past experience has indicated that even though it may take several years or sessions, certain major legislative trends, once identified and initiated, seem eventually to result in legislation. As examples of the former situation, we can mention the Occupational Safety and Health Act, the Toxic Substances Control Act, the Tax Reform Act of 1976, the Civil Rights Act, and many others. The point is that having some insights into these in advance and identifying those whose time might not yet have come, but will come, can be helpful to the forward-thinking marketing manager.

Although the possibilities are many and not all will agree with any particular list (because everyone has personal perspectives and vested areas), the following is at least representative of probable legislation.

The Planned Economy

At some time the gathering momentum toward national economic planning will probably occur, despite present controversy. Its exact form and shape is, of course, impossible to detail. What is important now is to watch carefully the developments in this area. Although this may seem absolutely impossible in our democratic society, we have seen other seemingly impossible situations come into being.

Controlled Growth

As a corollary to, but possibly independent of, a planned economy may be outright controlled growth policies, programs, and plans. Obviously, these could be incorporated in the totality of national economic planning but need not be. There are already clear possibilities for this to happen both overtly and, in a sense, covertly in such existing statutory authority as granted to EPA. This took its most recent form in the controversy generated over growth and expansion limitations attendant to EPA's implementation of the Clean Air Act with respect to nondetermination provisions in the law. Clearly, there are similar possibilities in the new EPA authority granted by two acts passed in the final hours of the 94th Congress—the Toxic Substances Control Act and the Resource Conservation and Recovery Act of 1976. Both of these have provisions that can affect national or local business development and growth. More direct controls are yet to occur through new legislation that might involve land and resources development and use.

Federal Business Chartering

Suggestions have already been made and there is strong support from Ralph Nader that certain, if not all, corporations should be federally chartered. Involved in such chartering would be the federal government's authority to determine the size and conduct of the business including authority for forcing divestiture. This has already been heard with respect to the petroleum industry, but among a number of other "targets" are steel, automotives, and textiles. For those who are interested and wish to read the arguments in favor of federal chartering, it is treated at great length in *Taming the Giant Corporation* by Ralph Nader, Mark Green, and Joel Seligman (W.W. Norton and Co., 1976).

Energy Allocation

Our recent experiences with energy shortages are still fresh in our minds. The primary effects on business; shortages and cost increases were of a nature and degree previously unparalleled and clearly unpredicated. OPEC is deliberating on the amount of another oil price increase, and its worldwide effects are predictable. The difficulties relating to this situation, its national and international ramifications and direct and indirect effects on marketing must be considered in long-term business planning.

Raw Materials Allocation

Although we have not recently seen problems of raw materials allocations (other than the oil crisis situation involving crude oil or oil fractions as raw materials for chemicals), this real problem lurks ominously just below the practical business surface. Many critical minerals and metals are in short supply. Our dependency on imports for some of them further complicates the situation; we may well encounter either price rises from supplying nations (as with oil, this has already occurred in some instances) or outright shortages. If the market does not accommodate and adjust to these situations, legislation will be enacted to mandate controls and allocations. For materials of national defense importance the federal government is already actively reviewing its stockpiles and making adjustments where necessary. Although business can afford only limited stockpiling, this is one possibility, at least for the short term and as a hedge while product substitution is attempted.

Consumer Protection Act

This bill was passed in the last Congress and would have already been enacted into legislation had it not been for a veto by President Ford, who considered the bill to be inflationary. There are many provisions in the act as proposed that go to the basic area of consumer protection from many viewpoints; several of them directly affect marketing and marketing activities. This bill is important to follow, for there is every likelihood that it will be reintroduced in the 95th Congress with a high probability of passage and enactment.

Consumer Class Action Bill

This proposed legislation would give all consumers automatic standing and allow them to file class actions in a change in legal standing of considerable importance to both the consumer and the businessman or marketing manager. This legislation has not been enacted, but it is strongly recommended and urged by consumer advocates such as Ralph Nader and may well pass in the 95th Congress. Another bill for marketing management to watch.

Are There More?

A quick look at President Ford's message to Congress of July 22, 1976, listing legislation that he wanted passed, as reported in the BNA Report (Table 11.1) of the same date, removes any doubt that there are more. President Carter's priorities may differ, but his list will probably not be shorter.

Many of these legislative proposals were not enacted into law, but we can expect them to reemerge in the 95th Congress. Remember, this is only the President's list, not that of the Congress itself. To all of this, too, lest we overlook it, must be added the plethora of state and local legislation and regulation.

Moreover, in the closing days of the last Congress at least two enormously significant bills were passed, they become law in 1977—the Toxic Substances Control Act and the Resource Conservation and Recovery Act of 1976. Both are

TABLE 11.1   PRESIDENT FORD'S MESSAGE TO CONGRESS, JULY 22, 1976, ON LEGIS-
LATION THAT HE WANTS PASSED DURING THIS SESSION

(TEXT)

TO THE CONGRESS OF THE UNITED STATES:

In the weeks remaining in this session of the 94th Congress there is an opportunity to write a legislative record of which we can all be proud. Over the past 23 months I have sent legislative proposals to the Congress dealing with many vital areas of national concern. Some of these proposals have been enacted, some are nearing enactment, but many others have been stalled in the legislative process.

Today I am calling on the Congress to turn its full and undivided attention to this unfinished agenda of legislative business. If you do, the record you will take to the people will be a good one.

The agenda is long, even though it does not include everything that should be passed by the Congress before it goes home. For example, I have not included here the appropriation bills which must be passed. Most of the agenda items have been debated at length by the Congress and the time for action has arrived.

The priority categories for action are familiar ones:
- tax reductions coupled with spending restraint
- crime control
- restoring the integrity of the Social Security System.
- catastrophic health care protection for those covered by Medicare
- restrictions on forced, court ordered busing
- revenue sharing and block grants
- regulatory reform
- energy
- indemnification of swine flu manufacturers
- the remainder of my defense program plus defense cost saving legislation
- and other legislation ranging from agriculture to the environment; from higher education to reform of the Federal retirement system.

In the agenda that follows, I have listed the specific legislation that needs to be passed by the Congress. I am convinced that the passage of these bills is in the real interest of all of the American people.

TAXES

Permanent Tax Reduction

This proposal would provide a $28 billion permanent income tax reduction effective July 1, 1976. Major provisions affecting individual income taxes include an increase in personal exemptions from $750 to $1,000, a reduction in

TABLE 11.1 *(continued)*

tax rates, and substitution of a flat standard deduction for the low income allowance and percentage standard deduction.

Estate and Gift Tax Adjustment Act

This legislation would raise the estate tax exemption from $60 thousand to $150 thousand and make all transfers of assets between spouses exempt from estate and gift taxes. The estate tax rate structure would be altered so that taxes on the largest estates would remain unchanged.

In addition, this legislation would make it easier to continue the family ownership of a small farm or business following an owner's death. This would be accomplished by liberalizing present rules governing installment payments of estate taxes attributable to a small family farm or closely-held business by providing a 5-year "grace" period before such payments must begin, reducing the interest rate on those payments, and by extending the installment period from 10 to 20 years.

Jobs Creation Incentive Act

This legislation would encourage construction of new facilities and expansion of old facilities in areas experiencing unemployment in excess of 7 percent in order to increase employment opportunities in these areas. The increased construction would be encouraged by allowing very rapid amortization for nonresidential buildings and capital equipment.

Broadened Stock Ownership

Tax incentives to encourage broader ownership of common stock by working men and women would be provided by this proposal. Taxes on funds invested in stock-purchase plans established by employers or directly by individuals would be deferred provided such funds are invested for at least 7 years.

CRIME CONTROL

Amendments to the Criminal Code

Amendments would provide for the imposition of a mandatory term of imprisonment in certain cases. A mandatory term of imprisonment would be imposed if the offender: (1) commits an extraordinarily serious crime involving kidnapping, aircraft hijacking, or trafficking in hard drugs; (2) commits a violent offense after previously having committed a violent offense.

A separate amendment would provide mandatory prison sentences for any-

TABLE 11.1 *(continued)*

one who uses a gun in the commission of a crime. This amendment would also ban the importation, manufacture, assembly, sale or transfer of cheap, easily conccalable handguns (the so-called "Saturday Night Specials").

Narcotic Sentencing and Seizure Act of 1976

This legislation would improve the ability of law enforcement officials to put traffickers of hard drugs into prison, take the easy profits out of drug trafficking, and improve the capacity of law enforcement officials to detect and apprehend drug's smugglers.

Major features of the proposal would require (1) minimum mandatory prison sentences for persons convicted of opiate (heroin and similar narcotic drugs) trafficking, (2) denial of bail to persons arrested for opiate trafficking, (3) the forfeiture under certain conditions of negotiable instruments used or intended to be used in illegal opiate trafficking, and (4) masters of boats — including pleasure vessels — to report their arrival to Customs authorities within 24 hours.

Crime Control Act

The Administration's proposal would extend the Law Enforcement Assistance Administration (LEAA) for five years, place LEAA under the general policy direction of the Attorney General, authorize LEAA to allocate up to $500 million annually to high crime impact areas, eliminate provisions in current law which require maintenance of previous LEAA spending for juvenile delinquency programs at the 1972 level, and place special emphasis on improving the operation of State and local court systems.

This legislation is designed to continue a vital Federal financial and technical assistance program to State and local governments so that they can improve their ability to enforce the law.

Justice Department Reorganization and Reform Act

The proposed legislation would provide a constitutional means of helping curb corruption in Government. It would establish within the Department of Justice a permanent Office of Special Prosecutor, whose head would be appointed by the President with Senate confirmation, and a Government Crimes Section in the Criminal Division to investigate and prosecute job-related criminal violations of Federal law committed by any elected or appointed Federal Government officer or employee.

A proposed Government Crimes Section in Justice would have responsibility for investigating criminal violations of Federal lobbying and campaign laws. This legislation would also require designated officers and employees of the Federal Government to file comprehensive annual financial statements.

TABLE 11.1 *(continued)*

SOCIAL SECURITY

Social Security Improvement Amendments

Two legislative proposals have been submitted to Congress to help insure a secure and viable Social Security system.

The "Social Security Amendments of 1976" would increase Social Security payroll contributions and thereby stop the immediate, short-term drain on the Social Security trust funds — which are now expected to pay out about $4 billion more in benefits each year than they take in.

The "Social Security Benefit Indexing Act" would correct a serious flaw in the method of computing benefits which, if left unchanged, would create severe long-range financial pressures on the trust funds. The two measures are necessary first steps to solve both the short and long-range financial problems of the Social Security system.

CATASTROPHIC HEALTH PROTECTION

Medicare Improvements of 1976

The proposed "Medicare Improvements of 1976" is designed to provide greater protection against catastrophic health costs for the 25 million aged and disabled Americans eligible for Medicare. An estimated 3 million beneficiaries would pay less in 1977 as a result of the proposed annual limits of $500 for hospital services and $250 for physician services.

The legislation would also provide for moderate cost-sharing for Medicare beneficiaries to encourage economical use of medical services and would slow down health cost inflation by putting a limit on Federal payments to hospitals and physicians.

BUSING

School Desegregation Standards and Assistance Act

The purpose of this legislation is to maintain progress toward the orderly elimination of illegal segregation in public schools while preserving community control of schools. The legislation would set guidelines for Federal courts concerning the use of busing in school desegregation cases.

It would require that courts determine the extent to which acts of unlawful discrimination have caused a greater degree of racial concentration in a school or school system than would have existed otherwise and to confine the relief provided to correcting the racial imbalance caused by those unlawful

308

TABLE 11.1 *(continued)*

acts. The legislation would also limit the duration of court ordered busing, generally to a period of no longer than five years.

GENERAL REVENUE SHARING AND BLOCK GRANTS

General Revenue Sharing: Extension and Revision of the State and Local Fiscal Assistance Act

This proposal would extend and revise the highly successful general revenue sharing program which expires on December 31, 1976. The program would be extended for five-and-three-quarters years, and the current method of funding with annual increases of $150 million would be retained.

The basic revenue sharing formula would be retained but the existing per capita restraint would be eased. Civil rights and public participation provisions would be strengthened while reporting requirements would be made more flexible.

Federal Assistance for Community Services Act

This proposal would improve and strengthen the program of social services established under Title XX of the Social Security Act. The $2.5 billion provided annually by the Federal Government would be distributed as a block grant to the States, with no requirement for State matching funds.

Most Federal requirements and prohibitions on the use of Federal funds would be eliminated. Services to low-income Americans would be emphasized. Federal funds would be focused on those whose incomes fall below the poverty income guidelines.

Financial Assistance for Elementary and Secondary Education

This proposal would consolidate 24 programs of Federal assistance to State and local education agencies for non-postsecondary education purposes into one block grant. Three-quarters of the Federal support would have to be used for disadvantaged and handicapped students, with greater flexibility for States to target funds among programs in accordance with their own priorities.

Administrative requirements on the States would be greatly reduced through reduction of Federal regulations and simplification of reporting procedures, and public participation would be required in the State planning process.

Financial Assistance for Health Care Act

This proposal would consolidate Medicaid and 15 categorical Federal health programs into a single $10 billion block grant to the States. The proposal is de-

TABLE 11.1 *(continued)*

signed to overcome some of the most serious defects in the present system of Federal financing of health care and to permit States to meet their citizens' health needs in a more effective manner.

It would achieve a more equitable distribution of Federal health dollars among States, and eliminate the present State matching requirements. It would also reduce Federal red tape, give States greater flexibility in providing for delivery of health care services to those with low income, and expand public participation in health planning.

Child Nutrition Reform Act of 1976

This proposal would establish a single comprehensive block grant to provide Federal funds for States to feed needy children. It would consolidate into a single authority the fifteen complex and overlapping child nutrition programs currently administered by the Department of Agriculture.

This new approach would concentrate Federal spending on the nutritional needs of poor children, while eliminating the substantial Federal subsidies now provided for non-needy children. It would also ease the heavy administrative burden being imposed on State and local governments by the complicated requirements and inflexible mandates of the present programs.

REGULATORY REFORM

Agenda for Government Reform Act

The Agenda for Government Reform Act would authorize a major review of Federal regulatory activities. It would require the President, over a four-year period, to submit specific proposals to the Congress for the reform of Federal regulatory activities affecting certain sectors of the American economy (e.g., transportation, agriculture, public utilities, etc).

It is designed to produce reforms to guarantee that government policies do not infringe unnecessarily on individual choices and initiative nor intervene needlessly in the marketplace, to find better ways to achieve our social goals at minimal economic cost, to insure that government policies and programs benefit the public interest rather than special interests, and to assure that regulatory policies are equitably enforced.

Aviation Act of 1975

The Aviation Act is designed to provide consumer better air transportation services at a lower cost by increasing real competition in the airline industry, removing artificial and unnecessary regulatory constraints and ensuring continuance of a safe and efficient air transportation system.

TABLE 11.1 *(continued)*

It would introduce and foster price competition in the airline industry, provide for the entry of new airline service; eliminate anti-competitive air carrier agreements; and ensure that the regulatory system protects consumer interests rather than special industry interests.

Motor Carrier Reform Act

The Motor Carrier Reform Act would benefit the consuming public and the users of motor carrier services by eliminating excessive and outdated regulations affecting trucking firms and bus companies. It would stimulate competition in these industries, increase their freedom to adjust rates and fares to changing economic conditions, eliminate restrictions requiring empty backhauls, underloading, or circuitous routing, and enhance enforcement of safety regulations.

Financial Institutions Act

The Financial Institutions Act is intended to remove Federal restrictions on the interest rates and services banks and savings and loan associations can offer to the public. It is designed to offer more competitive returns to small savers and a more diversified range of services to all banking customers.

ENERGY

New Natural Gas Deregulation

This bill is designed to reverse the declining natural gas supply trend as quickly as possible and to insure increased supplies of natural gas at reasonable prices to the consumer. Under the proposal, wellhead price controls over new natural gas sold in interstate commerce would be removed.

This action will enable interstate pipelines to compete for new offshore gas and encourage drilling for gas onshore and in offshore areas.

Alaskan Natural Gas Transportation System

This bill was designed to expedite the selection and construction of a system for the transportation of natural gas from the North Slope of Alaska to the lower 48 states through the establishment of new administrative and judicial procedures. The bill is necessary because of expected prolonged litigation of any Federal Power Commission decision and to assure that all necessary considerations are brought to bear in selecting a system.

The bill wound enable reaching a decision on this vital issue by no later than October 1, 1977 while still providing adequately for the detailed technical,

TABLE 11.1 *(continued)*

financial and environmental studies that must be completed to assure a decision in the public interest, with participation by both the Congress and the Executive.

Nuclear Fuel Assurance Act

This legislation would authorize the Energy Research and Development Administration to enter into cooperative agreements with private firms wishing to finance, build, own and operate uranium enrichment plants and authorize work on an addition to a government-owned enrichment plant. Existing capacity is fully committed.

Additional capacity is needed to meet domestic demands for fuel for commercial nuclear power plants and to enable the U.S. to maintain its position as a leading world supplier of nuclear fuel and equipment for peaceful purposes. This legislation would permit a transition to a private competitive uranium enrichment industry, ending the government monopoly and avoiding the need to spend Federal funds for capacity that can be provided by private industry.

Commercial Pricing for Uranium Enrichment Service

This legislation would permit the Energy Research and Development Administration (ERDA) to revise the basis for establishing its prices for uranium enrichment services to domestic and foreign customers.

It would enable ERDA to include cost elements in its price which should be associated with a commercial-industrial activity (e.g., provisions for taxes, insurance, and return on equity). The bill would end an unjustifiable subsidy by the taxpayers to domestic and foreign customers.

Synthetic Fuels

The Administration supports legislation to amend the Energy Research and Development Administration's existing authorities to provide $2 billion in loan guarantees during 1977 for the commercial demonstration of synthetic fuel production from coal, oil shale, and other domestic resources.

A total of $6 billion in loan guarantees is expected to be necessary over the 1976 to 1978 period in order to reach the 1985 objective of 350,000 barrels per day of synthetic fuel production capacity. With the enactment of the Energy Independence Authority legislation these ERDA projects will be transferred to the Energy Independence Authority.

Winterization Assistance Act

This proposal would establish within the Federal Energy Administration, a grant program for States to assist low income persons, particularly the elderly, in

TABLE 11.1 *(continued)*

winterizing their homes in order to reduce the long-term consumption of energy.

The combined savings in fuel, estimated to be thousands of barrels a day, would not only lessen America's dependence on imported fuels, but would also lower heating bills of low-income persons and families.

Building Energy Conservation Standards Act of 1975

This proposal would establish thermal (heating and cooling) efficiency standards for all new homes and commercial buildings to conserve energy. It is anticipated that this program will save the equivalent of 350,000 barrels of oil per day in 1985. Standards would be promulgated by HUD and primary responsibility for enforcement would be with State and local governments through building codes.

Utilities Act of 1975

This bill is designed to help restore the financial health of electric utilities. It would eliminate undue regulatory lags involved in approving proposed rate changes and assure that rates adequately reflect the full cost of generating and transmitting electricity. Though many States have already adopted similar programs, enactment of the bill will extablish certain standard regulatory procedures across the Nation. Resulting in more equitable treatment of utilities.

Federal Energy Administration Extension Act

The Administration has proposed a simple extension of the Federal Energy Administration for 18 months. This will provide the continuity needed to insure FEA's ability to implement the complex programs contained in the Energy Policy and Conservation Act of 1975 and to adequately administer oil price controls.

Energy Independence Authority of 1975

This Act would establish a $100 billion Energy Independence Authority, a self-liquidating corporation designed to encourage the flow of capital and provide financial assistance, through loans and loan guarantees, to private enterprise engaged in the development of energy sources and supplies important to the attainment of energy independence but which would not otherwise be financed.

This bill also seeks to expedite and facilitate the Federal regulatory and licensing process and to hasten the commercial operation of new energy technologies subsequent to the research and development phase.

313

TABLE 11.1 *(continued)*

Nuclear Powerplant Siting and Licensing Procedures

This legislation is intended to shorten and improve the licensing process for nuclear facilities by allowing licensing procedures for reactor sites and standardized reactor designs to be completed at an earlier point in time.

It would require the Nuclear Regulatory Commission to assure expeditious reactor siting and licensing hearings consistent with the public safety, exclude from consideration any issue which has either been decided or which could have been raised and decided in previous proceedings, and coordinate planning and scheduling of siting and licensing procedures with State agencies.

Electric Power Facility Construction Incentive Act

This legislation is designed to provide tax incentives to stimulate the construction of new electric power generating facilities other than petroleum fueled generating plants.

Construction costs of electric utilities would be reduced through changes in the investment tax credit and allowances for amortization and depreciation. These provisions would encourage utilities to reactivate their plans for the construction of nuclear plants and coal-fired plants that were cancelled or deferred in 1974 and 1975.

Energy Facilities Planning and Development Act

This bill is designed to expedite the development of energy facilities. The Federal Energy Administration would be required to develop a National Energy Site and Facility Report with appropriate Federal, State, Industry and public input.

Information in this report would be utilized by the Federal Government, the States and Industry in developing and implementing plans to insure that needed energy facilities are sited, approved and constructed on a timely basis. At the Federal level, FEA would be responsible for coordinating and expediting the processing of applications to construct energy facilities.

Natural Gas Emergency Standby Act

This legislation would provide a limited exemption from the regulation of natural gas in interstate commerce. It would grant the Federal Power Commission authority to allow companies which transport natural gas in interstate commerce to meet the natural gas requirements of their high priority users by purchasing natural gas (a) from sources not in interstate commerce and (b) from other companies on an emergency basis free from the provisions of the Natural Gas Act, except for reporting requirements.

TABLE 11.1 *(continued)*

Clean Air Act Amendments

The Administration favors legislation which would stabilize auto emission standards at the levels specified by EPA for model year 1977 for three years and imposes stricter standards for two years thereafter. With respect to significant deterioration and stationary source standards, changes are needed to achieve a better balance among environmental, energy and economic needs.

DEFENSE

Proposed changes to the Defense budget will be transmitted to the Congress in a separate message. These changes will include revided authorization and appropriation requests. These changes will:

1. Request approval of vital Defense programs deleted in Congressional action thus far.
2. Request delection of unneeded increases the Congress added to the Defense program.
3. Request approval of a series of legislative proposals which would produce major economies without impairing our national defense capabilities.

In addition to changes in the Defense budget, the Congress should enact the following legislation.

Military Construction Appropriation Authorization, Fiscal Year 1977

This legislation authorizes fiscal year 1977 appropriations for new construction for Defense, the military departments and the Reserve Components. On July 2, 1976, H.R. 12384 was vetoed because it contained a provision which would have seriously restricted the Executive's ability to carry out certain military base closures and reductions.

Congress should reenact this otherwise acceptable legislation without the objectionable base closure provision.

Uniformed Services Retirement Modernization Act

The Administration's legislation proposes substantial revisions to the uniformed services nondisability retirement system designed to increase its effectiveness both as an element of the compensation system and as an element of the personnel management system. These revisions would be phased in gradually with appropriate provisions for saved-pay. Major features of the proposal include

• increased multipliers for members with long service (over 24 years)

TABLE 11.1 *(continued)*

- an early retirement annuity for members who retire short of a full career (less than 30 years) with an increased annuity when they would have reached 30 years of service.
- use of the highest average basic pay for one year instead of terminal basic pay in computing retirement annuities.
- integration of military and social security retirement benefits at age 65.
- payments to both voluntary and involuntary separatees who leave before completing 20 years of service.

Restraint Items Requiring Permanent Legislation

1. Wage Board pay reform.
2. Phase out commissary direct labor subsidy.
3. Eliminate 1% "kicker" from retired pay adjustment computation.
4. Eliminate administrative duty pay for Reserve and National Guard Commanders.
5. Reduce the number of annual paid drills for the National Guard.
6. Eliminate dual compensation of Federal employees for National Guard and Reserve annual training.
7. Revise cadet and midshipman pay policy.

INTERNATIONAL

Bretton Woods Agreement Act Amendments

This legislation would authorize the United States to accept fundamental amendments to the Articles of Agreement of the International Monetary Fund. The amendments to the Articles generally concern: members' exchange arrangements; reduction in the role of gold in the international monetary system; changes in the characteristics and uses of the special drawing right; and simplification and modernization of the Fund's financial operations and transactions. The bill would also authorize the United States to consent to an increase in its quota in the Fund equivalent to 1,705 million Special Drawing Rights.

Protection of Intelligence Sources and Methods

This legislation is designed to protect intelligence sources and methods from unauthorized disclosures. It provides for criminal and civil sanctions against those who are authorized access to such intelligence information and who reveal it to unauthorized persons.

The bill contains provisions to prevent damaging disclosures of intelligence sources and methods in the course of prosecution and also includes safeguards to

TABLE 11.1 *(continued)*

adequately protect the rights of an accused. Injunctive relief would be provided in those instances in which unauthorized disclosure is threatened and serious damage to intelligence collection efforts would result.

Foreign Intelligence Surveillance Act

This legislation is designed to ensure that the Government will be able to collect necessary foreign intelligence while at the same time providing assurances to the public that electronic surveillance for foreign intelligence purposes will not be abused.

The proposed bill would provide a procedure for seeking a judicial order approving the use, in a particular case, of electronic surveillance to obtain foreign intelligence information. It also would establish standards that must be satisfied before any such order could be entered. The bill follows the framework of existing law governing such surveillance undertaken for criminal law enforcement purposes, with appropriate adjustments to meet the special needs and purposes of foreign intelligence investigations.

Export Administration Act Extension

This legislation would extend the Export Administration Act from September 30, 1979. The Act authorizes the President to regulate exports of U.S. goods and technology to the extent necessary to protect the domestic economy from an excessive drain of scarce materials, to further the foreign policy of the United States and to control exports when necessary for purposes of national security.

The Administration also has requested that the maximum civil penalty under the Act be raised from $1,000 to $10,000 and that criminal penalties be raised from $10,000 to more meaningful levels.

Financial Support Fund

This legislation would authorize the President to accept membership for the United States in a new, $25 billion Financial Support Fund agreed to by the Organization for Economic Cooperation and Development (OECD).

The Fund would be available for a period of two years to provide short to medium-term financing to participating OECD members faced with extraordinary financing needs. The proposal for the Fund was developed as part of a comprehensive response to the economic and financial problems posed by severe increases in oil prices.

The Administration's proposal would permit U.S. participation in the Fund by authorizing the Secretary of the Treasury to issue guarantees. The bill would authorize appropriations of such sums as are necessary to meet obligations on guarantees issued by the Secretary but not to exceed an amount equivalent to approximately $7 billion.

TABLE 11.1   *(continued)*

International Bank for Reconstruction and Development (IBRD); increased United States participation

This legislation would authorize the Secretary of the Treasury as the United States Governor to the IBRD (World Bank) to vote for an increase of $8.4 billion in the authorized capital stock of the Bank. It would also authorize him to subscribe, on behalf of the United States, to an additional 13,005 shares of capital stock and authorize appropriations of approximately $1.57 billion for the increase in United States participation.

Implement Agreement Between the United States and Turkey

This proposed joint resolution would approve the new Defense Cooperation Agreement with the Government of Turkey and authorize the President to implement the Agreement.

Economic Coercion Act of 1975

This proposal would prohibit any business enterprise from using economic means to coerce any person or entity to fail to do business with or otherwise to discriminate against any United States person on the ground of race, color, religion, sex or national origin. The prohibition would be enforced by civil actions brought by aggrieved persons or by the Attorney General.

Increased Participation in the Asian Development Fund

This legislation would authorize appropriations of $50 million which would permit the United States to make the first of three scheduled contributions to a multi-donor replenishment of the Asian Development Fund.

AGRICULTURE

U. S. Grain Standards Act Amendments

The Administration proposed a bill to amend the United States Grain Standards Act to improve the grain inspection system. Specifically, the bill would:

- retain the Federal, State and private grain inspection system now in effect, but authorizes USDA to perform original inspection on an interim basis during suspension or revocation proceedings against an official inspection agency, or where other qualified agency or person is not willing or able to provide service;

TABLE 11.1 *(continued)*

- authorize USDA to conduct monitoring activities in foreign ports for grain officially inspected under the Act;
- eliminates the potential for conflict of interest from the present grain inspection system;
- require official inspection agencies to comply with certain training, staffing, supervisory and reporting requirements;
- provide for the suspension or revocation of official inspection agencies for violation of the Act;
- provide for the triennial designation of all official inspection agencies; and,
- require the payment of grain inspection fees which would make the program largely self-supporting.

Federal Crop Insurance Act

The Administration proposed a bill to amend the Federal Crop Insurance Act and to repeal the disaster payment provisions for feed grains, cotton, and wheat under the Agriculture Act of 1949.

The proposed amendments would permit the Federal Crop Insurance Corporation to offer insurance on a nationwide basis on feed grains, cotton, and wheat and thus provide the producers of those commodities with protection from the financial losses attributable to crop failures.

It would also permit the Corporation to reinsure policies written by private insurance companies thereby expanding the availability of this valuable service. This program would save an estimated $250 million in government outlays annually and place the cost of and responsibility for maintaining crop insurance on the producers who would benefit from it.

Restructure Agriculture Conservation Program

The Administration proposed a bill to update the conditions under which the Federal Government provides financial assistance to agricultural producers for needed soil, water, woodland, and wildlife conservation and environmental enhancement measures on agricultural lands.

Specifically, the bill would:

- provide for financial assistance to those agricultural producers *who are financially unable* to fully carry out needed conservation practices; and,
- *limit financial assistance* under the Act to *enduring type* practices pertaining to soil, water, woodland, and wildlife conservation on agricultural lands and *emphasize long-term agreements* as opposed to *annual or short-term* conservation practices.

TABLE 11.1 *(continued)*

ENVIRONMENT

Federal Water Pollution Control Act Amendments

The 1976 amendments proposed to the Act would affect future funding of the waste water treatment grant program.

They would focus Federal funding on the construction of treatment plants and associated interceptor sewers; eliminate the eligibility of that portion of each project designed to serve reserve capacity for future population growth; and authorize the Administrator of EPA to extend the July 1, 1977 deadline for compliance with secondary treatment and water quality standards on a case-by-case basis for periods not to exceed six years.

In addition, extensions of appropriation authorizations were proposed for FY 76 and FY 77.

Comprehensive Oil Pollution Liability and Compensation Act

The Comprehensive Oil Pollution Liability and Compensation Act of 1975 would establish a $200 million domestic fund which would be available to compensate individuals who suffer damages from oil spills in U.S. waters. The bill would create a uniform nationwide system of strict liability for oil spill damages and a standard procedure for settlement of claims. It would also implement two international conventions which deal with oil pollution caused by tankers on the high seas.

INCOME ASSISTANCE

National Food Stamp Reform Act

This proposal would concentrate food stamp program benefits on those truly in need, significantly improve program administration, and correct abuses and inequities of the current program. A standard deduction would replace the present set of complex itemized deductions; eligibility would be limited to those whose net income is below the poverty level; families would be required to spend 30 percent of household income for stamps; a more realistic measure of actual income over the preceding 90 days would be used to determine eligibility; categorical eligibility for public assistance recipients would be eliminated; and able-bodied recipients would be required to seek, accept, and retain gainful employment.

TABLE 11.1 *(continued)*

Work Incentive (WIN) Program Amendments of 1976

The purpose of the Work Incentive (WIN) program is to help recipients of Aid to Families with Dependent Children (AFDC) shift from welfare to self-support through employment. The proposed WIN amendments would redesign the program to help more AFDC applicants and recipients move into the mainstream of the economy with greater efficiency and less cost to the taxpayers.

It would revise WIN to ensure that employable AFDC applicants and recipients in WIN areas are exposed to job opportunities, and will actively search for and accept suitable jobs. The legislation would extend to AFDC applicants the employment services presently provided only to AFDC recipients—i.e., direct placement and labor market exposure—and would terminate the less effective work and training components of the WIN program.

Aid to Families with Dependent Children (AFDC) Amendments of 1976

This proposal would simplify the administration of the Aid to Families with Dependent Children (AFDC) program and focus the resources devoted to this program on the most needy. For example, it would standardize the disregard for work-related expenses, thereby eliminating one of the troublesome inequities of the AFDC program, and it would eliminate the dual work registration requirement for unemployed fathers which would remove an extra burden on the individual and reduce administrative work.

It would also require that an applicant for AFDC under the enemployed fathers program apply for and accept any unemployment compensation benefits to which he is entitled. Currently, as a result of a Supreme Court decision, an individual who is eligible for unemployment compensation benefits has the option of applying for either unemployment compensation benefits or AFDC benefits. An individual's first recourse should be to unemployment benefits for which his employer has contributed and to which he is entitled.

Low Income Housing Contributions

This proposal would amend the definition of "income" used in determining eligibility and maximum rental charges under the low-income public housing program, to conform the criteria used in public housing to those used in the lower-income housing assistance program under section 8 of the United States Housing Act of 1937.

Present law provides for a number of exlusions from income, among which are exclusions for minor children, extraordinary medical or other expenses, and a flat deduction of 5 percent of the family's gross income (10 percent in the case of elderly households). The amendment would require exclusions only for the

TABLE 11.1 *(continued)*

number of minor children in the household and for the extent of medical or other unusual expenses.

This would promote equity between tenants and public housing authorities and between tenants and Federal taxpayers.

Unemployment Compensation Amendments

This proposal would expand coverage under the regular unemployment insurance system to additional groups of workers and would make urgently needed changes to strengthen the financing of the system. The permanent extended unemployment insurance program would be made more responsive to changes in the economy.

A National Commission on Unemployment Compensation would be established to comprehensively study the system and proposed changes, and make recommendations for further improvements.

VETERANS

Medical Insurance for VA Hospital Care

Many veterans who receive free medical care at VA hospitals have health insurance. This proposal would require the insurance companies to reimburse the VA for hospital care provided to veterans who do not have disabilities resulting from active military service.

The proposal reflects the Administration's belief that the Federal taxpayer should not bear the cost of treating people with no service-connected disabilities when to do so will benefit only third parties, including insurance companies, who are legally liable for the disability or injury necessitating such treatment.

Termination of Veterans Educational Benefits

This proposal would terminate VA education benefits for those men and women who decide in the future to enter the peacetime All-Volunteer Force. The educational assistance programs for veterans, from their inception, were designed as readjustment benefits for those who served during wartime.

They were never intended to be a continuing benefit and both the World War II and Korean conflict GI Bill programs were terminated within a reasonable period after the cessation of hostilities. The Vietnam conflict officially ended in May 1975; the draft, in June 1973. With the advent of a peacetime, All-Volunteer Force, GI Bill educational benefits are no longer appropriate for those who enter military service in the future.

TABLE 11.1 *(continued)*

OTHER

Indemnification of Swine Flu Manufacturers

This proposal is essential to implementation of the National Influenca Immunization Program. Current law bars the Federal Government from agreeing to indemnify vaccine manufacturers for losses from injuries which may result from the Federal Government's activities in the immunization program. The Administration proposal would enable HEW to agree to indemnify the manufacturers against claims attributable to inoculation with the vaccine, except claims arising out of the negligence of the manufacturer.

Student Loan Amendments

This proposal would correct certain abuses in the Federal guaranteed student loan program that have resulted in high default rates under that program.

Specifically, the proposal would amend Title IV of the Higher Education Act to eliminate proprietary schools as eligible lenders, and amend the Bankruptcy Act to make student loans nondischargeable in bankruptcy during the five-year period after the first installment becomes due. The proposal would also prohibit borrowers who default on guaranteed loans from receiving a basic educational opportunity grant or any further guaranteed loans.

Federal Impact Aid Amendments of 1976

This bill would reform the impact aid program by targeting funds only on those school districts that are truly adversely affected by Federal activities. It would provide support to local education agencies only for those children whose parents both live and work on Federal property.

These people do not pay property taxes, and the Administration believes that the Federal Government has a responsibility to help pay the cost of educating their children, but not to help pay the costs of educating other children whose parents pay local property taxes.

Comprehensive Health Professions Education Act

The Administration's proposal would provide Federal support to those medical and dental schools that agree to meet certain conditions.

Unlike prior programs of Federal assistance which were directed towards increasing the aggregate numbers of doctors and dentists in the Nation, the Administration proposal would shift the emphasis of Federal support for health professions schools from merely increasing enrollments to addressing national problems of medical specialty and geographic maldistribution.

TABLE 11.1 *(continued)*

The proposal is designed to produce more primary care physicians and to provide greater access to health professionals.

Higher Education Act Amendment and Extension

This bill would extend for four years those higher education programs which have demonstrated their effectiveness in meeting the postsecondary education needs of the Nation. The bill would extend the most effective student assistance programs, namely, the basic educational opportunity grant program, the work-study program, the State student incentive grant program, and the guaranteed student loan program.

Programs to strengthen developing institutions and the Teacher Corps program would also be extended. The bill would also simplify and clarify the requirements relating to accreditation and institutional eligibility.

Closure or Transfer of Public Health Service Hospitals

This proposal is one of several Administration initiatives designed to reform Federal financing and direct delivery of health care. It would authorize HEW to transfer to community use or close the eight Public Health Service hospitals which are underutilized and which essentially serve only one occupational group.

The proposal reflects the conclusion that maintenance of a Federal hospital system for some 200,000 merchant seamen is an inappropriate and inefficient use of resources, particularly in light of low hospital occupancy rates, the excess supply of hospital beds, the availability of alternative health care facilities, and the substantial capital investment which would be required to continue operation of the hospitals.

Repeal the 1% Add-on in the Cost-of-Living Adjustment of the Civil Service Retirement System

Federal civilian and military retirement systems automatically increase benefits to compensate for changes in the Consumer Price Index (CPI). Since 1969, these automatic adjustments have included a 1% add-on which has been compounded with each subsequent CPI adjustment.

This bill would eliminate the 1% add-on provision in the civil service retirement law which has been progressively overcompensating Federal retirees for changes in the cost of living. The Congress has passed legislation to eliminate the 1% add-on in the military, foreign service, and CIA retirement systems, but only if it is also eliminated for the civil service retirement system.

TABLE 11.1 *(continued)*

Wage Board Pay Reform

The basic principle governing Federal blue-collar employees' pay rates is that they should be comparable with prevailing rates and pay practices in the non-Federal sector in the same locality.

This bill would eliminate aspects of present law governing wage board pay rates that are inconsistent with that principle and therefore result in Federal blue-collar workers earning more than their counterparts in the private sector. Among other things, the bill would eliminate use of wage rate data from outside the local area involved.

It would also eliminate the present requirement for each grade to have five steps, and would substitute a step-rate structure that would accord with the predominant industry practice.

Increased Authorization for Certain Small Business Loan Programs

This legislation would increase the total amount of loans, guarantees, and other obligations which the Small Business Administration (SBA) may have outstanding at any one time. These revised ceilings will permit SBA to increase the number of loans made to those small business who otherwise would be unable to obtain in the private sector

Federal Procurement Act

A number of recommendations made by the Commission on Government Procurement—including proposals to consolidate the basic Federal procurement acts and modernize the provisions for awarding contracts—would be implemented by this bill.

Reorganization Act Extension

This proposal would extend the President's authority to submit plans for the reorganization of executive agencies to the Congress.

This authority expired on April 1, 1973. The legislation is designed to restore the authority necessary for the President to propose reorganization in order to foster both efficiency and flexibility in the structure of the Executive branch.

Stockpile Disposal

This legislation would authorize disposal from the national stockpile and supplemental stockpile of industrial diamond stones, antimony, tin, and silver. The

TABLE 11.1   *(continued)*

amounts of these four materials recommended for disposal are in excess of adequate stockpile requirements, and their sale would result in estimated receipts of $746 million in fiscal year 1977.

Patent Modernization and Reform Act

This legislation would substantially strengthen the American patent system by improving the strength and reliability of issued patents through procedural reforms in the patent examination and issuance process.

It would also simplify procedures for obtaining patents, make more complete and precise the disclosure of information about technology contained in patents, and add new provisions concerning enforcement of patients.

Winter Olympic Games Assistance

This legislation would authorize Federal financial assistance for the construction of certain permanent, unique sports facilities needed for the 1980 Winter Olympic Games at Lake Placid, New York.

The total amount of special Federal assistance under both existing authorities and this legislation would not exceed $28 million plus the financing of certain increases in construction costs.

These are important legislative proposals dealing with matters of the National interest, and I urge the Congress to move with dispatch to enact them.

GERALD R. FORD

Source: Daley Report for Executives DER, No. 142, Bureau of National Affairs, Inc., Washington, D.C., July 22, 1976. Used by permission.

extremely complex laws of far-reaching business importance. Their effects can reliably be predicated to be wider and they are typical of laws that will have both direct and indirect consequences on marketing.

Summary

Several facts emerge with crystal clarity.

1. Regulatory reform may well not take the form or substance that many seem to think it will. As Senator Gary Hart said at the first National Forum on Busi-

ness, Government and the Public Interest, sponsored by the American Management Association: "It is easier to get government in, than out."

2. Even if regulatory reform does come along, bringing some relief, it may be too little and too late. The time for marketing managers to act and prepare is now—based on worst case assumptions.

3. Recent reform and reorganization efforts may provide some benefits, but they should be looked upon with a degree of skepticism.

4. Several important new statutes have been enacted in the latter part of 1976 and the effects of these, while not yet felt, can be predicted to be significant, posing new and as yet not fully appreciated concerns and problems.

5. The basket of pending federal and state legislation is overflowing, with seemingly no one in government saying, "let's simultaneously repeal some existing statutes, do away with some existing agencies, departments, or commissions."

WHAT CAN AND WHAT SHOULD BE DONE

All of this may seem overwhelming and it is easy to slip into a fatalistic or pessimistic mood. However, that is neither realistic nor desirable. The world is a place of constant change, and while we have been examining many aspects that have their negative effects, there are many that are equally positive. One of the results is that while we are living through a transitional, and perhaps even painful, period, we can and must make our contribution to it. What is right must be reinforced and what is wrong altered. Our concerns here have included not only the specifics of marketing but, as needed, we have touched upon some of the deeper and more fundamental aspects of social organization, social structure, culture, and choices that we all must make. One of the choices is to look to improvement of the total social dynamic, which includes broader aspects of social events as well as narrow elements that more clearly apply only to the marketing function.

Earlier we indicated that we would have some suggestions to make pertaining to the preservation of a "free market"—although perhaps not so free as we once knew it—and to the satisfaction of social objectives while preserving our democratic structure with its inherent individual rights and privileges. The actions taken to accomplish this derive from recognition of the need for a change and the commitment to change, not only by business but by the government and the public interest activists as well. In an earlier speech addressing this need, as presented at the first National Forum on Business, Government and the Public Interest (sponsored by AMA, December, 1976, Washington, D.C.) I summarized this concept:

TIME FOR A CHANGE

There is a mood upon us. A mood that we can sense even if we cannot know its meaning, nor necessarily how to accomplish what it impels us to do. Each time has to it a meaning, a purpose, and those means which seem designed to allow of accomplishing that purpose.

There was a time for America's development and growth. A time for its assertion as an international power and as the exemplar of industrial development and growth. A time, in effect, for business dominance. Later, there was a transition, a period of quiesence, as it were. Later yet arose a time of dissatisfaction amongst the many who, rightly or wrongly, perceived that they were controlled and directed by the few. The consumer awash in the battle against the monolithic corporation. The individual controlled by the government.

Today there is a sense of yet another time. A disquietitude that perhaps has had its latest and most notable expression in the presidential election. A time for a change.

Months ago when authoring *Business, Government and the Public Interest,* well before it evolved into the basis for the present forum, the objective was to attempt the visualization of such change, its purpose and accomplishment. Perhaps then, and certainly now, there was an underlying recognition that herein lies an approach to the solution of the nagging feeling that most of us have: something is wrong; what has been done to make it right has yet to work; and something new is needed. While we may not yet clearly see what that something new is, perhaps it lies in what we will attempt to accomplish here together. The evolution of that next step. A step whose time may well have come. A time to set aside past dissatisfactions and disagreements. Past partisanship and biases. A time, rather, in which to examine the vast potentials of working not singly but together. Not in autonomous diametrics, but in far sighted cooperation

There are, obviously, no glib nor easy solutions to the all-too-many problems. However, the very fact that we are all assembled together here, pays testimony to the fact that we, consciously or not, acknowledge these problems and, more importantly, look with realistic expectation to their solution.

In approaching a forum of this type, there is an obvious tendency to fall back on past approaches. To use this platform to air grievances and attempt to redress old inequities, real or imagined. All have their personal set of examples, the past stories of regulatory excesses, or the corresponding instances of corporate insensitivities, the exaggerated insistances of the public interest activists. It is a temptation, however, that must be resisted. For it is just such past experiences, which validate how futile they, in fact, are in the identification and accomplishment of positive solutions, how short they fall in attaining the social weal.

The dynamic forces which not only are the basis of our society, but which rightfully control and direct it, are, in the broadest sense, the government, the business community, and those groups which have been identified as representing the public interest. And truly, it matters not at all in which order we tabulate them, for all are equally important, but more importantly, equally interdependent. How then can the true challenge be met? How can society, national and international, be served? How can our national promise be realized?

Many of us here have reached an age where more than half our lives have been spent in whatever pursuits we may have considered necessary, valuable, and fulfilling. Many are far younger and have yet to make their dedication. While many have examined their personal convictions, some have yet to do so. But we all must be wary. Roles are too easy to ascribe. Images too easily conjured up. What is the true nature of any individual may be far from what is his or her role or image in society at large. What this tells us is that there is no exclusivity on altruism or ultruism.

We have a commonality. We all play each other's roles in one instance or another, and we all have each other's sensitivities or insensitivities in one instance or another. Realizing that can help us greatly in approaching the seemingly insoluble problems of energy, conservation, social reform, equality, economics, survival, and growth that confront us. Recognizing this also reveals that truly no one individual, or correspondingly, no one group, has the omniscience to see fully and clearly not only the positions of all others but the solutions that are optimum for us all.

Times, and what is appropriate for them, come and go as all too unfortunately do societies, what they stand or stood for, what they accomplished or hope to accomplish, and with that perhaps too their opportunity for accomplishment. We as a nation accomplished much. We as a nation can yet accomplish more. Not only for ourselves, but for the world. Whether from the public interest, government or business sector, we all desire the same end. We all aspire to the same objective. The question that confronts us then is how to accomplish this objective for all without subordinating the basis and valid concerns and prerogatives of each.

It is a foregone conclusion that, overly simplistic as it may seem, the time may perhaps be right to change to mutual problem exploration and solution rather than to continue the separatism that seems to have been, and is, the role that each plays. Perhaps, like the role of the individual—the role of the person—that of the dominant social factors, too, is far too strictured and confined, far too preoccupied with playing out its self-assigned posture than looking deeply at the issues and rising above this parochialism to what is, perhaps, a more visionary than attainable attitude of problem identification, goal setting, and solutions through informed, mutual analysis, evaluation, prioritization and commitment.

Herein lies the nucleus of the alteration. Mutual problem identification. Mutual goal setting and mutual solutions. This forum provides nothing more than an initial step in this direction. It may be a faltering step. Faltering as it may be, however, it is taken with the conviction that the second step will be stronger, and the third stronger yet. With each step comes added strength, added purpose, and with that a new direction.

The time for a change is here. The need for a change is apparent. The challenge to change there. Fortunately, our human intellect has already demonstrated our ability to meet all of these requirements; for man is, if nothing, creative, innovative and adaptable. We have always struggled to improve our lot, to advance the human condition, to control our destiny. There is no reason to believe we cannot meet these latest challenges with the same creativity that has been applied to past, even if seemingly from our contemporary perspective, less pressing and complex problems. We proceed here, for the next three days, from the firm conviction that this can be, and will be, accomplished.

Business, government, and the public interest as separate institutions, insofar as they can be or ever were separate, have had their time. That time is past. In the future lies the time of interaction, interaction and joint effort from which will follow the eventual resolution of difficulties which we now perceive to be insurmountable. It is manifestly naive to think that merely bringing these elements together will automatically provide solutions. This will not be an easy task. Past apprehensions and suspicions are not easily allayed. Past animosities not easily overcome. The accomplishment is, however, more than worth the effort.

It is my contention that did we not already perceive both the need and the feasibility, then we would not be gathering at this forum together to take the first step.

In more specific terms, this philosophy can be translated into several recommended actions that should be undertaken. These were advanced in my AMA Management Briefing, *Business, Government and the Public Interest* and bears repetition.

GOVERNMENT ACTION

1. Recognize the legitimacy of the interest advocated by both the public and business so that a reasoned balance can be attained in the development of legislative action.
2. Recognize that priorities are required for legislative action. While our economy is vast, it also is finite. Not all things can be done for all interests simultaneously.
3. Do not permit legislation to be considered or enacted in a vacuum that considers only a particular bill or regulation but fails to view it in the context of other statutes and regulations (both existing and proposed). The cumulative effects have been ignored or underestimated far too long. Similarly, such review should carefully consider the ability of existing law and regulation, properly enforced, to solve a problem before additional legislative burden is imposed.
4. Retain control of legislative branch prerogatives and stop the trend, now practically an irresistible force, driving decision making into the judiciary, with the consequent establishment of national goals, objectives, policies and priorities by the Court and not the Congress.
5. Provide for more comprehensive analysis of proposed legislation, both as to need and effect before enactment. The adage of prevention rather than cure applies to legislative and regulatory excesses as well, amendments are feasible, but they are no substitute for reasoned legislation and regulation.
6. Not only critically review existing legislation and practices but also, as President Ford has suggested, examine the equally fundamental question of regulatory reform.
7. Critically reexamine the effects of past legislation and regulatory actions, with particular emphasis on determining whether, in fact, the public has been served.
8. Provide an egalitarian forum for legislative and regulatory development—an open exchange for all concerned parties, not what all too often turns out to be an adversary procedure in which industry is usually put on the defensive.
9. Provide for full-scale economic analysis of all legislation, both before and after pas-

sage. The latter should take two forms: economic review of the legislation to determine if it is cost-effective and beneficial and analysis of each regulatory action within the statute before promulgation.

10. More clearly delineate congressional intent in any given legislation in order to contain both the agency or department in its actions as well as the courts in any of their deliberations and decisions. The basic authority of the people is vested in the Congress, and the expression and execution of this authority should remain there. At the very least the delegation of congressional authority should be more carefully circumscribed.

BUSINESS ACTION

1. Become more aware of its responsibilities both to its employees and to society.
2. Encourage joint legislative developments and attempt to circumvent diametric oppositions.
3. Voluntarily acknowledge problems and issues and proceed with self-imposed regulation.
4. Commit company to policies and programs of business and social reform where justified and valid.
5. More effectively present its viewpoints to both the Congress and the public. All too often the message is not taken nor is it in a readily comprehensible form when it is taken. One of the problems lies in failure to translate the business argument into terms and dimensions that can be understood, appreciated, and accepted by those outside the business community who are unfamiliar with business problems.
6. Develop and subscribe to industry codes of conduct, thus taking the concept of voluntary regulation one step further.
7. Engage in active government and consumer education programs.
8. Expand its efforts to regain credibility with government, the public interest groups, and, of ultimate importance, the public.
9. When presenting its viewpoints, regardless of the forum be better prepared and better able to defend its position.
10. Become more involved and active. The idea of showing no profile, while perhaps tempting, is impractical or unrealistic. I am not recommending hyperactivity but rather a balanced approach.
11. Just as industry informs government when it does not agree, industry should also advise when it does agree and take a more active role in supporting valid legislation and regulation.

PUBLIC INTEREST GROUPS ACTION

1. Recognize that ours is a technologically dependent society and that technology and all it implies are implicit to the order, structure, and duration of that society. Technology,

then, controlled as and where required, is an inherent part of the public interest and welfare. To envision them as separable is impractical and unrealistic.

2. Appreciate that industry and government do have a public interest and are assuming public responsibilities despite many allegations to the contrary.

3. Recognize that what industry says and does is not automatically incorrect or at best suspect.

4. Develop a better understanding of techno-economically dependent society in which complex problems require equally complex solutions.

5. Look to joint problem identification, priority setting, and solution, not dichotomy and polarization.

6. Recognize scientific and technical problems as such rather than treating them on an emotional basis.

7. Realize that while citizens' suits, petitions, class action, and similar legal rights are desirable within our system, there must also be some limitation and control just as there are in other areas. If not, these actions will become counterproductive and will not serve their intended function; certainly they will not benefit the public.

COMBINED ACTION

The central theme to solution of the problems discussed is obviously the recognition of mutuality of interest and cause and effect implicit in the social dynamic involving the interaction of government, business, and the public interest activists. From this it should be apparent that if action is to be beneficial and ultimately in the interest of all (although the effect may differ in degree on any one segment at a given time) it must derive from a common ground and objective. What is most sorely needed, then, is action based on objectivity and with ordered priorities, something that can only be accomplished through mutual identification and development—partnership.

A hasty attempt to redress all the real or imagined ills of this world, particularly those attributed to the business community, accomplishes little, frustrates many, and results more in confrontation than solution, more antagonism than action, and more intransigence than progress. In the long run, the public benefits very little.

This criticism could also be leveled at government and business as well as the public interest groups. If the ultimate objective is the welfare of the people, then the public interest and public welfare must demand a broader interpretation and mandate balanced advocacy and action by all three parties. This can only be accomplished through "partnership." As we achieve a more mature society there can be no doubt that this will happen.

WHAT MARKETING CAN DO

It can reasonably be argued that some, if not all, of these suggestions go beyond the authority and purview of the marketing function. This is certainly the case with many, although someone must take the initiative—not only individually, but organizationally.

Regardless of whether this does or does not occur, there are several actions that the marketing executive can initiate immediately which are within the realm of his responsibilities and to the interests of his function as well as his company. Most of them have been scattered throughout this book, here we have assembled them into one convenient summary, along with some others that may not have appeared before.

50 Things You Can Do: Positive Action for the Marketing Manager

1. Establish new organizations and assigned responsibilities.
2. Develop new strategies.
3. Revise market research outlook, objectives and perspective (perceived value).
4. Revise economic outlook and objectives.
5. Establish a new marketing outlook (Z factor, GEEM factors).
6. Make advertising and promotion more factual.
7. Establish a positive government/public interface.
8. Establish flexible programs and management to decrease response time.
9. Develop contingency products, processes, marketing plans.
10. Do projective cost and price determinations.
11. Undertake continuous/periodic product and account rationalization.
12. Minimize introduction of imitation products and concentrate on extending longevity of existing products.
13. Explore product substitution.
14. Explore process alterations, substitutions.
15. Identify sensitivity and vulnerability factors.
16. Change packaging to minimize risk/liability.
17. Change labeling to minimize risk/liability.
18. Establish product-by-product profit objectives.
19. Establish account-by-account profit objectives.
20. Reexamine and, if need be, establish new profit criteria.
21. Reexamine nature of business and product line; look to spreading risks.
22. Establish new R&D criteria.
23. Reexamine planning and establish new planning operations, especially contingency planning.
24. Develop and present legislative and regulatory positions.

25. Establish internal and external informational systems.

26. Establish new teams for compliance, internal and external coordination.

27. Carefully evaluate trade, professional, and trade associations and use their expertise and position effectively.

28. Develop new system of distribution, storage, inventory.

29. Look to tighter controls, not only cost but price accounting and return on investment.

30. Monitor risk and liability closely.

31. Look at competition differently (nearest equivalent product, perceptual value, value analysis, vested interest).

32. Monitor court decisions carefully (de facto legislative decisions are being made in the courts).

33. Watch personal liability carefully.

34. Participate actively in studies, surveys (industry, associations , or external).

35. Utilize consultants in areas where in-house expertise or experience does not exist or is limited.

36. Be objective in presentations; look to benefits and cost effectiveness, options, alternatives.

37. Develop scientific compliance programs.

38. Develop appropriate records for documentary purposes.

39. Watch legislative developments carefully (there is opportunity for amendment).

40. Work with and through the media.

41. Develop cost accounting systems to capture accurate costs on product-by-product basis.

42. Watch cost allocation system; it can be deceptive.

43. Remember who is to be served—the public. Legislators move on the same premise.

44. As always, carefully explore and establish short- versus long-term interests and the options that ensue.

45. Establish a specific government relations function—whether a full-time new position or added responsibility to an existing position.

46. Identify your informational needs and develop the required informational systems to satisfy them.

47. Do not forget internal communications. Information is of no use unless distributed.

48. Obtain top management support. Considering criminal and civil personal liability, this should not be difficult.

49. Always look to whatever positive aspects and opportunities might exist.

50. Keep a prayer book handy.

BEGINNING

Usually the end of a book has a section titled "Conclusion" rather than "Beginning." However, this *is* just the beginning—the beginning of a new marketing era.

All things good or bad do come to an end. As Omar Khayyam said in the *Rubaiyat*, "And this too shall pass away." What will pass away here is not the legislation, or the regulation, but perhaps the elements of both that are overly restrictive, counterproductive, and detrimental. From the business side, what may pass away is the attitude that the government and the public have no right and no "business" in their business. Eventually a harmonization of interests will ensue. The most difficult task of all is to recognize, provide for, and advance the rights and interests of all without jeopardizing the basic and specific interests and rights of each. The rights of the corporation at law have a precise meaning and significance. This is not, however, the right or privilege that really concerns us here. The rights and privileges of some abstraction, while of academic interest, do not reflect the concerns of the public, or the government, or for that matter, each and every one of us who one day is a marketing executive and on that same day is a consumer, or even possibly through his private activities a bureaucrat in his own right.

This balancing will come. The harmonization will occur. The intervening period may be vexing, and in some cases no doubt more than vexing, painful. It is a period of adjustment and a period of learning for all. What is emerging is not only a new way of looking at things, but a new way of doing things.

Business is a social force. Business is a social need. Business without any other embellishment has a social value. All of these will, of necessity, be recognized even if not in the terms that we, for the moment, have come to accept. In many respects business has the opportunity and obligation now, as never before, to fulfill its role in helping to shape this future—an opportunity and an obligation that will, no doubt, be met, just as have been previous opportunities and obligations. Just as *business* will do this, so too, will marketing.

We can look to some long-term relief from our current and immediately foreseeable problems. There is here, as in most things, a pendulum effect. Force and reactions swing first to one extreme and then to another. Eventually they come to rest somewhere in between. Because this is a dynamic process, the in between is always ahead of the center; the trend line, if healthy and beneficial, is always upwards—upwards in terms of social and public benefit and social progress. Therefore, while there will be some alterations in specific, some alleviation in trend will be more to public benefit, participation, and interest. Although no one can pretend to provide a blueprint of the future, least of all a blueprint for corporate conduct, it all seems to reduce itself to four elements:

Recognize
Organize
Integrate
Participate

Those individuals, and those organizations that do will not only survive but prosper—even if by *prosper* we mean a different prosperity than many of us have come to expect or accept as prosperity.

Marketing was created in times of change. It was created in response to demands which at their time must have appeared just as difficult, just as incomprehensible, just as challenging, and in some cases perhaps just as unnecessary. Marketing will respond to new concerns as it did in the past—with creativity, imagination and vigor. It had better.

Sources

ACT News, Action for Childrens Television, Inc., Vol. 6, No. 1, Fall 1976.

Almanac Congressional Quarterly, The, 1973, 1974, 1975.

America, Inc. (Morton Mintz and Jerry S. Cohen), Dell Publishing Co., Inc., New York, 1971.

American Economic System, and Your Part in It, The, The Advertising Council and The U.S. Department of Commerce in Co-Operation with U.S. Department of Labor, 1976.

Americans Speak Out on Inflation . . . Politicians . . . Bureaucracy, *U.S. News & World Report,* September 13, 1976.

American Politics. A Systems Approach (Stephen V. Monsma), Holt, Rinehart & Winston, Inc., New York, 1969.

Behind the Decline in New Drugs, *Chemical and Engineering News,* September 22, 1975.

Big Government vs. the Little Guy (Sen. James L. Buckley), *Reader's Digest,* August 1976.

Business End of Government, The (Dan Smoot), Western Islands Publishers, Belmont, Mass., 1973.

Business, Government, and the Public Interest (George S. Dominguez), American Management Association, New York, 1976.

Business Policies, No. 142, B-11, Bureau of National Affairs, Inc., Washington, D.C.

Business, Society, and Environment: Social Power and Social Response (K. Davis and R.L. Blomstrom), McGraw-Hill Book Co., New York, 1971.

Buson-Marsteller Backgrounder for A.M.A. Conference, *Business, Government, and the Public Interest,* September, 1976, unpublished paper.

Capitalism and Freedom (Milton Friedman), Phoenix Books, The University of Chicago Press, 1962.

Congressional Record, The, U.S. Government Printing Office, Washington, D.C., various issues.

Consumer Legislation Report, Soap and Detergent Association, New York, various issues.

Courting Industry's New Board Member: Government, *Industry Week,* October 18, 1976.

Daley Report for Executives, Bureau of National Affairs, Inc., Washington, D.C., various issues.

Economics of Crisis, The (Eliot Janeway), Weybright and Talley, Inc., New York, 1968.

Everybody Pays the Price of Over-regulation, *Industry Week,* December 20, 1976.

Federal Rathole, The (Donald Lambro), Arlington House, New Rochelle, N.Y., 1975.

Federal Register, U.S. Government Printing Office, Washington, D.C., various issues.

Free Enterprise as A Catalyst (Roger C.B. Morton), *NAM Reports,* November 17, 1975.

General Information Bulletin, Soap and Detergent Association, New York, various issues.

Generous Juries Cost You a Bundle, *Chemical Week,* November 24, 1976.

Government Mandated Price Increases (Murray L. Weidenbaum), American Enterprise Institute for Public Policy Research, (Washington, D.C.) February, 1975.

Government Rules, Problems, Opportunities, *Chemical and Engineering News,* March 22, 1976.

Greening of America, The (Charles A. Reich), Bantam Books, Inc., New York, 1970.

Humphrey-Hawkins Bill—Boondoggle or Economic Blessing?, *National Journal,* June 2, 1976.

Impact of FDA on Industrial R. & D. (L. H. Sarett), Chemtech, January, 1975.

Management Tasks—Responsibilities Practices (Peter F. Drucker), Harper & Row, Publishers, New York, 1973–1974.

Mark and Engels. Basic Writings on Politics and Philosophy (edited by Lewis S. Feuer), Doubleday—Anchor Original, Garden City, N.Y., 1959.

Marketing in a Shortage Economy (George S. Dominguez), American Management Association, New York, 1974.

Modern Economics (Robert D. Leiter), Barnes & Noble, Inc., Outline Series, Division of Harper & Row, New York, 1968.

More U.S. Chemical Patents Going to Foreigners, *Chemical and Engineering News,* September 22, 1975.

New Industrial State (John Kenneth Galbraith), Houghton Mifflin Co., Boston, 1967.

New Trends That Will Affect Your Profits, *Nation's Business,* February 1976.

New Wave of Government Regulation of Business, The (Murray L. Weidenbaum), *Business and Society Review,* Fall 1975.

Our Depleted Society (Seymour Melman), Holt, Rinehart & Winston, Inc., New York, 1965.

Product Management (George S. Dominguez), American Management Association, New York, 1972.

Regulatory Agencies (Phillip M. Crane, M.C.), *The Journal of Social and Political Affairs,* Vol. 1, January 1976.

Report of the Commission on Federal Paperwork, A, *Occupational Safety and Health,* July 6, 1976.

Taming the Giant Corporation (Nader Green Seligman), W.W. Norton & Co., Inc., New York, 1976.

Tapping a Gold Mine of Information (Matthew J. Lesko), *Industry Week,* August 2, 1976.

Too Much Government by Decree (John Barron), *Reader's Digest,* May 1975.

U.S. Fact Book, The, 1976 Edition, Grosset & Dunlap, Inc., A Filmways Co., New York, 1976.

U.S. Government Manual, 1976 Edition, U.S. Government Printing Office, Washington, D.C., 1976.

Washington Information Directory 1975–1976, Quadrangle–The New York Times Book Co., New York, 1975.

What Business Leaders Are Doing to Polish a Tarnished Image, *U.S. News & World Report,* September 13, 1976.

Who's Best at "Wrecking Free Enterprise" (C.W. Borkland), *Government Executive,* November 1975.

Why Business Has a Black Eye, *U.S. News & World Report,* September 6, 1976.

INDEX